# KGB

# KGB

## Death and Rebirth

**Martin Ebon**

PRAEGER

Westport, Connecticut
London

**Library of Congress Cataloging-in-Publication Data**

Ebon, Martin.
    KGB : death and rebirth / Martin Ebon.
      p.  cm.
    Includes bibliographical references and index.
    ISBN 0–275–94633–9 (alk. paper)
    1. Soviet Union. Komitet gosudarstvennoĭ bezopasnosti—History.
    2. Russia (Federation). TSentral 'naia sluzhba razvedki—History.
    3. Intelligence service—Soviet Union—History.   4. Intelligence
    service—Russia (Federation)—History.   I. Title.
    JN6529.I6E26   1994
    327.1'247—dc20       93–5398

British Library Cataloguing in Publication Data is available.

Library of Congress Catalog Card Number: 93–5398
ISBN: 0–275–94633–9

First published in 1994

Praeger Publishers, 88 Post Road West, Westport, CT 06881
An imprint of Greenwood Publishing Group, Inc.

Printed in the United States of America

The paper used in this book complies with the Permanent
Paper Standard issued by the National Information Standards
Organization (Z39.48–1984).

10 9 8 7 6 5 4 3 2 1

# Contents

# Abbreviations

Where initials are based on foreign-language identification, they are followed by English translations.

| | |
|---|---|
| AIDS | Acquired Immune Deficiency Syndrome |
| BBC | British Broadcasting Corporation |
| CHEKA | All-Russian Extraordinary Committee for Combating Counterrevolution and Sabotage |
| CIA | Central Intelligence Agency (United States) |
| CIS | Commonwealth of Independent States |
| CSS | Committee for State Security (Armenia) |
| EC | European Community |
| ECO | Economic Cooperation Organization (Middle East, Central Asia, South Asia) |
| FAGCI | Federal Agency of Government Communications and Information |
| FIS | Foreign Intelligence Service |
| FSA | Federal Security Agency |
| GPU | State Political Directorate |
| GRU | Chief Intelligence Board (of the Soviet Army) |
| ISS | Inter-Republican Security Service |
| KGB | Committee of State Security |
| KNB | Committee for National Security (Kazakhstan) |
| MGB | Ministry of State Security |

| | |
|---|---|
| MGIMO | Moscow Institute of International Relations |
| MP | Member of Parliament (Great Britain) |
| MVD | Ministry of Internal Affairs (or Ministry of Interior) |
| NATO | North Atlantic Treaty Organization |
| NKVD | People's Commissariat of Internal Affairs |
| NSA | National Security Agency (United States) |
| NSS | National Security Service (Ukraine) |
| OGPU | United State Political Directorate |
| OMON | Special Security Unit (of the Soviet Ministry of Internal Affairs) |
| PPI | Pergamon Press, Inc. |
| RSFSR | Russian Soviet Federated Socialist Republic |
| SDNS | State Directorate for National Security (Armenia) |
| SSR | Soviet Socialist Republic |
| SUK | National Security Committee (Georgia) |
| USSR | Union of Soviet Socialist Republics |
| VAAP | Copyright Agency of the USSR |

# Memo to the Reader

Let's dispense with the easy metaphors, first of all. Yes, the KGB was declared officially dead on October 24, 1991; but then it was immediately reborn. We can compare this rebirth to a new incarnation, like the rise from the ashes of Egypt's legendary Phoenix bird, and even, quite correctly, to the division of an amoeba into different parts that quickly begin a life of their own. And, for a final cliché, let's quote a distinctly non-Russian proverb—*plus ça change, plus c'est la même chose*—although even in France, the more things change they do not remain precisely the same. All of this applies to the evolution of the KGB. And here, just for the record, is its full name: Komitet Gosurdarstvennoy Besopasnosti, or Committee of State Security.

This "Memo to the Reader" takes the place of a more formal "Introduction" because there should be a mutual understanding between author and reader, from the start. This is not a history of the Soviet secret service, not an account of KGB wickedness or derring-do in the past. Rather, you are about to read an account of what has happened, of late, to the heirs of Vladimir Ilyitch Lenin's All-Russian Extraordinary Committee for Combating Counterrevolution and Sabotage, or Cheka for short. Devoted Russian secret police officers used to proudly call themselves "Chekists." In addition, we will look into the future of the various "nouveau" KGB organizations, scattered throughout the former Soviet Union.

To begin with, let us do away with a bit of gothic mystique: the KGB was never a faceless, monolithic, omniscient, omnipotent operation. It employed skilled people, but also men of limited imagination and capabilities. In this book, the personalities of recent and current top Russian intelligence officers will be examined, including that of Vladimir A. Kryuchkov, who was appointed Chairman of the KGB by President Mikhail Gorbachev, and then masterminded an abortive coup attempt in August 1991, winding up in prison and put on trial in 1993. Naturally, we are also interested in Gorbachev's own KGB connections, including his indebtedness to onetime KGB chief and Soviet head of state, Yuri Andropov. The interplay of ambitions and the impact of personal characteristics—perhaps more than administrative changes—dramatize the death and rebirth of the KGB.

Within the labyrinth that is the agency's history, it boggles the mind just to list the acronyms of the KGB's predecessors. The roll call begins with the CHEKA, which lasted from 1917 to 1922, continues with the GPU (State Political Directorate), which functioned in 1922 and 1923, and then goes to the OGPU (United State Political Directorate), which lasted from 1923 to 1934. Perhaps the most ruthless secret police force operated under the initials NKVD (People's Commissariat of Internal Affairs) from 1934 to 1946, the years of Joseph Stalin's show trials and mass purges before and after World War II. Finally, all so-called security matters were merged into the MVD, the Ministry of Internal Affairs, under Lavrenti Beria, Stalin's notorious secret police chief, from 1946 to 1954, the year after Stalin's death.

From 1954 on, the KGB as such has been on the scene, going through a series of internal and external changes, expanding and contracting, constantly involved in the Soviet leadership's positions on domestic and international events. From the ebullient heavy-handedness of Nikita Khrushchev to the corrupt bonhomie of Leonid Brezhnev, the KGB maintained its influential role and organizational solidity. Together with the leadership of the Communist Party and the armed forces, the KGB was regarded as one of the three major pillars holding up the state structure.

The reader should be aware that he or she has just reached a crucial point in this "Memo." Here is the reason: the Communist Party officially ceased to exist after the August coup, and the armed forces were weakened following defeat in Afghanistan, because of budget problems, leadership crises and internal morale problems. For these reasons, certain questions must be asked. Does the KGB, such as it is and has remained, represent the strongest element of power in Russia today? And what is the role of the secret police, sometimes still bearing the KGB name, within the power structures of other former Soviet republics, from Ukraine to Kazakhstan, from Latvia to Georgia?

Amoeba-like, the KGB split into several parts. But, to the world at large, clearly most important was the continuity of its international espionage, or intelligence, operations. Early in 1992, what used to be the KGB's legendary First Chief Directorate became an independent spin-off, Russia's Foreign Intelligence Service (FIS). The foreign intelligence setup had been a Russian operation right along, financed largely by Russia and staffed almost exclusively by Russian personnel (other "ethnics" were regarded as unreliable). The question on everyone's mind, throughout the years of the Gorbachev regime, was this: could the KGB really be "reformed," or were its clandestine habits so ingrained that, no matter what its public protestations, it would retain its tactics of extralegal surveillance, communications interception, infiltration of institutions, disinformation, and illicit manipulation, at home and abroad?

The easy answer to this is that there is no easy answer. Moreover, within the various KGB spin-offs, people didn't really know themselves what was going to happen next, or who, and what policy, would come out on top. Still, it had always been like that. Oldtimers could recall one shake-up after another, mixed signals from competing authorities, innumerable rules and regulations handed down to Residents abroad, plus wave after wave of revelations and denials, triumphs and defeats, medals, defections, scandals uncovered and scandals covered up. The not-so-easy answer provided in this book is that, "Yes, not much has changed; but beware of snap judgments. We are dealing with an ongoing process, called history. Our world is forever changing, and a well-established intelligence agency knows how to change along with it."

One radical interpretation, that the KGB only underwent a facelift, was presented by Yevgeniya Albats, news analyst for the weekly *Moscow News* in a full-page article, "KGB-MSB-MBVD: Substantive Changes?" (no. 2, 1992). The author took the position that, except for a brief period following the August 1991 coup, the KGB was able to consolidate its position rapidly. Signs on doors were changed, but activities behind the doors remained much what they had been before, the article suggested. While department heads were removed, their places were taken by deputies in the same mold. Vadim Bakatin, who directed the KGB during four crucial months—and whose impact is analyzed in detail in this book—admitted that he had been "conservative in changing the leadership." Albats suggested that Bakatin was forced to go slow in making personnel changes because of "the hatred which security people felt for him."

As for the purely temporary spin-offs of major KGB segments, such as the Border Guards, communications facilities, and the Security Service that protects high officials—why were these done so quickly? Well, just after the abortive August 1991 coup, people in Moscow were in a vengeful mood; right in front of the KGB building, they tore down the statue of Felix Dzerzhinsky, whom Lenin had picked as head of the CHEKA. According to Andrei Oligov, chief of public relations for Russia's Federal Security Agency (FSA), the immediate successor of the KGB's domestic operations, the quick parcelling-out was a tactical move, calculated to defuse public anger. Oligov said that, "to soothe public unrest and prevent the lynching of KGB people, the vandalizing of buildings and plundering of archives, it was decided to announce that the Committee would be quickly disbanded and split into independent departments."

What wasn't planned was the rapid falling-away of regional KGBs in such states as Kazakhstan and Belarus, and particularly in Ukraine. Anti-Russian sentiment in the newly independent states was often directed at the KGB, long regarded as a Russian weapon to enforce colonial-type controls, even provoking violent incidents that played into Moscow's hands. Inevitably, in the long run, interregional rivals must set one national KGB successor agency against another, at least in such places as Armenia and Azerbaijan, which have been at war with one another. Elsewhere, for instance in Georgia and Tajikistan, national KGB organizations have had to adjust to rapid changes in government leadership, which demanded either switches in loyalty or the replacement of KGB officers, at least at the top level.

The role of Russia's Foreign Intelligence Service under the diplomat-scholar-journalist Yevgeny Primakov became extraordinarily wide and complex. While the FIS pledged cooperation with its ex-partners within the Soviet framework, the potential for a "need to know" about what goes on inside them may well call for outright spying. This becomes intricate, because it could involve former KGB colleagues in newly independent X-istan being employed by FIS, while X-istan's own KGB looks for old or new friends within—believe it or not—the FIS. And so, intelligence would meet counterintelligence, which meets countercounterintelligence! All of this is deniable, and is, of course, denied by all concerned. Nevertheless, frictions and clashing political-economic interests of the successor states are all too obvious, and intelligence agencies are quick to spot needs, opportunities, and gaps in someone else's security armor.

The KGB has been reborn in many forms, most formidably as Russia's new Ministry of Justice. The new intelligence operations may employ fewer people than in the past, at least during periods of budget cuts. But the latest acronyms are, when all is said and done, a historic continuation of earlier reorganizations, from CHEKA to MVD. Ideologies fade; but as the twentieth century comes to a close, national identities have tended to sharpen. Russia itself remains a great power, struggling toward new self-assertion. From Riga to Vladivostok, the lands of Euro-Asia eagerly proclaim their individualities. What was only one intelligence service is now divided into a multitude of ambitions and activities, relentlessly engaged in an intelligence renaissance.

The author of this book is indebted to the generous help of friends and acquaintances, some of them dating back to World War II and its aftermath, who have supplied information and criticism. On a topic as controversial as this book's, it is appropriate to note that the author did not receive financial support from any government agency or foundation at home or abroad, nor did this project originate anywhere outside the author's own initiative. Credit should be given to a vital but little-known source of information on world affairs: the Foreign Broadcast Information Service (FBIS), located in Springfield, Virginia, which publishes almost daily reports of media extracts from major regions, including the former Soviet Union (now under the label "Central Eurasia"). The FBIS began its work about half a century ago, monitoring enemy broadcasts during World War II, and has continued this valuable service for government officials, scholars, and other individuals and agencies ever since. Much of the material used on the following pages is based on FBIS reports. The author also wishes to acknowledge the expertise and help of the Munich and New York offices of Radio Free Europe/Radio Liberty, whose researchers and librarians have, for years, excelled in expertise and generous support. Finally, this book would not have been possible without the untiring assistance of my patient, multilingual wife Chariklia S. ("Koutsie") Ebon.

# Part I

## The Coup That Failed

# 1

# Three Days in August

On Sunday afternoon, August 18, 1991, President Mikhail Gorbachev was sitting, informally dressed, in a study at "Zarya," his summer home on the Black Sea shore, near the Crimean town of Foros. The Gorbachev family was guarded by a top secret unit of the KGB, the Presidential Bodyguard. At ten minutes to five, Gorbachev was confronted by a delegation of Moscow plotters; they demanded that he either resign or surrender presidential authority to his deputy, Gennadi Yanayev. Among the group that presented him with this ultimatum were two close associates: Lieutenant General Yuri Plekhanov, chief of the Presidential Bodyguard; and, much to Gorbachev's surprise and irritation, his personal assistant and chief-of-staff, Valery Boldin.

The split that, during this crisis period, characterized much of Soviet society, its leadership, the KGB, and the armed forces, emerged quickly within the Presidential Bodyguard. Defying Plekhanov's orders, loyal guards formed a protective circle around the Gorbachev family. Recounting these events, the President said, "We were completely isolated, by sea and by land. Thirty-two bodyguards remained with me, those who had decided, as it were, to stay until the end. They divided defense functions among themselves. Family members were spread around, and all of them were protected." The loyal guards took up positions within the vacation villa. They also provided the expertise to put into operation several radios that were on the premises. Gorbachev recalled, "We found some old receivers in the servants' quarters and were able to set up antennas." With these additions, the radio sets were able to pick up Russian-language broadcasts by the British Broadcasting Corporation (BBC), Radio Liberty (the U.S.-operated transmitters with studios in

Munich, Germany), and the "Voice of America," broadcasting from Washington.

The roles of Plekhanov and Boldin—two trusted associates—corresponded to the treachery committed by such men as KGB Chairman Vladimir Kryuchkov and Defense Minister Dmitri Yazov, whom Gorbachev had personally appointed to their positions. When representatives of the conspirators appeared at the Fornos villa, Plekhanov provided an air of legitimacy. As Gorbachev saw it, "Plekhanov, the head of the KGB administration, was with them. Otherwise, my guards would not have let them pass." Gorbachev discovered that all telephone connections had been cut; he and his family had been effectively imprisoned, and, as the President put it, they underwent "seventy-two hours of total isolation." In contrast to the still-loyal bodyguards, KGB guard units surrounding the compound refused all of Gorbachev's requests "that my communications be restored" and "an airplane be brought immediately, so that I might return to Moscow."

Five of the loyal bodyguards later appeared on the Moscow Central Television (on September 10, 1991): Oleg Klimov, Boris Kolentsov, Valery Cherkasov, Andrei Belikov, and Nikolai Tektov. The men recalled that, down at the Gorbachev villa, their first intimation of trouble came when bodyguards who tried to leave the compound were intercepted by armed Border Guards, another KGB branch. Men who wanted to go off duty were asked to hand over their weapons. This made them suspicious, and they remained at their posts.

As news of the Moscow coup spread, the bodyguards were put to a decisive loyalty test. One commander, Vyacheslav Generalov, made an erratic, violently anti-Gorbachev speech. Generalov warned the guards against "protecting a traitor" and threatened that, by continuing their protection, the men would themselves "become traitors." Told of this, the puzzled TV interviewer said, "I heard that Generalov was a good man. He was even described as being first-class. What went wrong with this man? Why did he turn against the President?"

Klimov replied, "He was like a suitcase with a false bottom. A scheming careerist. A man not to be trusted. By 1800 [6 P.M.] everything had been decided for us. And when the President called us in, a little after 9, I was able to assure him that thirty-two of us bodyguards at the *dacha* [villa] had decided to stay with him to the end." The limited strength of this defense unit was described by Kolentsov: "We did not have a very large force, or many weapons; just a few individual [machine] guns. I do not think these weapons played a decisive role at the time. We protected only the house of the President and his family. This building was the final barrier. If any physical attack had taken place, we would have stood our ground until the end. The President would have been the last. No one had any doubt about that."

Lieutenant General Plekhanov sought to disrupt the guard unit's morale further by removing Major General Vadim T. Medvedev, its commander. Medvedev told investigators that the Moscow group turned up at the dacha unannounced: "They simply told me: 'Report to Mikhail Sergeyevich that a group has arrived for talks with him.' So I did just that. And he asked: Why? Where from? I said I had no idea. That's all there was to it." Plekhanov then told Medvedev, "Get your things together, and go home." When the commander refused, Plekhanov said that these were Kryuchkov's orders. Medvedev, wise in the ways of KGB bureaucracy, asked for written instructions. "So they wrote out an order," he said. "After that I got my things together and went. That's all." Plekhanov put him on a plane and shipped him off to Moscow.

Plekhanov's dubious role might presumably be rationalized by his position in the chain of command, leading down directly from KGB Chairman Kryuchkov. His defense lawyers could advance the timeworn explanation that Plekhanov was "only following orders" when he joined the "delegation" representing the Moscow conspirators. No such explanation would serve Valery Boldin, Gorbachev's assistant and confidant through much of his career. Moscow speculation inevitably centered on the possibility that the KGB had planted Boldin deliberately in Gorbachev's office, or that he had become a KGB recruit earlier, while working as a journalist or party official. Valery Ivanovich Boldin, born July 9, 1935, began his career in 1953 as a radio technician with the Moscow-Ryazan Railroad Administration. In 1960 he worked as a reporter and literary critic for *Pravda*, the Communist Party daily. A year later, he joined the staff of the Communist Party's Central Committee. Boldin returned to *Pravda* in 1969; he advanced to membership of the paper's Editorial Board, dealing mainly with agricultural problems.

Finally, in 1981—once again with the party's Central Committee—Boldin became Gorbachev's right-hand man; at first, he specialized in agriculture, but eventually he gained his boss's full confidence and remained with him while Gorbachev became party chief and, finally, the country's President. The weekly *Moscow News* (September 15–22, 1991) in a devastating profile of Boldin entitled "Traitor No. 1," noted that he consistently "avoided the limelight," camouflaged his own opinions, "kept away from the political scene in the same way he avoided cameras," but tended to gloat about his manipulative powers behind the scenes. The paper quoted the views of an unnamed man in the presidential office that many who had originally been "undecided about joining the plot" decided on betrayal when they found out "Boldin was among the plotters." Viktor Loshak, the article's author, concluded, "How much he must have hated the boss who addressed him simply as Valery and summoned him with just a nod or a wink!"

A writer in *Izvestia* (August 24, 1991) commented, "One thing is clear: He [Boldin] is a member of Gorbachev's inner circle. Owes him every-thing. Betrayed him." The same article quotes one of Gorbachev's as-sistants, Vladimir Yegorov, as providing these scathing comments: "Boldin was Mikhail Sergeyevich's assistant from the time he moved to Moscow. A typical apparatchik. Not a bad organizer, probably. All con-nections and contacts with the President went through him, were in his hands. He had the best access within Gorbachev's office. Reserved and unsociable. It was always a mystery to everyone just what was on his mind. That he was a schemer—that is beyond doubt; there's no other opinion on this." The article concluded that a great deal concerning the August coup, as well as other events, might be "explained by the fact that this Grey Eminence stood right next to the President." In sum: the Ultimate Insider and calculating opportunist, who miscalculated his op-portunities this time, however.

While Gorbachev was being held incommunicado in the Crimea, pro-tected by loyal KGB bodyguards and isolated by disloyal KGB Border Guards—just what was the KGB machinery doing elsewhere? Historian Yuri Afanasyev, an outspoken reform advocate, was traveling in Hun-gary at the time. Speaking on the Budapest Kossuth Radio (August 19, 1991), Afanasyev doubted that "the KGB and the army have fallen into the hands of the Committee, the putschists; on the contrary, I expect the polarization to begin in the Army, as well as in the KGB."

Lieutenant General Nikolay Britvin, chief of the Military Political Di-rectorate of the KGB Border Guards, told *Izvestia* (August 23, 1991) that their troops were placed on an "increased readiness" alert. Did this mean that the KGB was ordered to prevent opponents of the coup from escaping arrest by fleeing the country, was ordered to seize them at the border? Asked whether the borders had actually been closed, Britvin replied, "Not quite. Our fellow citizens could still travel abroad, if they had appropriate documents and visas. However, I would like to specify that the Border Guards did not determine whom to let out of the country and whom to let in." He added that the Border Guards "did not receive written instructions" concerning tightened border control—which, at the very least, suggested lack of administrative firmness on the part of the KGB's top command.

The public and the investigators were also concerned about the conspirators' possible plans to round up actual or potential opponents of the coup, within the country. Did the KGB prepare extra prison capacity prior or during the coup? The question was answered by Alexander Fokin, chief of the agency's Tenth Department, in charge of the KGB's detention centers and prisons. Fokin told *Izvestia* (August 27, 1991) that he had received no instructions pointing to the arrest of "any additional contingent of prisoners" during the crisis period. Yuri Rastvorov, director of the notorious Lefortovo Prison, confirmed this statement. Rastvorov said that before, during, and after the coup attempt the prison (with a capacity of more than two hundred) was undergoing such routine summer maintenance as repainting. As the paper put it, "After the putsch, there was minor cosmetic repair work in the cells."

Another indication of indecision, opposition, or division within the KGB was provided by Major General Oleg Kalugin, the KGB's most prominent critic prior to the August coup. Kalugin told the Moscow paper *Rossiskaya Gazeta* (August 28, 1991) that friends within the KGB had warned him of imminent arrest. He was tipped off by "people from the Seventh KGB Directorate," and so "I went underground on August 19th, and I was already in the White House [the Russian Federation Building] on August 20th." Kalugin saw the warning as indicating a "serious split in the KGB."

The KGB's Seventh Directorate, one of whose members had warned Kalugin, was in charge of its specially trained commandos known as the "Alpha Group." These units—generally referred to as "antiterrorist" squads—were trained for use against hijackers and kidnappers, and in other civilian crisis situations where selective violence might be required. During the August coup, Alpha was ordered to attack the so-called White House, the Russian Federation Building, where Boris Yeltsin and much of the organized resistance to the coup had established headquarters.

A decisive factor in the failure of the coup was the assumption of its leaders that their orders would be unquestionably executed. In the case of Alpha, the news agency Tass reported (August 26, 1991) that the group's combat readiness was increased on Sunday, August 18. The report quoted Mikhail Golovatov, then deputy chief of the group, as stating that Alpha had been ordered to undertake covert reconnaissance of the Russian White House on August 19, by infiltrating it, and to take the building "by force" at 3 A.M. on the night of August 20–21.

Golovatov recalled the group's misgivings: "There were about five-hundred armed people in the building, so it was likely that, if an operation were undertaken, it would lead to a great deal of bloodshed." Golovatov said, "We were simply flabbergasted by the order"; and he added, "The commanders of the group were sitting together when the order was received. We immediately decided not to carry it out, although we knew very well what the consequences might be. We then called the sub-unit heads together and asked for their reactions to the order. It is to the credit of our colleagues that they decided not to carry it out, as it was illegal."

According to this oddly bland account, the whole Alpha staff was then called together and within twenty minutes decided "unanimously" not to attack the Russian Federation Building. For their part, the deputy group commanders pledged that they would "not lead them." Golovatov emphasized that this decision was, after all, a grave and difficult one, representing outright disobedience: "For servicemen, especially of our unit, this was unprecedented. Nothing like this had ever happened throughout the existence of the Alpha group, dating back to 1974."

Boris Yeltsin, whose life would have been endangered by an attack on the Russian White House, and Mikhail Gorbachev, who was told of the Alpha decision after his return from the Crimea, paid tribute to the group's refusal to carry out the attack order. Still, the group's top leadership was implicated in the coup attempt. According to Golovatov, Alpha's chief at the time—General Viktor F. Karpukhin—originally insisted that the order be carried out. In effect, Alpha undertook a successful mutiny. Karpukhin publicly denied that KGB Chairman Kryuchkov had given Alpha or any other "special purpose groups" specific orders. *Komsomolskaya Pravda* quoted Karpukhin (August 24, 1991) as saying, "I personally received no orders from Kryuchkov, and consequently obeyed no orders." Nevertheless, Golovatov—who succeeded Karpukhin—provided the following analysis of preparations for an attack:

"Firearms and ammunition had been issued to the men. We knew the layout of the offices of the White House, and we knew the RSFSR [Russian Soviet Federated Socialist Republic] presidential bodyguard that we would face. All that was left to do was climb into our vehicles and take up positions to begin operations. Storming the building would have meant the beginning of combat operations. This could have led to terrible bloodshed. Our group had the required training, while the defenders of the White House, as we found out later, would have stood their ground to the bitter end. But they would have been no match for the professionals. To put it bluntly, we could have finished the job within twenty to thirty minutes."

Golovatov added that storming the White House would have provoked fighting between opposing Soviet Army units. He concluded that "a large part of the KGB, if not the bulk of it, did not back the putschists." Yeltsin, in an interview on the Russian Television Network (August 25, 1991), said the KGB had a "very detailed blueprint" for a takeover of the White House, including use of antitank weapons and grenade launchers. He said the plan included "a hail of fire from all sides," simultaneously directed against the first and second floors of the building, followed by an assault on himself, "the President, and if there were any chance of his [Yeltsin's] escaping, shoot him on the spot," followed by seizure of eleven other key people.

Yeltsin confirmed that the plan ran up against the "super-disciplined" Alpha Group, which refused to have any part in it. This reaction, he said, was "something totally unexpected by the whole KGB leadership," but neither propaganda nor "threats of trials and shootings" could change the minds of the commanders of Alpha's subunits. As he reconstructed events, the planned assault kept being postponed, from 6 P.M. to 8, to 10, to 1 A.M., and finally to 3 A.M., until "they finally realized that it was too late, because so large a crowd had assembled that it would have been difficult even to get near the building."

With the assault on the White House called off, and opposition led by Yeltsin grown overwhelming, the coup plotters sought to negotiate a compromise with Gorbachev. To this end, Kryuchkov canceled a scheduled appearance before the Supreme Soviet and decided that his group should fly down to Foros on August 21. An armed group of Gorbachev loyalists, headed by Russian Vice-president Alexander Rutskoi, arranged for a rival flight designed to head off the conspirators and rescue the Gorbachevs. The Kryuchkov-Yazov group, which included Plekhanov, who was then still (technically) the head of the Presidential Bodyguard, arrived three hours ahead of the loyalist contingent. But—with communications restored, and warned by a Yeltsin telephone call—Gorbachev refused to meet the coup group. The loyalists were greeted warmly by Gorbachev's hardcore bodyguards.

In the confusion that resulted from the overlapping arrival of the two delegations, the dramatic rescue of the Gorbachev family, and the presence of uniformed and armed personnel loyal to the President, a dazed KGB Chairman Kryuchkov was separated from the other plotters, frisked for weapons, and placed on a Moscow-bound presidential plane. Together with Plekhanov and Boldin, Kryuchkov was taken to Interrogation Unit No. 4 in northeastern Moscow, for detention pending trial. There the three were joined by eleven other accused plotters; the group included seven members of the conspiratorial committee.

The very next day (August 22) the KGB Collegium, a committee of senior officers, stated that the agency's administrators and staff were "deeply upset" that the KGB's collective "honor has been besmirched" by its Chairman's involvement in the plot. The statement also said:

"The conspiracy, which has been broken by decisive actions of the democratic forces of the country, cannot be evaluated in any other way than as an attack against constitutional organs of power, which the KGB is dedicated to defend. The KGB of the USSR has nothing to do with these anti-constitutional actions . . . . The Collegium of the KGB calls on leaders of security organs to act on the basis of the evaluation of the attempt provided by USSR President [Gorbachev] and in accordance with the Constitution, laws and decisions of the President."

It was a hasty, cautious, and somewhat bewildered attempt at last-minute damage control.

# 2

# Bewildered, Rigid
# Mastermind

How could Vladimir A. Kryuchkov, whom Gorbachev appointed head of the KGB in 1988, turn against his benefactor three years later—edge his country toward civil war, bring personal disaster upon himself, and destroy all he believed in? Here, the head of the world's most-feared secret police, a veteran of twenty years' service, totally miscalculated his country's basic mood! Here, a top-level intelligence agency administrator failed to employ clear-cut conspiratorial plans, orders, and controls!

In the end, Kryuchkov's personality puzzled Gorbachev himself. When, after the August 1991 coup, he was asked why he had ever chosen Kryuchkov in the first place, Gorbachev confessed that he was "very impressed" by the fact that Kryuchkov appeared "less professional" than the other secret police veterans he had considered for the post of KGB chief. Gorbachev acknowledged that being a professional in the secret services might be "good in one sense," but added that, "in another sense, these are dreadful people, these professionals." Gorbachev had assumed that years of activity in international affairs had given Kryuchkov a broad view: "It seemed to me that his political horizon, the fact that he had some contacts with external intelligence, foreign intelligence, created a certain wider comprehension—I thought I recognized in him a person with a certain level of cultural erudition, an ability to engage in dialogue."

And, indeed, during the years he served as head of the KGB, Kryuchkov did encourage dialogue about the history, image, status, practices, functions, and future of the agency. The changes that took place after the failed August coup were, to a degree, foreshadowed during the

Kryuchkov years. Soon after he took office, he began a public relations campaign designed to change drastically the domestic and international views of the KGB, and he played a major role in conveying this message through talks, testimonies, and interviews.

Much of what Kryuchkov said during this period implemented the concepts of *perestroyka* [restructuring] and reflected what might be termed "loyalty under pressure" to President Gorbachev's political principles. And yet, it was possible to detect four dissonant themes in Kryuchkov's utterances: (1) that the Communist Party of the Soviet Union was, and had to remain, the guiding center in terms of ideology and functions; (2) that the Soviet Union, as a Union, was close to sacrosanct, and that certain efforts toward independence on the part of the different republics were illegal to the point of treason; (3) that independent business and financial initiatives were nearly or totally equivalent to criminal activity; and (4) that subversive pressures from abroad, including efforts by foreign intelligence agencies, were at least partly responsible for the Soviet Union's economic instability, ethnic violence, and threat of political-economic disintegration.

The very career elements that had persuaded Gorbachev to entrust Kryuchkov with his important position may also have been instrumental in anchoring these dogmatic viewpoints in his mind and personality. His outlook had inevitably been shaped by early Marxist indoctrination, Communist Party activities, years in criminal prosecution, a mixture of Soviet diplomacy and liaison with Communist parties abroad, and finally a career of two decades within the ranks of the KGB itself.

Vladimir Alexandrovich Kryuchkov was born on February 20, 1924, in Stalingrad (now Volgograd). In an interview with *Pravda* on December 30, 1990, he said that his first job had been decided "by circumstances." He recalled that early in World War II, "at the age of 17, I had to drop out of school and go to work at a defense plant." According to his official biography, Kryuchkov was employed as a metal-plater from 1941 to 1942 at the No. 221 Plant of the Commissariat of Defense in Stalingrad, then briefly at the No. 92 Plant in Gorky, and once again, until 1943, in Stalingrad. He must have witnessed the devastation of his hometown after the Soviets' costly defeat of the German Army; he was an organizer with the Communist Youth League—the Komsomol—at the No. 25 Construction Unit in that city. In 1944 and 1945 he served as first secretary of the Komsomol at the local Barrikady District. He became a Communist Party member at the age of eighteen.

After the war, in 1946, Kryuchkov became second secretary of the

Komsomol's Stalingrad city committee. He had little to say about his father, and told *Pravda* only that the elder Kryuchkov was "a worker." But he spoke warmly about his early "mentor," Ivan Lomov, Communist Party secretary at the Stalingrad construction project, whom he described as "a man of amazing kindness, integrity, decency and honesty." He recalled that Lomov "did not have much formal education but his life experience and natural abilities more than compensated for this lack of education." Kryuchkov paid further tribute to Lomov as having been "simply unique in his fatherly concern, his desire to help, while at the same time being a demanding mentor." Clearly, the paternal influence of this devoted party functionary had a lasting impact on Kryuchkov's personality and outlook.

In 1945 and 1946, Kryuchkov began the study of law at the Saratov Juridical Institute. He was to continue these studies through correspondence courses with the All-Union Juridical Institute, graduating in 1949. Eventually, after attending the USSR Foreign Ministry's Higher School for Diplomats from 1951 to 1954, Kryuchkov graduated with a degree in international law. Meanwhile, his life veered from a blue-collar career into the judiciary, beginning with successive positions as prosecutor and investigator with the Office of the Public Prosecutor in Stalingrad from 1946 to 1951; these hectic postwar years were a period of civil unrest, coupled with a high crime rate. Following his training period at the Foreign Ministry, Kryuchkov became third secretary in the ministry's Fourth European Department, which dealt with Czechoslovakia and Poland.

Kryuchkov's first assignment abroad was crucial for his later career. He served as third secretary at the Soviet Embassy in Budapest, Hungary, from 1955 to 1959. This period overlapped with the stay in Budapest of Yuri V. Andropov (b. 1914–d. 1984), who later became head of the KGB, General Secretary of the Soviet Communist Party in 1982, and subsequently President of the USSR. Andropov outranked Kryuchkov in Budapest; he started as counselor and chargé d'affaires in 1953, and served as ambassador from 1954 to 1957. Kryuchkov told *Pravda* simply that he "met" Andropov in 1955, but avoided details concerning place and circumstance. He praised Andropov's "intellect, his enormous knowledge, his amazing capacity for work and his ability to find nonstandard solutions to complex problems—all of this enriched everybody who worked with him." The year after Kryuchkov arrived at his Budapest post, the Kremlin crushed Hungary's attempt to steer a relatively independent course. On November 4, 1956, Soviet troops invaded the country and put an end to the uprising; the East European nation's reformist Communist leaders were subsequently killed.

Kryuchkov told his interviewers, "Incidentally, it was through Yuri Vladimirovich [Andropov] that I became acquainted with Mikhail Sergeyevich [Gorbachev]." To varying degrees, Gorbachev and Kryuchkov owed their prominence to the fact that, earlier in their careers, they were among Andropov's protégés. Ever the non-"professional," Kryuchkov even suggested that he might have preferred another line of work. "The Chekist career was not of my choosing," he said. "In 1967 Yuri V. Andropov was assigned to work in the state security organs. I went with him, to work for the KGB."

But both Andropov and Kryuchkov first spent several years in the Central Committee of the Communist Party—specifically, in its Department of Liaison with Communist and Workers' Parties of Socialist Countries (Eastern Europe). Andropov became head of this department in 1957. Kryuchkov joined him two years later, specializing in Hungarian matters. In 1962, Andropov rose to the position of a secretary in the party's Central Committee; from 1965 to 1967, Kryuchkov served as his aide. Then on May 19, 1967, when Andropov was given the post of KGB director, he took Kryuchkov with him. For the next four years, Kryuchkov had the title of Head of the Secretariat, KGB.

Under Andropov's tutelage, Kryuchkov was placed in charge of the KGB's foreign intelligence operations, including the agency's covert activities. This important part of Kryuchkov's career began in 1971. He headed the KGB's First Chief Directorate (External Operations) for fourteen years, from 1974 until 1988 when Gorbachev made him the agency's Chairman (director). Andropov had appointed him Deputy Chairman in 1978. In the early 1970s, Kryuchkov was said to have served as the KGB's chief officer, or Resident, at the United Nations in New York. In 1987, he was a member of the delegation that accompanied Gorbachev to Washington for a summit meeting with President Ronald Reagan.

Looking back on Kryuchkov's career—as Gorbachev did in 1988—one might very well assume that this was a worldly wise, sophisticated man, aware of the inevitability of changes within the Soviet Union and the Communist-governed nations. And yet, Kryuchkov appears to have remained ambivalent about Gorbachev's policies, as well as about the man himself. On the one hand, as his public statements indicated, he recognized a need for substantial changes; on the other hand, he feared what seemed to him the subversive-anarchic impact of these changes on the society of which he was a part.

In line with the appearance of personal openness, of the KGB's efforts at showing a "human face," Kryuchkov even answered questions about his personal life. During an appearance on Moscow Television (June 24, 1989), he spoke briefly about his wife Yekaterina (although he did not give her name), his sons, one grandson, and a granddaughter, "whom I love very much." He added, "Yes, I am a family man, but unfortunately I have very little time to spend with my family." He acknowledged that he devoted to work between fourteen and sixteen hours daily, allowing himself only four to five hours of leisure on Sundays: "The only thing that saves me is an exceeding constructive and positive attitude toward physical exercise." He said that he tried to swim for an hour each morning and that, "like a true Russian," he loved skiing and the theater, including the plays of Berthold Brecht. Perhaps thinking back to his days in Budapest, Kryuchkov said, "I like Hungarian literature a great deal."

Another TV interview (August 10, 1990) showed Kryuchkov outside a country house, identified as an "out-of-town KGB residence." Asked about official privileges due to his rank, Kryuchkov replied (with what was surely designed to be disarming candor), "I've discussed this question with my wife. I cannot think of any privileges that I enjoy. I receive my salary. There is a car that takes me to work and back, and which is absolutely indispensable to me. In the first place, I would not be able to get to work otherwise. Secondly, this car is equipped with special communications facilities, and so it has to be a large car. If similar equipment could be installed in a smaller car, I would be happy to accept it— although, I admit, the car I now have makes everything a good deal easier." He also said, "I pay for my apartment. I pay for holiday vouchers, although, I must admit, not at full cost. I cannot give you the exact figures right now; but I do not pay full price, and neither does my wife. In addition, I am entitled to travel clear across the country, once a year, free of charge, stopping wherever I like. I have, however, never taken advantage of this right, although, of course, I do not have to pay when I travel otherwise." Asked about the residence at which the interview took place, Kryuchkov identified it as "a guest house, a service house, used by one of the sub-units of the KGB," mainly to accommodate visiting delegations.

Kryuchkov advanced the public position that the KGB was both subject to the law and an agency engaged in implementing the law. Since his appointment as KGB director, he favored establishment of a parliamentary oversight committee, as well as a law outlining the functions and limitations of the security apparatus. Early on, Kryuchkov said that, in creating an oversight committee, "I think we will borrow some of the experience of the Americans." Throughout his tenure, he never missed an opportunity to state that the new KGB Law would be governed by principles of human rights. In taking the initiative and urging the Supreme Soviet to establish an oversight committee, Kryuchkov was able to assure the draft of a law satisfactory to the KGB's own interests.

With such a legal framework virtually completed, *Pravda* (April 5, 1990) put the following question, rather politely, to Chairman Kryuchkov: "How do you picture the mechanism of oversight over the activities of state security organs by representative bodies of authority, and what will be the limits to *glasnost* [openness] within this oversight?" Kryuchkov's legal background showed when he answered:

"The mechanism of oversight over the activities of state security organs by representative bodies of authority will be provided both by existing legislation and the draft Law on the USSR KGB. It specifies that the USSR KGB is accountable to the Congress of USSR People's Deputies, the USSR Supreme Soviet, the President of the country, and the USSR Council of Ministers. The chairman of the USSR KGB submits an annual report on the activities of the USSR KGB to the Supreme Soviet. The USSR Supreme Soviet Committee for Defense and State Security Questions periodically hears reports from leaders of the USSR KGB and its structural subdivisions. Information about the activities of the USSR KGB and organs and troops under its jurisdiction can be obtained by USSR people's deputies in accordance with their status, that is, by means of requests and written questions. Oversight functions will obviously also be carried out by the Presidential Council, one of whose main tasks will be the elaboration of measures to ensure the country's security."

Underneath Kryuchkov's public emphasis on the KGB's role as guardian of the law as well as servant of the law, one could perceive increasing personal frustrations. His numerous public statements reflected impatience with limits of the law and restrictions on law enforcement. What may be termed "emotional hostility" toward all forms of spontaneous economic activity also found frequent expression. His earlier visits abroad had obviously failed to give him a feeling for the vagaries of a free market. Appointed by Gorbachev to head the KGB, Kryuchkov at first seemed to act on the assumption that, by their training and background, the two men shared basic convictions. And in fact, Gorbachev's continued professions of loyalty to socialist concepts must have buttressed this assumption.

Yet, by the fall of 1990, Kryuchkov—together with Defense Minister

Dmitri T. Yazov, and others—clearly began to feel that Gorbachev was ill-advised in associating with a succession of political and economic reformers (among them Vadim Bakatin, then head of the Interior Ministry). Public attention was drawn to the possibility of a coup when a series of troop movements took place near Moscow in the days centering around September 10. Among the units involved were regiments of the army, the Vitebsk Airborne Division of the USSR KGB Border Guards, and the Interior Ministry's Dzerzhinsky Division. Kryuchkov and the top military spokesmen assured the public that such troop movement activity was merely routine, and they brushed off rumors of a planned coup.

During the coming months, Kryuchkov became increasingly vocal in public, appearing on domestic and foreign television programs and giving a series of newspaper interviews. On December 11 he made a strikingly aggressive speech; in terms reminiscent of Cold War rhetoric, he warned of internal and external threats. Oddly, the title of his talk—"On Instructions of the USSR President"—implied that he was speaking on behalf or even at the urging of Gorbachev. He cited an "increasing flow of appeals," presumably by the public, that the KGB take "decisive actions to defend the law and maintain order." He saw a "threat of the collapse of the Soviet Union." In a clear reference to regional independence movements, he warned that "national chauvinism" was causing "death and outrage to human dignity," with "millions of lives being broken." Kryuchkov said the KGB possessed information that lists had been compiled, pinpointing people "liable for neutralization if the need arises." In other words, he warned of a planned uprising that would include the mass murder of previously selected individuals.

Kryuchkov alleged that "some extremely radical political tendencies" were not spontaneous or homegrown, but were carefully planned and had received "lavish moral and material support from abroad." He accused subversive elements of a combined effort to "undermine our society and our state, and to liquidate Soviet power." He judged some of the "mass media" to be guilty of "instigating and aggravating the moral and political climate in the country with concentrated attacks on the basic foundations of Soviet power." Kryuchkov pledged the KGB's "duty to prevent any interference in our internal affairs by foreign special services and by those foreign organizations and groups which, with their support, have conducted secret campaigns against the Soviet state for decades and continue to do so." He concluded by saying that "KGB bodies and troops" had "no other interest than the interests of the people." And he added, "We envision no road other than the road of democratic renewal of our socialist fatherland."

Vladimir Kryuchkov engaged in a second round of attacks shortly afterward: on December 22, in a long and detailed address to the Fourth Congress of People's Deputies he laid down what was, in effect, a popular doctrine of Communist conservatism at the time, a virtual justification for the coup attempt that was to follow eight months later, and a valid guideline for any long-range opposition to substantial political and economic reforms. While the KGB chief devoted much of his talk to the need to counter outright criminality, he linked such activity with independence movements and free-market functions. In the mind of undiscriminating listeners frustrated by shortages of food and consumer goods, the targets listed by Kryuchkov could easily blur into an undifferentiated mass of subversions, or, as he put it, "destructive forces."

Once again, as in his earlier speech, Kryuchkov alleged that foreign intelligence agencies ("special services") were engaged in hostile activities: "Despite a warming in international relations, one can observe a considerable increase in the activity of certain Western special services in collecting information about the development of the political situation in the USSR, about our defense and scientific-technical potential, the size of strategic reserves of raw materials, fuel, foodstuffs, and foreign currency reserves. The aforementioned special services, and foreign anti-Soviet centers connected with them, are working out new forms and methods of their work regarding the Soviet Union, and they are modernizing their strategies and tactics."

One particular passage in his speech aroused considerable chagrin outside the USSR, where aid in the form of food was being assembled to counter serious shortages: "The actions of a number of our foreign partners are, basically, akin to economic sabotage, and this is creating quite a few difficulties, as we strive to improve the economic situation in the country. Take, for example, the quite large purchases of foreign food being made by the Soviet Union. Unfortunately, not all our trading partners are conscientious. For example, taking advantage of our mismanagement, they deliver impure and, sometimes, defective grain, as well as products with an above-average level of radioactivity or containing harmful chemical admixtures. According to data at our disposal, about 40 percent of imported grain is weed-infested and about 10 percent is substandard. Do not forget that we are paying hard currency for this!"

Kryuchkov asked this rhetorical question: "Do all the negative features and vices of the capitalist market really have to become an automatic part of our life?" And: "By what right do billions of rubles pass from the pocket of honest toilers into the pocket of swindlers?" He concluded with further appeals to "discipline and the law," and reiterated his warnings of a "disordered society."

The image of the KGB as the law-abiding guardian of the law was also projected by Kryuchkov in comments on the secret police's history. He told the weekly *Literaturnaya Gazeta* (January 23, 1991) that the "mass repressions of the thirties, forties and early fifties" had been a violation of humanitarian principles. He said that, "as early as 1954," during the regime of Nikita Khrushchev (whom he did not name), "state security began to review cases" of "enemies of the people." Kryuchkov acknowledged that these reviews had been "truncated and incomplete"; he added with emphasis, "—But, nevertheless!"

He also stated, "In recent years we have been engaged in complete rehabilitation. An immense amount of work has been done. The real scale of the repressions has become clear. Up to this point, the most diverse figures have been given for the numbers of repressed—from 20 million to between 60 and 70 million. In reality, during the thirties, forties and early fifties, 3,778,234 people were convicted, of whom 786,098 were executed. When I first presented these figures, no one would believe me." When told by an interviewer that these totals sounded extremely low, Kryuchkov insisted that they were "the real figures."

By this time, Gorbachev had yielded to pressure from the Kryuchkov–Yazov group. In December, the reformist Bakatin had been replaced by Boris K. Pugo, who had served as head of the KGB in Latvia and was known as a hard-line opponent of Baltic independence. An Andropov appointee, Pugo was a political ally of Kryuchkov. President Gorbachev also named Gennadi I. Yanayev, an undistinguished Communist Party administrator, to serve as vice-president. His position within the country's leadership thus strengthened, Kryuchkov continued to press for a slowdown in reforms, and sought to advance his policies behind law-and-order rhetoric.

At this stage, Kryuchkov publicly applauded Gorbachev's position. Five months before the 1991 coup attempt, while being interviewed by Japan NHK General Television Network (March 7, 1991), Kryuchkov said that the President had "reacted responsibly" in the face of "divisiveness." Asked whether Gorbachev was likely to retire in the near future, Kryuchkov said that "literally thousands of telegrams have been received by the President, supporting Gorbachev's political course."

From our perspective of being able to consider the developments of later that year, Kryuchkov's reaction to a question concerning a possible anti-Gorbachev coup has a distinctly professional ring. He said, "As far as a coup is concerned, in order for something like this to actually happen, a number of conditions would have to exist. There would have to be an organization, with forces and individuals willing to take risks, resting on a solid social basis. However, that is something the KGB has not observed. That is why I can say that, so far, we can guarantee that this will not happen." In other interviews, the question of a possible coup came up again and again, but always with the assumption that the KGB would act as a watchdog against such a conspiracy, rather than as an active participant or initiator.

Two months before the coup, Kryuchkov delivered yet another combative speech. On June 17, during a closed session of the USSR Supreme Soviet, he warned that Western intelligence agencies were using "agents of influence" to destroy the Soviet Union. He cited an alleged U.S. Central Intelligence Agency plan, dating back to 1977, designed to train such agents to occupy key positions within the Soviet government for subversive purposes. He said that the CIA had, "in recent times," worked on "plans for optimizing hostile activities aimed at the breakup of Soviet society and disorganization of the socialist economy."

Kryuchkov's talk implied that advocates of perestroyka had, in effect, acted in the interest of destructive Western forces and were thus guilty of treason, directly or indirectly. He said that the West was offering economic aid on conditions of structural changes in the Soviet Union that amounted to a dismantling of the nation. "Among these conditions," he said, "is the carrying out of fundamental reforms in the country, not as they are envisioned by us, but as dreamed up across the ocean." Among these demands he cited "cuts by the Soviet Union in defense spending below tolerable limits, the cutting of relations with countries friendly to us, concessions on the so-called Baltic question, and so on."

*Komsomolskaya Pravda* (July 5, 1991), in a shrewdly prophetic satirical comment on the Kryuchkov speech, said that "the relevant conclusion" to be drawn from his warnings would lead all the way to the top of Soviet leadership. The article suggested, "Any politician who opposes the 1980 model of the USSR is undoubtedly an Agent of Influence. Right up to the country's President, who launched perestroyka."

In the end, after the abortive coup, Gorbachev and Kryuchkov continued to speak of each other more in sorrow than in anger. Each had seen the other as something of a mirror image of himself; had projected his own principles and aims upon the other; had hoped against hope that the other one would act as he, himself, would have acted. After all, they had so much in common! Kryuchkov told his interrogators that he had hoped to convince Gorbachev—while the President was down vacationing in the Crimea—to "give up his position" at least for a time, with the understanding that "he might return later." Kryuchkov had hoped that his old colleague from back in the Andropov days might see things his way. Gorbachev, in turn, had misjudged his KGB chief. He confessed to an interviewer for *Literaturnaya Gazeta* (December 4, 1991), "To me, to a significant degree, what mattered, aside from what I knew myself, was that Andropov had supported him." He spoke of Andropov as "a man of great intellect, resolutely set against corruption." How, then, had this prompted Gorbachev to put his trust in Kryuchkov? This is what Gorbachev said:

"I was associated with him [Andropov] for a long time. I would not say we had a very close relationship, but I knew him well, and we used to meet regularly. And that is why I took on Kryuchkov, of whom Andropov had a high opinion. Anyway, where do you find people for that sphere? Andropov's attitude toward Kryuchkov was decisive for me."

Yes, Gorbachev admitted, Yuri Andropov had not been perfect: "I don't want to idealize him." Gorbachev realized that Andropov's "ideological views and his involvement in combating dissidence" had been "shortcomings." And so Gorbachev's inability to break with the past, with a tradition of ruthlessness and illegality, had clouded his judgment. Out of respect for the opinions of a dead spymaster, he had hired a man who misunderstood and finally betrayed him.

# 3

# Ever-New Image Making

Following a totally unprecedented invitation, leaders of fifty-six Russian parties, representing the whole political spectrum, assembled at Moscow's former KGB headquarters, 12 Lubyanka Street, on June 11, 1992. They had been invited by Andrei Chernenko, director of the Public Relations Office of the Russian Ministry of Security, successor to the KGB's domestic operations. The crowd filled the huge conference room used previously by the KGB Collegium, the agency's inner circle. It fell to Vladimir Zhirinovsky—head of the Liberal Democratic Party, and a Russian nationalist firebrand—to quip, "There is, after all, one force in this country that can bring us all together!" Public relations director Chernenko left no doubt that he called the meeting to redress the Ministry's still tainted ex-KGB image, to reassure the political leaders of its no longer sinister position—and to dramatize a need for the Ministry's active role and continued existence.

The political leaders were assured that the Ministry did not, as of old, keep them under surveillance, nor did it tap their telephone wires. "Operational investigatory work," they were told, required the approval of the Russian General Prosecutor (roughly equivalent to the U.S. Attorney General) and was only ordered if a person represented "a threat to matters that fall within the competence of security organs." Asked whether former KGB officers were continuing to work within the new Ministry, the party leaders were told, "Yes, they are!" The officer added that, while "a whole host of leading workers from the USSR security organs have been dismissed, the majority of ordinary operational staffers are continuing to serve; after all, it takes from five to seven years to train a high-quality senior officer."

The briefing officers recalled that various former KGB intelligence operations had been separated: "Foreign intelligence, the government communications system, government protection, and a number of para-military structures have been separated-out as independent state institutions." The party leaders were reminded that originally, following the coup attempt of August 1991, the Border Guards had also been separated from the KGB; however, "the complex situation regarding Russia's borders made it necessary to revert to the time-tested position whereby border troops were an integral part of the security organs." Consequently, they became reattached to the KGB's domestic successor, Russia's Security Ministry.

While the KGB's public relations efforts reached a crescendo during the Gorbachev years, they began even earlier. As far back as 1984, the agency sponsored a competition for the best books, motion pictures, and television shows on internal security and foreign intelligence activities. The weekly *Literaturnaya Gazeta* (May 16, 1984) announced that the KGB was offering prizes for such artistic creations glorifying its work, aimed at the celebration of its seventieth anniversary in 1987.

Somewhat stiffly, in 1988 the KGB's twenty-first conference approached the challenge of a new openness. Meeting on December 17, top officials discussed ways of putting the agency's best foot forward. Though it was not used to endearing itself to the public, the KGB cited incidents that might be publicized, such as help to earthquake victims or the rescue of children from a hijacked plane. Lending authority to the meeting was the presence of the KGB's former director, Victor M. Chebrikov, then a member of the Politburo. His successor, Vladimir Kryuchkov, delivered the keynote address.

Characteristically for the period, much emphasis was still placed on the role of the secret police, the "heroic Chekists" as the "shield and sword" of the Soviet state. Loyalty to the Communist Party was dutifully emphasized, although rather uncomfortably phrased: "All party decisions and work on their fulfillment are geared to enhancing Communists' responsibility for the performance of their service duty, to defend the revolutionary transformations of the Soviet state and society." In the next breath, the KGB sought to prove the continued need for its existence: "It is a fact that the West's special services have not curtailed their subversive activities in the face of our restructuring. On the contrary, it has in some ways become even more energetic and sophisticated, primarily in terms of the acquisition of state and military secrets. In the last few years USSR KGB organs have exposed and instituted criminal proceedings against more than twenty dangerous agents of capitalist countries' intelligence services who had engaged in espionage."

Kryuchkov made increasing efforts to trim the KGB's sails to the winds of glasnost. He told *Izvestia* (May 6, 1989) that his agency had adopted "a very important resolution" entitled "KGB and Glasnost." He promised that "our future activities will not be as secret as they were until recently." He qualified such new openness this way: "While observing our professional principles, without which the Committee [of State Security] work is inconceivable, we will brief the public more widely on our work. We plan to report on the major and important operations conducted by our service." The next day, *Pravda* reported that the KGB Collegium had decided to engage in an internal reeducation program, while noting "the Soviet people's legitimate and growing interest in KGB activities." It announced the appearance of a column, "The USSR KGB Reports and Comments," in the weekly *Argumenty i Fakty*, as well as wider coverage of KGB activities on television programs. The KGB Collegium added:

"At the same time, the process of broadening *glasnost* in the activities of USSR KGB organs and troops still does not fully accord with the demands of the times and needs to be deepened and filled with specific content. The lack of public information about the tasks and rights of state security organs, and about the nature and the specific results of their activity, sometimes creates a false picture of the work of Chekists, dulls working people's sense of vigilance, and contributes to the emergence of various kinds of rumors and fabrications."

Cautious as this approach was, it clearly encountered internal resistance. For too long, the KGB had treated the public with disdain, created a mysterious image behind a wall of secrecy, and regarded reports on its actual activities as near-heresy. The KGB Collegium now took great pains to denounce the "excessive restraints with which leaders of certain subdivisions undertake a direct dialogue with a mass audience," and declared that "their attempts to avoid meetings with the public on the pretext of the secret nature of Chekist work, are inadmissible."

The KGB leadership outlined what were, in effect, directives for increased public relations contacts. These included future meetings of KGB officers with groups of workers, with "ideological establishments, creative unions, the public of higher educational institutions, and the mass media." Among themes to be advanced were such noble efforts as "sociopolitical measures organized by the Chekists," as well as the establishment of "rooms and museums of Chekist-military glory, to cover in great depth the history and the contemporary activity of KGB organs and troops, and to organize news conferences, 'roundtables,' and thematic debates in labor collectives on a regular basis."

The KGB's ventures into public relations managed to be at first overly cautious, and then folksy to the point of cloying. Early in 1989, correspondents for the military paper *Krasnaya Zvezda* were invited to visit the premises of the traditionally notorious Lefortovo Prison. In a three-article series entitled "KGB Investigates: How State Security Organs Work Today," readers were taken inside the building at 3A Energeticheskaya Street, home of the KGB's "Investigation Department." They were told that the place—one of sixteen jails built by Catherine the Great—no longer served as a prison, but did contain "interview cells."

Readers were assured that, while KGB investigators might occasionally display "shortcomings" in their work, they no longer practiced ruthless methods similar to "the distortions of the thirties, forties and early fifties." The reporters were told that the KGB's interrogation unit was firmly guided by "Soviet laws and under the supervision of the USSR Prosecutor's Office and, to a certain extent, the Chief Military Prosecutor's Office." Reporting on the visit in the paper's issues of March 10, 11, and 12, the correspondents—quite in awe of it all—acknowledged that they had been strictly supervised: "During our entire stay in the Investigation Department, neither of us was left unattended by KGB staffers for a single second. And not because they did not trust us. It is just there are no exceptions to the rules; they carry out instructions to the letter—that is their style!"

Later that year, the foreign press was invited to a preview of a fifty-five-minute film called *The KGB Today*, clearly designed to make the much-feared agency appear ever-so human. The film presented the KGB in such a homey manner that some scenes caused a good deal of hilarity among viewers. At one point, Colonel Igor N. Prelin, the KGB's press officer, guided the cameras into the Lefortovo Prison's kitchen where both vegetarian and nonvegetarian dishes were being prepared. Prelin dipped a huge spoon into a vat of porridge and complimented the cook on his method of cooking pearl barley, using the *bain-marie* method. In another scene, the film's narrator complimented a KGB captain on the style of his haircut. Colonel Prelin, a twenty-seven-year veteran of the service, summarized the KGB officer's complex role in verse, as follows:

*We wage a war with no rules,*
*A snowstorm with no end.*

*We share a battle with a foe*
*Or get a bullet from a friend.*

The film, which Kryuchkov praised as accurately reflecting "life, work and struggle of the KGB"—although "not in all aspects"—created a precedent by showing the inside of the KGB main building, complete with marble staircase, conference rooms, and Chekists undergoing self-defense training. In later years, these once-hidden interiors, including the office occupied by Felix Dzerzhinsky, founder of the secret service, were to become public exhibits—for a fee, and only for a limited time.

The PR campaign went into high gear with the opening of the USSR KGB Center of Public Relations on September 11, 1991. With offices on the third floor of the Lubyanka building, and under the direction of the appropriately suave and accessible General Alexander N. Karbainov, the Center survived numerous changes in names, structure, and personnel during the following years. The public relations office implemented directives of the KGB Collegium, including installation of a small museum of espionage items that dramatized KGB ingenuity and the stealth of foreign "special services."

Throughout the year, the KGB's public relations campaign had gained momentum. Perhaps its oddest by-product was the selection, in October, of a "Miss KGB," allegedly chosen during a beauty contest organized by "younger officers" of the agency. The winner, twenty-three-year-old Katya Mayorova, was widely shown tying a bulletproof vest around her upper body. Mayorova had been on the KGB staff for six years, since leaving high school. She was quoted as saying, "I'm glad I won! Not that I feel like a real beauty queen. It's sheer entertainment, after all. I had the time of my life, and the audience enjoyed it, too." The contest was not limited to physical appearance, but included shooting, wrestling, and walking with a dancing step while wearing a bulletproof vest weighing close to fifteen pounds. Mayorova promptly gave press and television interviews, projecting the image of the "modern KGB"—telling her audiences she had started work as a secretary, she underwent an all-around training that included using a Makarova handgun, but she also loved the Beatles and played the guitar.

Over and over, to domestic and foreign audiences, the KGB emphasized that its bloody record was a thing of the distant past, and that its staff now worked strictly within the law, protecting the citizenry, and fighting crime and subversion. Officers—from Kryuchkov on down—gave interviews, provided one guided tour after another, answered questions on television shows, and began to put their new message into print through articles, magazines, and books, at home and abroad.

One of the KGB's most comprehensive public relations presentations at that time was given by General Karbainov to the Istanbul (Turkey) newspaper *Milliyet* (November 26, 1990). Karbainov acknowledged that, in the past, the KGB had not even served to function as "a state security organ" but simply to "strengthen Stalin's personal rule," and had regarded itself as "above the state and even the Communist Party." He confessed that "there remains the impression that the methods used in Stalin's era are still being used today." To counteract this negative image, Karbainov said, "we must open ourselves to the people as much as we can. We must inform the citizens on the concrete results of the work we do. We must explain why the people need us."

In other words, the KGB was engaged in a PR campaign to justify its own continued existence, and it used all available means to ingratiate itself with opinion-making levels of Soviet society, and with the community as a whole. For example, on November 15, 1990, KGB officials participated in a meeting of the Association of Victims of Illegal Oppression, using the opportunity to state that the agency's Fifth Directorate—designed to combat "ideological subversion"—had been abolished; a new subdivision—to "protect the Soviet constitutional system"—had replaced it.

Under the title "Ecology and the KGB," Moscow Television (December 23, 1990) interviewed V. Leshin, the head of a unidentified KGB subunit. The interview developed a xenophobic slant when Leshin stated that the KGB's protection of the "ecology" dealt with the alleged delivery of Western equipment containing "concealed defects." Leshin, echoing Kryuchkov's much-publicized charge against foreign aid deliveries, said the KGB sought to "prevent sabotage" through Western shipments of "equipment, technology and produce of animal and vegetable origin" that contained agricultural pests, as well as "agricultural plant diseases and weeds." Leshin sought to bolster the need for KGB vigilance by using the term "biological and chemical terrorism" as a danger to the environment.

A more benign view of ecological matters was presented by Major General E. N. Yakovlev, director of the KGB's Intelligence Analysis Section. He told *Pravda* (December 20, 1990) that, in 1985, Western intelligence services showed concern over "problems of sources of fresh water and its utilization." This prompted KGB analysts to examine the Western viewpoint that "gigantic projects to irrigate waterless areas, and particularly to divert rivers, are not cost-effective." For years, just such projects had been under way in the Soviet Union, designed to divert northern rivers as part of a highly ambitious and controversial irrigation project. According to General Yakovlev, the KGB analysts used the Western findings, applied them to the situation in the USSR, and warned against the high risks of such projects in terms of water loss and ecological changes. Yakovlev said that the KGB submitted its findings to the USSR Council of Ministers, but encountered "several unpleasant moments," with reactions from the various institutions being for the most part "abusive." Nevertheless, the projects were abandoned, and (according to this version) the good guys—the ecology-minded KGB—triumphed!

Other KGB public relations campaigns during this period dealt with several cases of alleged "economic sabotage," and with the arrest on July 1, 1986, of one V. Potashov, a former employee of the USSR Academy of Science, as an alleged CIA agent, and his imprisonment for thirteen years in June 1987. The image of the KGB as a corps of crime-busters was emphasized in a September 29, 1990, meeting between agency officials and teachers functioning as "propaganda workers." Radio Moscow noted that this meeting "marked the beginning of the new school year in the political education system. The new teachers learned many new things about the present-day security bodies. Activities in intelligence and counterintelligence and the fight against terrorism were discussed." But, the report added, those present were "most interested in the fight against organized crime."

During 1991, and as the August coup attempt approached, the KGB's public relations campaign developed cracks and began to emphasize negative themes. Early in the year (January 23), the KGB Public Relations Center announced that sixty-four KGB officers in the city of Sverdlovsk had published an open letter in a newspaper (*Rossiskaya Gazeta*, November 29, 1990), claiming that, despite its protestations to the contrary, the agency continued to present "a potential danger to the democratic transformation" of the country. The protesters charged that the KGB still managed to put the interests of the Communist Party above those of society as a whole, and that it successfully evaded supervision (oversight) by the Supreme Soviet.

The PR office reported that several of the daring letter-signers had been "invited" to a January conference, apparently in Moscow, to set them straight on the KGB's new policies. The conference leaders decided that the Sverdlovsk KGB was out of touch with developments and "poorly informed" about changes within the KGB practices, and that local "discipline was slack." The PR office concluded its announcement with the assurance that the Sverdlovsk whistle-blowers would be called to order: "Confidence was expressed that Sverdlovsk's security officers, with a sense of great responsibility, will make a sober and principled analysis of the atmosphere prevailing in the collective, will do everything necessary to consolidate their ranks to ensure our motherland's security, and will honorably fulfill their duty toward the Soviet people."

On a popular note of public enlightenment, the KGB opened a pavilion at the *Pravda* Festival, which the daily paper held on May 3 and 4. The pavilion operated under the slogan "KGB without Secrets." The KGB public relations men announced wittily that, "despite these times of market forces, entrance is free." The booth featured video displays of KGB derring-do, lectures about the fight against organized crime, and tributes to the heroism of secret agents during World War II. Several displays and lectures dealt with the operations of "Western subversion centers."

By mid-year, emphasis on the threat of foreign intelligence operations increased. Lieutenant General Vadim Kirpichenko, First Deputy of the KGB's Foreign Intelligence Department, stated in a lengthy interview with the *Novosti* press service (June 4, 1991) that "it is more difficult for Soviet secret agents to operate in the United States than for their American counterparts to work here." He based this claim on the assumption that recent changes in Soviet society had "created conditions that make it easier for Western secret agents to establish contacts with Soviet citizens." By contrast, he maintained, "such radical changes have not occurred in American society." That such a trend would call for more KGB action was a point made (May 24, 1991) in an interview with the press service *Interfax*. Anatoli Klimenko, identified as a senior counterintelligence officer, put it this way: "Foreign intelligence services see the current situation in this country as extremely favorable. Naturally, this strengthens the role of the Soviet counter-intelligence service."

The need to counteract foreign espionage was also emphasized during an unprecedented "open house" at the USSR KGB Higher School, 4 Pelshe Street in Moscow, on July 7, 1991. It was a Sunday, and curious youngsters crowded the main hall of the eight-story brick building that covered two city blocks. The KGB Higher School was founded in 1930, and the young visitors were given a dramatic history of the KGB's achievements. They were told by Anatoly I. Petrovich, Candidate of Technical Sciences, that U.S. intelligence had a budget of more than $20 billion, and that "of the more than forty spy satellites in space, some monitor radio relay links within the [Soviet] Union, including intercity telephone conversations."

The youngsters saw demonstrations on how to monitor telephone talks with the aid of an ordinary radio receiver, how to utilize a television set for monitoring work, and how a conversation can be recorded through a wall five meters thick. The visitors were taken to the school's living quarters, its sports hall, and its one-million-book library. In keeping with the KGB's theme that its staffers were just regular folk, the visitors were invited to apply for jobs with the agency, told that its five-year course included from three hundred to five hundred students per semester, and that most applicants were between seventeen and twenty-five years old.

Into the midst of this goodwill campaign burst KGB chief Kryuchkov's speech of June 17, to a closed session of the Supreme Soviet, charging that the Soviet Union was being changed, or virtually destroyed, by the imposition of "fundamental reforms in the country, not as they are envisioned by us but as dreamed up across the ocean." He warned that the CIA sought to foster "hostile activities aimed at the breakup of Soviet society and disorganization of the socialist economy."

Within two months, Kryuchkov emerged as the key figure in the August coup attempt, the KGB was renamed and subdivided—and its public relations staff was facing unprecedented problems. General Karbainov, interviewed almost immediately by the Italian daily *La Repubblica* (August 24, 1991), was quick to admit, "Of course, we have our faults and our responsibilities. But we ordinary aides of the Committee [of State Security] were dragged into this terrible business by the KGB chiefs, without ever having made any decisions, without ever having been consulted, and in many cases without agreeing with the decisions that were being made."

Vadim Bakatin, who replaced Kryuchkov, was easily his own most valuable public relations asset, projecting the image of a truly modernized and purified secret service. Bakatin himself gave interview after interview, anticipating a truly "democratic" KGB—if not immediately, at least in the foreseeable future. The doors of the Lubyanka building were thrown open even more widely than before, although at a price! For several weeks, visitors, reporters, and television crews roamed the KGB headquarters, or at least parts of it. Eventually, for a fee equivalent to U.S. $35, anyone could join a guided tour of the onetime *sanctum sanctorum*. The tour, which lasted three hours, was conducted by such knowledgeable guides as retired counterintelligence officer Vladimir Ivlev and Lieutenant Colonel Valery Vozdvizhensky. It covered the KGB Museum, the "Dzerzhinsky Room" (complete with the agency founder's Communist Party membership card), as well as the offices used by Yuri Andropov.

The KGB guides claimed that the agency needed the currency the visitors brought, but some officials became too grasping for the representatives of foreign media. Jean-Jacques Vidal-Huber, of Brussels-based Way Press International, wrote Bakatin (November 26, 1991) that Super Channel, a European TV company, had to pay $400 for an interview with KGB Vice-chairman Nikolai Stolyarov. Under this arrangement, Super Channel purchased the "organizational-consultative assistance on the part of the KGB Public Relations Center for filming of an interview with the USSR KGB Vice-Chairman." But Vidal-Huber felt distinctly shortchanged by the deal; he wrote, "The Center's 'assistance' was limited to a visit, with the accompaniment of a guide, to Yuri Andropov's former apartment, several fleeting moments spent at a 'museum' consisting of several old photographs depicting the feats of KGB agents in their fight against their American counterparts, and a 20-minute interview with Vice Chairman Stolyarov, who, incidentally, quoted from a number of documents." The TV team had also been promised that on the next day it might film the inner courtyard of the Lubyanka in daylight. However, Vidal-Huber wrote, "despite my insistent requests, our 'assistant' from the KGB was unable to take us there again, and ultimately disappeared without a trace."

With the dissolution of the Soviet Union, and the further reallocation and renaming of KGB departments, such ventures in KGB exhibitionism came to an end. On February 28, 1992, the guided tours of the headquarters offices and of the Museum were abruptly discontinued. A duty officer named Victor Berinov told disappointed visitors, "We have new bosses, and they are making new decisions." One such decision, apparently, was in favor of new decorum and old secrecy.

In due course, each KGB successor agency established its own public relations office. When the domestic operations of the KGB were finally reestablished as the Russian Ministry of Security, the ministry quickly set up its own PR office, with Andrei Chernenko as its director. In one of his first press conferences, Chernenko had to parry questions about the alleged sale of KGB archives and the apparent continuation of telephone wiretapping. During the following months, the Ministry's Public Relations Office had to deal with a variety of delicate questions, including the purge of personnel accused of corrupt practices. Chernenko was particularly agitated by rumors that the Ministry was keeping under surveillance a number of opposition members of the Russian Federation Supreme Soviet. He said that there existed a "campaign to discredit the security organs, planned by highly intelligent people, and we assume not on Russian territory."

Chernenko was asked whether Kryuchkov had been "possibly correct, after all," when, back in 1991, he said that some people were acting as "agents of influence" in the service of foreign powers. As quoted in *Pravda* (September 30, 1992), this was Chernenko's reply: "I will answer that question somewhat differently. We have unequivocal, verified information that it was clearly said, at a foreign intelligence community's plenary conference, that the priorities for intelligence activities proper, against Russia, take second place to priorities for activity relating to the further and final collapse of the Russian special services."

In order to reassure a wider public about the functions of the Security Ministry, Chernenko had appeared on a TV show over the Ostankino network (July 30, 1992). The thirty-minute program, "The Lubyanka through the Eyes of the Lubyanka," contained a video record of Ministry officials meeting with the diverse group of party leaders on June 11, shots of the Lefortovo investigative center, and interviews with several agents. Chernenko explained the purpose of this program as follows:

"We would like you, through seeing the faces of our staff members, and the work in which we are engaged, to realize that the various fabrications alleging that the state security bodies and the Army structures are preparing some kind of coup, and are attempting to weaken the presidential power structure and parliament, have nothing in common with reality. The main thing is that, in the final analysis, politicians come and go, while the state remains. What kind of state remains depends to a great extent on the people with whom I work."

Such Kryuchkov-type rhetoric, coming from the KGB's domestic successor agency's PR spokesman, was not echoed by his foreign intelligence counterparts. At first, when the KGB's First Chief Directorate was transformed into the Soviet Central Intelligence Service, its PR chief was a man who may well have done double-duty for the KGB abroad. Yuri Kobaladze, a graduate from the Moscow Institute of International Relations, had served as a radio reporter in Great Britain from 1977 to 1984, and covered Gorbachev's travels to Malta, the United States, and France. In commenting on the CIA during a television interview (December 6,

1991) Kobaladze spoke with an air of collegial concern, emphasizing a need for greater mutual understanding:

"American intelligence is interested in the processes which are taking place in our country. They really should know, in order to predict correctly, in order to provide a correct evaluation and forecast to [their] leadership, so that the leadership makes fewer misjudgments. There is a kind of stabilizing factor in this mechanism. We should follow the same methods. We should know what is happening there. There are some areas in which we are finding common fields of interests, for example, in international terrorism. We may even cooperate here and in the non-proliferation of nuclear weapons."

Despite his obviously diplomatic demeanor, Kobaladze was replaced by a former journalistic colleague of Yevgeny Primakov, the new chief of the Russian Foreign Intelligence Service. On November 18, 1991, Primakov named Tatyana Samolis to direct his agency's Public Relations Center. Samolis confessed that the appointment was "completely unexpected," and said she had "never given any thought to the existence" of intelligence agencies. She had gone to work for *Pravda*, where she met Primakov, right after graduating from Moscow State University. She spent eighteen years on the editorial staff of the Communist Party's newspaper, much of the time working with letters to the editor, which suggested article topics. In 1986 she wrote an article suggesting that the Communist Party might be "purified" by ridding itself of corrupt influences. Eventually, in her last article for *Pravda*, "Tragedy without Optimism," she stated that the party was beyond renewal. According to a biographical sketch released by the Tass news agency on the day of her appointment, she left *Pravda* "after long and painful considerations." Primakov promptly offered her the PR job at the foreign intelligence office. At that time she had been married for twenty-five years to a journalist of Lithuanian ancestry, and had a son who studied at the Asia and Africa Institute, Moscow State University.

It fell to Samolis to provide a brief PR version of the Russian parliamentary bill on foreign intelligence. According to her summary (June 19, 1992), the bill contained the following key elements:

1. Foreign intelligence is a constituent part of ensuring security of Russia.
2. Intelligence activity is carried out by special state agencies set up for this purpose.

3. Bodies of foreign intelligence are designed to defend the security of individual, society, and the state from outside threats.

4. General guidance over the bodies of foreign intelligence shall be carried out by the President of the Russian Federation.

5. Results of intelligence activity shall be reported to supreme bodies of state power and administration of Russia.

6. Control over the activity of foreign intelligence shall be exercised by the Supreme Soviet of the Russian Federation.

Samolis concluded the announcement with an assurance that was eminently suitable for a public relations presentation: "Methods of work used by intelligence should not infringe on the rights and freedom of citizens or run counter to applicable democratic legislation."

Overall, an analysis of the basic public relations themes advanced before as well as after the August 1991 coup attempt reveals that their essentials remained remarkably constant. These themes can be summarized as follows:

1. Espionage and secret police functions are a universal tradition, and Moscow is merely following a worldwide practice in maintaining a multifaceted intelligence structure.

2. The KGB used to act as a guardian of law and order; now, with an economy in chaos and society in upheaval, the existence of its successor agencies is ever more essential.

3. While other pillars of society—such as the Communist Party—have disappeared, and the armed forces have been experiencing moral and organizational disarray, the KGB successor agencies, including the Border Guards, have gained a heightened importance in maintaining social structures.

4. The KGB successor agencies are pledged to uphold the law, and they themselves have pledged to operate strictly within the law.

5. With alleged subversion (supposedly aided from abroad) a threat to the nation, and domestic crime rampant, a vig-

ilant secret police must act as a bulwark against lawlessness and anarchy.

6. The KGB's successor agencies have broken with the despicable practices of Soviet secret police agencies of the past, and the excesses of that tradition should now, at last, be forgotten.

# 4

# The Gorbachev–KGB Connection

A head of state needs inside information; he needs the kind of confidential data that enables him to anticipate events, in order to act on the basis of maximum knowledge. In other words, he depends heavily on the briefings supplied by the secret services. Also, and perhaps inevitably, heads of state tend to be increasingly isolated, despite their frequent travels and many high-level contacts. And for this reason, they are in danger of getting a distorted, preselected view of the world around them.

During the years and months preceding the August 1991 coup attempt, Mikhail Gorbachev ran the risk of becoming an information prisoner of the KGB. Its foreign intelligence services fed him supposedly reliable information that the United States was even preparing a possible nuclear attack; its domestic network provided Gorbachev with a daily dose of news of social disintegration, economic breakdown, near-anarchy. On the instructions of Vladimir Kryuchkov, Gorbachev was being manipulated into a state of mind so agitated as to endorse the establishment of a nationwide "state of emergency"—all but inviting the planned power takeover under KGB direction.

Gorbachev—though often a master of elusive generalities—was quite precise about this period and its dangers when he spoke on Japan's NHK General Television Network (February 12, 1992): "They tried to make me suspicious of the West whenever I agreed to cooperate with them or concluded some kind of agreement. Such information had a definite purpose. I was aware of the kind of thing the KGB did, and I knew that among reports received from the KGB was information designed to put pressure on the President [that is, Gorbachev himself]."

Kryuchkov's presidential disinformation apparatus worked in tandem with Defense Minister Dmitri T. Yazov's. To make sure that he received carefully orchestrated information from separate sources, Gorbachev recalled, "demagogue information was spread through different channels, aimed at hurting the integrity of the Soviet Union's foreign policy." Gorbachev noted that "information supplied to me by the various armed forces' departments was to the effect that the West was making the best of the given situation to expand its arms, or something like that."

The effort to manipulate President Gorbachev encompassed the KGB's domestic apparatus and its connections within the Communist Party's Central Committee. As Gorbachev remembered the procedure, it usually began with a statement by the Central Committee "objecting to my policy"—a statement then handed to local party offices. Next, he said, "they held meetings in these places and discussed the statement. After the discussions, the protest statement was put to a vote, and I was informed of the result of the voting. The purpose was to put some kind of pressure on me."

Gorbachev also found that military intelligence was echoed by the KGB's First Chief Directorate, its foreign intelligence branch. He told the Moscow TV program *Chief Editors' Club* (February 7, 1992) that the KGB used to time its dire warnings about alleged U.S. war preparations to coincide with domestic crises that put Gorbachev under special stress. He recalled that, "at a certain stage, in perfect timing with growing confrontations within society and in the party," he could "predict what the Chief Intelligence Directorate would send me—absolutely, absolutely!—to show that American Imperialism was continuing to arm itself and preparing for war, in order to attain military superiority, exploiting our specific difficulties."

Although, in retrospect, Gorbachev was able to analyze this pattern of manipulation, he nevertheless yielded to pressures from the Kryuchkov group in late 1990 and early 1991; the result was a shift in top-level personnel and policies that satisfied this group, at least temporarily. Yet, to speak of the Kryuchkov group as a separate unit, or of a distinctly separate KGB elite, would mean to separate it unduly from Gorbachev himself. Extremist critics even went so far as to accuse Gorbachev of secret participation in the August coup, of merely playing a part in a well-rehearsed historic charade. One participant on a Moscow television panel even charged that the President had discussed the planned coup with a plotter beforehand; Gorbachev threatened to sue the man for libel. Anti-Gorbachev conspiracy buffs were corrected by Yevgeny Lisov,

Deputy Chief Prosecutor of the participants in the attempted coup, who told a news conference in Moscow (January 21, 1992) that Gorbachev had given the conspirators "no hint, either directly or indirectly, that he was with them." Lisov did, however, suggest that the Kryuchkov group's perception of Gorbachev had led it to believe that he would, sooner or later, go along with them. The prosecutor said, "However, his long relations with members of the conspiracy, who were his closest associates, and some special features of his character, gave them, in our view, the right to think that sooner or later, after one, two, three days, they would be able to draw him to their side."

According to these findings, it seems fair to conclude that serious misconceptions were mutual: Gorbachev had misjudged the men he appointed to top positions, mainly Kryuchkov; and, of course, Kryuchkov & Company misjudged Gorbachev's response to their campaign of manipulation and to their final attempt using emotional extortion. Gorbachev ultimately refused not only to be under KGB house arrest at Foros, but to be pressured into becoming an actual KGB coconspirator. And yet, through much of his career, there had been a Gorbachev–KGB connection, which at times had been demanding, directive, and decisive.

It is worth recalling that Gorbachev was heir to the organization and ideological inheritance of Yuri Andropov, who served as KGB chief from 1967 to 1982. Andropov's career illustrated that, despite organic rivalries between various Soviet or Russian government departments, remarkable interchanges were routine. At one time or another, Andropov worked in the Foreign Ministry, the Communist Party's Central Committee, and the KGB. And he finally succeeded Leonid Brezhnev as actual head of the Soviet state, which position Andropov held until his death in February 1984.

Gorbachev's long association with Andropov apparently left lasting impressions on his general outlook, his choice in associates, and even on his terminology. (He did not, alas, inherit Andropov's brevity of speech!) When referring to Andropov's high intellectual capacity and his battles against corruption, Gorbachev may have thought in terms of his own aspirations, his efforts to achieve aims that Andropov had originally set. In fact, if one reads some of Andropov's speeches, they sound remarkably like "Early Gorbachev." For instance, on November 22, 1982, Yuri Andropov said, "Evidently, these forces of inertia and old habits still have their effects. Or perhaps some people simply do not know how to tackle the job. It is necessary to think what kind of encouragement should be given to these comrades. The main thing is to speed up work in improving the entire sphere of economic management—administration, planning and the economic mechanism. Conditions have to be provided—both economic and organizational—that will stimulate qualitative production work, initiative and enterprise." It was apparently during Andropov's tenure as KGB chief that Gorbachev—although not actually enlisted by the KGB—was approached by Andropov's deputy, Semen K. Tsvigun. Gorbachev told *Komsomolskaya Pravda* (November 7, 1992) that Tsvigun had told him, in 1968, "It is a pity we lost you— we could do with someone like you in the organization." Gorbachev quickly added, "Anyway, I then found out what the KGB was like, what a terrifying system the KGB was. And for a long time I discussed it privately with my closest colleagues. I was waiting for the right moment to reorganize the system. It was difficult then, and not much has changed even now."

During his first years in power, Gorbachev's policies did, in fact, seem little more than a fresh implementation of Andropov's blueprint. He had apparently come to power with KGB backing. Andropov had followed Brezhnev; Konstantin Chernenko had followed Andropov; and when Chernenko died in March 1985, a crucial vote in the Politburo decided the choice of his successor. Yegor Ligachev (later an opponent of Gorbachev's policies) mentioned this power play when he spoke at the Nineteenth Communist Party Congress in July 1988. According to Jeremy R. Azrael in his booklet *The KGB in Kremlin Politics*, "Ligachev identified Chebrikov as one of the three members of the leadership whose outspoken support of Gorbachev turned the political tide in the latter's favor." Azrael added that Ligachev's statement "lent additional credibility" to a report by Russian historian Roy A. Medvedev that "it was not until Chebrikov made it clear that the KGB was firmly on Gorbachev's side, and was prepared to play political hardball on his behalf, that Gorbachev's opponents withdrew their support" from rival candidates.

Like other leaders before and after him, Gorbachev faced the risky task of using the secret police while avoiding the danger of being used by it. His predecessors had sought to clip the secret police's wings— ever since Secret Police Chief Lavrenti Beria, after Stalin's death, sought supreme power for himself. The rival leaders arrested Beria, tried him secretly, and had him shot. Boris Yeltsin—although harassed by the KGB for years—nevertheless made sure that its domestic operations continued, full-fledged, as the Russian Ministry of Security. During Gorbachev's regime, the KGB underwent a series of mixed cosmetic and substantive changes; but it remained a major force in society, and its leaders maintained a decisive influence on their nation's destiny.

Chebrikov, who had been KGB chief under Andropov and Chernenko, lasted with Gorbachev for three years. What led to a break between the two men closely resembled the issues that prompted Kryuchkov, Chebrikov's successor, to attempt the 1991 coup. Chebrikov's speeches from 1985 to 1988 sounded very much like Kryuchkov's during much of 1990 and 1991. The difference was that Kryuchkov operated on two levels: he paid lip service to liberal principles, including a reform of the KGB itself; at the same time, he felt that the country was under attack from without and within, and needed authoritarian control from the top. In September 1987, as Chebrikov celebrated the 110th birth of Felix Dzerzhinsky, founder of the secret police, he denounced the alleged efforts of "imperialist special services" to convert "Soviet people to the bourgeois understanding of democracy." He also accused Western intelligence services of using dissidents to commit "illegal actions" in order to "stir up yet another big fuss about alleged Soviet human rights violations." Clearly, Chebrikov disapproved of such Gorbachevian actions as the freeing of the distinguished dissident Andrei Sakharov, who had been under KGB house arrest and exile from Moscow.

When it came to a parting of their ways, *Pravda* carried the brief formal notice that "Comrade Gorbachev, M.S." was thanking "Comrade Chebrikov, V.M." for his "many years of active and fruitful activity in the party organs." Albert L. Weeks, in an article entitled "Gorbachev and the KGB" in the quarterly *Global Affairs* (Winter 1990), noted that Chebrikov's fortunes had fluctuated greatly during the months preceding his dismissal. Weeks observed that "the abruptness and terseness of the announcement of Chebrikov's retirement suggested an attitude of 'good riddance' on the part of the Gorbachev-led Politburo." Weeks assumed, as Gorbachev himself obviously did, that the replacement of Chebrikov by Kryuchkov would strengthen the President's hand and remove potential KGB threats to his position. Weeks said that "by this latest maneuver" Gorbachev had "succeeded in advancing himself well along the road to the assumption of one-person authority." Adding a note of caution, Professor Weeks wrote that Kryuchkov, "for now at least," seemed "content to play the role exclusively of policeman and intelligence chief, instead of a self-styled *eminence grise*. The latter status clearly had been Chebrikov's ambition in playing his erstwhile influential role as overseer of political and legal reform, as well as the new spokesman for the Kremlin's nationalities policy."

As it turned out, once Kryuchkov had moved from foreign intelligence to overall KGB direction, he quickly outdid his predecessor in trying to outflank Gorbachev and in placing his own hands on the country's controls. When more or less subtle pressures on the President failed to have their desired results, Kryuchkov and his fellow conspirators first pushed for governmental reorganization, but finally decided to kidnap Gorbachev and try to persuade him with threats and politicoemotional blackmail.

Just how thorough the precoup pressure had been, Gorbachev's own files revealed. After the abortive coup, investigators opened a safe that had been handled by the President's conspiratorial chief-of-staff, Valery Boldin. The Moscow paper *Rabochaya Tribuna* reported (January 7, 1992) that documents found in the Boldin safe showed the KGB had kept Gorbachev's political opponents under surveillance. The paper suggested that the KGB used these surveillance reports to manipulate Gorbachev "into an irreversible process of confrontation with Boris Yeltsin, and then to force him [Gorbachev] to head an antidemocratic coup, or at least to support a junta in one way or another." While the paper said that Gorbachev "did not once make use of material obtained by illegal means," it suggested that the information—which Kryuchkov channeled through Boldin—"created additional motives for confrontations within the Russian leadership and the general disintegration of power in the country."

The Moscow paper commented that discovery of the KGB's Yeltsin surveillance reports in Gorbachev's safe could explain "the dubious behavior of Boris Yeltsin, who literally drove Mikhail Gorbachev from his Kremlin office, even prior to the date agreed between them." Yeltsin himself told foreign journalists in Moscow (September 7, 1991) that he was shocked to realize that the KGB had kept him under constant surveillance since 1989. He said that files, films, and tapes had been discovered that provided the following information:

"All phones were tapped, absolutely all of them. Internal surveillance, outside surveillance, constant monitoring, full reports, and so on and so forth. Wherever I was, wherever I went, the KGB was constantly shadowing me—moreover, it was on the direct instructions of Kryuchkov that all of this was done. Now that all these safes have been opened, it is frightening to think that I was listened to wherever I went, even when I became President of Russia. Even then, all my phones were tapped, and I was under surveillance. That is what is frightening."

Alexander Rahr, Russian affairs specialist at Radio Free Europe/Radio

Liberty, who wrote "Gorbachev under Investigation" in the *RFE/RL Research Report* (February 14, 1992), observed that "Yeltsin did his utmost to make Gorbachev's departure as humiliating as possible." He gave these details: "While Gorbachev was still in power, thinking about his resignation speech, Yeltsin deprived him of everything but his Zil limousine and his personal bodyguards. [Six months later, annoyed at Gorbachev's continuing criticism, Yeltsin had his luxurious Zil replaced by a standard Volga sedan.] He sent his men to the Kremlin to count the computers, television sets, telephones, and other furnishings of value in Gorbachev's offices. Yeltsin also seized Gorbachev's presidential communication system in the Kremlin. Gorbachev was told to hand over to Yeltsin his 'black briefcase' containing nuclear codes and to quit no later than mid-January. On the day Gorbachev resigned, Yeltsin issued an edict privatizing Gorbachev's state-owned apartment in Moscow. Although he had promised earlier that Gorbachev's resignation would be handled 'in a civilized manner,' Yeltsin unceremoniously occupied Gorbachev's personal office in the Kremlin before the latter had even had time to clean out his desk. When Gorbachev came to his office on 27 December to remove personal papers, Yeltsin was already sitting in his chair; Gorbachev was forced to work in the office of his former chief of staff"—that is, the treacherous Boldin, keeper of incriminating KGB documents.

Was Gorbachev doing the moral and ethical thing when he collected KGB reports on Yeltsin and other high-level officials, and even on parliamentary delegates? Were these reports, of themselves, proof of any wrongdoing on his part? These questions troubled the coup investigators—who quickly found themselves stonewalled in their inquiries. Their dilemma was described by Lev Ponomarev, chairman of the Supreme Soviet's Commission Investigating the Causes and Circumstances of the August Coup. He told *Izvestia* (February 8, 1992) that Gorbachev's personal archive had, "unfortunately," come "under the control of the leader of the Russian president's [Yeltsin's] administration, Yuri Petrov, and access is no longer possible." Another dead end was reached by the investigators when they sought access to the files of the KGB foreign intelligence department, formerly directed by Kryuchkov. Ponomarev described their frustration: "After we tried to gain access to the First Chief Directorate's archives, Yevgeny Primakov himself came to the White House [seat of the Russian government], sidestepping the whole Supreme Soviet leadership. As a result, those archives have simply remained inaccessible to us."

A few days earlier, Foreign Intelligence Service chief Primakov had assured a parliamentary inquiry that "the intelligence service, as part of the former KGB, was not involved in the coup last August." But the investigators had their own reasons to feel put off by Primakov's refusal to permit a study of his department's files. Ponomarev recalled that one set of documents—complete with Gorbachev's handwritten notes—had mysteriously disappeared, literally overnight: "At one time our experts found, in the archives at Lubyanka, a First Chief Directorate document containing instructions on how the behaviour of USSR and Russian people's deputies, while traveling abroad, was to be observed: Whose money they live on, whom they meet, where they go, and so forth. This document, moreover, had comments written on it, in Gorbachev's own hand. The next day, the document vanished without a trace. The experts were later able to get hold of a copy of it; but, now, without Gorbachev's notes."

Once again, there arises the question of Gorbachev's use of KGB services, of his almost unavoidable concern with information that may be secretly obtained—but also his interest, as a practicing politician, in the day-to-day affairs of other political figures, whether allied or in opposition. (And there also arises the intriguing question of whether other Kremlin leaders used to receive KGB reports on *Gorbachev's* activities, correspondence, telephone calls, and personal contacts. Very likely, the answer to this question must be, "Yes, certainly!") Still, to what degree was Gorbachev personally responsible for KGB activities? One very forceful answer was given by Dr. Boris M. Pugachov, one of the experts employed by the parliamentary investigation commission. He told Moscow's Mayak Radio Network (February 4, 1992) that the commission had "carefully studied the correspondence between the President of the USSR [Gorbachev] and the leadership of the KGB during the eighties and nineties. Our conclusions are: attempts to exert pressure on the democratic forces, attempts to remove the democratic forces from the political arena, were being hatched by the Committee for State Security in the autumn of 1990. Kryuchkov repeatedly sent letters to Gorbachev, the aim of which was the introduction of a state of emergency and the use of acts of force and repressive actions against the democratic forces."

Pugachov offered a virtual indictment of Gorbachev: "We are deeply convinced that Gorbachev was informed about all these actions. Moreover, we came to the conclusion that Gorbachev bears political responsibility for the lack of control over the activity of the state security organs and for the clandestine activity that they carried out for a year to overthrow the legitimate bodies of power—this is Gorbachev's direct political responsibility. We found documents testifying to large-scale surveillance of Union and Russian deputies abroad, and it is striking that the most careful surveillance was of the deputies closest to Gorbachev." Pugachov alleged that, as President of the USSR, Gorbachev "was informed about" the "anti-constitutional activity" of the KGB and that he "took no steps" to stop it. Pugachov added that, throughout 1990 and 1991, the KGB "intercepted letters sent through the mail, examined correspondence and bugged telephone conversations; there were also secret searches of apartments of people active in political parties and movements, which is generally impermissible."

Of course, what Pugachov was describing might well be regarded— by realists or cynics—as precisely the kind of activity to be expected from a well-entrenched secret police, whether or not it engages in a public relations campaign or proclaims that it desires nothing more than to operate strictly within a framework of legality. To what degree President Gorbachev could be held directly responsible for activities that were, in a sense, deeply ingrained in Russian and Soviet society would remain in doubt. Such questions aside, the investigative commission was specifically concerned with his role, if any, in the August coup. Although Pugachov used the term "we," he appeared to express a purely personal opinion.

At this point, the conspirators' "perceptions" of Gorbachev's response to their collective fury over domestic disintegration and international retreats turned out to have been purely subjective. Very likely, Kryuchkov and his coconspirators engaged in vaguely wishful thinking, assuming that, when all was said and done, Gorbachev would go along with them. After all, he had come to see their point in late 1990 and early 1991. And now, in the summer of 1991, the dissolution of the Soviet Union was at hand; the Red Apocalypse had arrived. There had been, throughout much of his career, an inevitable Gorbachev–KGB connection, with all the ups and downs of a long relationship. Finally, the Moment of Truth had arrived. Except that it turned out to be a Moment of Tragic Misconceptions.

# Part II

Months of Transition

# 5

# KGB "Camelot": Bakatin Interlude

As soon as Gorbachev found himself back in his Kremlin office, he faced a crucial question. Who was now going to run the KGB? One thing was obvious: it had to be a top loyalist, someone who had defied the August conspirators from the start. An inviting but unorthodox choice was Vadim Bakatin, the former Interior Minister. Gorbachev had removed Bakatin from this ministerial position the previous fall, replacing him with the former KGB chief of Latvia, Boris K. Pugo, who became a major coup plotter. For about a year, Bakatin had been at odds with KGB director Kryuchkov. Their feud went beyond the traditional rivalry between the Ministry of Interior (or, early on, the MVD) and the KGB. According to Bakatin's outspoken criticism, much of what the KGB did was either illegal or superfluous. Could such a declared opponent of the KGB function as its director?

On August 22, 1991, Gorbachev called Bakatin to the Kremlin. He was met by a group of nine members of the State Council, including presidents of the major Soviet republics: Boris Yeltsin of Russia, Nursultan Nazarbayev of Kazakhstan, Islam Karimov of Uzbekistan, and Askar Akayev of Kyrgyzstan. Bakatin later recalled that they offered him the job, and he accepted the KGB assignment, in a euphoric atmosphere of "post-putsch enthusiasm." The Soviet leaders seemed to share an aggressive anti-KGB sentiment. Yeltsin suggested to Gorbachev that Bakatin should be empowered to reorganize the KGB. Bakatin cautioned the assembled leaders to remember that he had previously called for elimination of the KGB: "Now it turns out that I have been summoned to destroy the Committee of State Security. What are you thinking of? I am simply—just read my speech—I spoke of combining the KGB and the Ministry of Interior. I spoke of separating the [foreign] intelligence service. On this, I had some—perhaps not totally specific, but still—I did have my own ideas."

A few days after his appointment, Bakatin recalled in a television interview (August 28) that the Soviet leaders had told him to go ahead and dismantle what he regarded as the KGB's intolerable power "monopoly." He proceeded to do so, despite strong internal KGB opposition. And while this period of reformist enthusiasm—this KGB "Camelot"— lasted only four months, it left at least a temporary imprint on the KGB's successor agencies. This imprint was, to a high degree, formed by the personality of Vadim Bakatin himself—a unique figure in Soviet and Russian society, a man seemingly quite unsuited to be the head of the world's most feared and ruthless secret police organization.

But Bakatin also served as temporary protection for the KGB's bureaucratic machinery, as a human shield for the old "sword and shield" of Kremlin power. While Bakatin spoke convincingly of reforming the KGB, its old-timers were able to use him as a fashionable facade. Looking back on his tour of duty, Bakatin admitted in an *Izvestia* interview (January 2, 1992), "Now I'm aware that I know far less about the KGB than I thought I knew before." He had also come to realize that he was outmaneuvered, in some areas, by the KGB establishment. "My mistake was that I was the only newcomer," he said. "Or almost the only one. Under KGB conditions, you need your own team immediately."

This position, or self-created image, of the reluctant outsider fitted Bakatin's background as a man from the provinces who felt ill at ease in Moscow. Although sardonic humor was not among his characteristics, he could have placed above his desk at KGB headquarters a plaque that read: "I'd rather be in Siberia!" This would have recalled Russian secret police practice, dating back to czarist times, of exiling prisoners to cold, remote Siberian villages. But it would also have testified to Bakatin's own dislike for life in Moscow, and to his fond memories of the Siberian town of Kemerovo. He spoke of this during a television interview (September 19, 1991), castigating life in the big city:

"People out there are human. You can live there as you cannot exist in Moscow. All you have here is a mechanical functioning—not friends, not anybody. But there you have a real childhood, a well-rounded existence. Here, I do not call it life. Therefore, I did not consider myself as a careerist, as someone who attaches himself to an upward movement at any price, as some do who engage in all kinds of intrigues, who seek attachments in order to further their advancement. I did not get involved in any of that."

If he didn't use personal connections, or "pull," how did Bakatin emerge as a member of the Moscow elite? And how did he manage to gain a reputation as an undisputed liberal and a respected administrator? Above all, deep-down, what was his attitude toward the KGB—past, present, and future? Bakatin's view of the KGB was illustrated in two instances. Outside his office at KGB headquarters in the autumn of 1991, only a grotesque stump of the giant monument to Felix Dzerzhinsky remained. The statue of the founder of the Russian secret police had been pulled down by an angry crowd. Bakatin held a low opinion of the secret police Dzerzhinsky launched, but he disliked the destructive violence that led to toppling the statue. He felt that symbols of the past should not be turned into targets in themselves. Bakatin told the weekly *Moskovskiye Novosti* (September 8, 1991) that he could not regard "vandalism" as an "expression of victory." His personal attitude toward Dzerzhinsky, he said, had matured into "total indifference."

The second illustration of Bakatin's position as KGB director emerged when, at his desk at the agency's headquarters, he perused files on the persecution of his grandfather. In 1937, Vadim Bakatin's paternal grandfather, a Siberian-born teacher, was accused of anti-Soviet activities; found guilty by a *troika*, a secret tribunal of three men; and executed at the city of Tomsk by a firing squad of the NKVD, a predecessor agency of the KGB. There is no known grave. As Bakatin examined the papers dealing with his grandfather's case, he found that they contained information on the individuals who had been guilty of manufacturing the case against him—of, in fact, contributing directly to his death. What, at this late date, were his feelings about them? Not feelings of revenge. Rather, feelings of sadness, and detachment. He summed it up: "I want no punishment for the people who did this."

Bakatin used his personal encounter with these fifty-four-year-old files to clarify his position on the fate of KGB archives. He declared that archives of purely historical value should ultimately be made available to historians, in order to respond, wherever possible, to the many unanswered questions to which KGB files might contain clues. But, he also stated, records that might lead to witch-hunts—to the pursuit of real or alleged informers—should be sealed and never be made public. Bakatin told a session of the Supreme Soviet (August 29, 1991) that "he had no objection, in general, to handing over all KGB archives that concern historic developments, such as those concerning the disagreeable events connected with repressions, the fight against dissidents, and so on."

Speaking with a good deal of emotion, Bakatin continued: "I will, however, object categorically, up to the point of resigning my position, if access is demanded to archives that deal with secret agents. Categorically! I am saying this, well in advance, to everyone here. Whether or not you confirm my appointment, that is for you to decide. These agents were, in fact, without guilt, and so were the so-called informers; while all of us lived in a society of total surveillance that permeated every aspect of life, beginning with the [Young] Pioneers [Communist children's units]—at a time when people were forced, as it were, to 'perform their duty honorably.' By now, it would be quite inappropriate if we were to recall who said what to whom, when and where. Therefore, that part of the archives must never be handed over to anyone. We would rather destroy it; but I should not like to see any such attempt at present—and some have already been made—to destroy these archives."

Defending KGB agents and informers naturally went against the grain of many individuals and families who had suffered grievously at the hands of the secret police. Bakatin's position was therefore politically risky, potentially unpopular, and characteristically daring. Still, his defiant position ultimately did not diminish his chances of Supreme Soviet confirmation to the position of KGB Chairman; the vote favored him 366 to 9. Nevertheless, and from the very start, Bakatin had to defend himself against attacks on his own integrity. After all, here was a man who not so long ago had favored total elimination of the KGB—and now he was at the head of it, undertaking, as it were, the Renaissance of one of the most vicious and despised organizations in modern history. In fact, during a Moscow press conference at the Ministry of Foreign Affairs (August 30, 1991), one reporter asked this provocative question: "Why has Vadim Bakatin, a man of integrity, honesty and respectability, everybody's blue-eyed boy, agreed to head an organization that has been tainted forever?"

Bakatin graciously denied that he regarded himself as "everybody's blue-eyed boy," but thanked the reporter for the appellation. He replied that "integrity" and "respectability," with which he had just been credited, were precisely the reasons that "prevented me from refusing the appointment." He explained: "I just couldn't turn it down. It is a tough job, and somebody, at some time, must clear away those mountains of debris which we, ourselves, have managed to pile up during the past seventy years. No one is likely to come along and correct these mistakes for us. And, as far as being 'tainted' is concerned; well, those stains will simply have to be removed."

Bakatin admitted, with a good deal of reluctance, that his family, too, had been quite upset by news of his appointment as KGB chief. Ironically, one of his sons turned out to be the most aggrieved—because this son already held a KGB job! The father—obviously concerned about creating a top-level precedent of nepotism—immediately fired him. Bakatin explained, "I do not think that I should have subordinates who are in any way related to me." In a wry aside on entrenched bureaucratic practices, the new KGB director noted that separating his son from this job proved to be an incredibly complicated process, requiring signatures on twenty-nine clearance papers. The Bakatins have two sons, both married; at the time of Vadim Bakatin's appointment as KGB chief, he had two grandsons.

Bakatin's wife Lyudmila, a doctor of medicine, was clearly upset by the prospect of having a KGB boss–husband. He confessed that she had wept when he first told her of his appointment, and cried, "Vadim, what will become of us now?" Bakatin (somewhat embarrassed) recalled, "I could not reassure her." He later told friends that the task of running the KGB often kept him at his office until after midnight; staff members, though, left their desks so punctually that he had great difficulty in getting departmental information late in the day. He observed during a Moscow television interview (September 19, 1991) that "no one seems to realize that this is, in fact, dangerous work, and what wife would be pleased to learn that her husband has a dangerous job?" In that interview, Bakatin reiterated that, when he told his wife of the appointment, "there was no great rejoicing. And, from the point of view of material benefits of one kind or another, I got nothing extra out of it. Well, I do not, of course, think that my wife is that sort of person; she is not concerned with these [financial] matters. She is more interested in me, naturally; and so, to put it mildly, she did not like it."

As a matter of fact, the early experiences of his wife, and of others he knew, hardened his determination to seal all nonhistorical KGB files. In her student days, Lyudmila Bakatin had been approached by secret police recruiters; and while she refused to become involved with the KGB, the very fact that she had been interviewed prompted the agency to set up a file on her, which continued to exist in its archives. Bakatin cited a similar, prominent case—that of onetime Lithuanian Prime Minister Kazimiera Prunskiene, to whom Bakatin referred as "a person I respect very much" and as "a courageous woman." He noted that her name, too, had turned up in a secret police card file, although this connection dated back to a time "when she was of Pioneer [children's] age, or some other—I do not remember—or of student age." He asked, "So what then? Are we now to look into every one of these cases? I do not think there is any need to stir up the subject. It is very sensitive, and these people are not the guilty ones. The system is guilty, of course."

Friends and family urged Bakatin to cut down on his Herculean schedule—his trying to clean the KGB stables, as it were. But he maintained that he had just concluded a long involuntary vacation, "forty days of idleness," during which he "enjoyed a brief illness and managed to write a short book." Bakatin's book dealt with his service as Interior Minister, cut short by the surprise appointment of Pugo. Book royalties helped pay for building a dacha, a country house, which Bakatin designed and helped to construct.

Of course, designing and building a dacha should have come easily to a former construction engineer, whose life began in a small Siberian mining town. Vadim Viktorovich Bakatin was born on November 6, 1937, at Kiselevsk, in Russia's Kemerovo *oblast* (administrative region). His father, Viktor Bakatin, was a mining engineer; his mother, a medical doctor. The young man graduated from the Novosibirsk Institute of Construction Engineering in 1960, and received his master's degree in construction the following year. For two years, he was foreman at the Kemerovokhimstroi Trust in Kemerovo, then worked his way up the ladder to positions as shop superintendent and chief engineer; he served as director of operations from 1969 to 1971.

Bakatin's work in civil engineering soon gave way to a career in politics and government. He joined the Communist Party at the age of twenty-six. Still in Kemerovo, from 1973 to 1975 he worked as chief engineer of the Housing Construction Combine. For the next two years he served as second secretary of the local Communist Party's municipal committee (or *gorkom*); then for another two years he ran the party's municipal construction department; and from 1977 to 1983 he was secretary for industrial affairs. Finally, during the administration of former KGB chief Yuri Andropov who became the top Soviet leader in 1982, Vadim Bakatin was brought from his provincial post to Moscow.

From 1983 to 1985, Bakatin's Moscow position was that of inspector in the Central Committee of the Soviet Communist Party, an administrative post that suggests responsibilities in personnel evaluation, selection, assignment, and control. Then, for barely two years, he was assigned to the city of Kirov, where he served as first secretary of the region's party committee. Next, Bakatin returned to his beloved, relatively serene Kemerovo. There too, he functioned as the party's regional administrator; but he stayed for just over a year. It was then, in the fall of 1988, that Gorbachev asked Bakatin to return to Moscow and take on the crucial post of Minister of Interior.

Lyudmila Bakatin recalled somewhat ruefully that time when Gorbachev summoned her husband to Moscow; "It was on October 2, a little more than a year after we had moved from Kirov. I was finally unpacking our books and lining them up on the shelf. And by October 17 we were supposed to move to Moscow!" Vadim Bakatin was surprised by Gorbachev's call. True, they had both worked under Andropov and had been regarded as members of his team. But when asked whether, during those earlier Moscow days, the two men had known each other well, Bakatin replied, "Not really. I had met Mikhail Gorbachev on only a few occasions, and none of those encounters had been long."

Bakatin was called to the telephone while attending a committee meeting at the Kemorovo party headquarters. He recalled, "I was told that Mikhail Gorbachev wanted to talk to me. Before that, he had telephoned three or four times to inquire about local coal production and crop output. This time, he began by asking, 'How are things going? How are the election meetings coming along?' I answered, of course; but then he switched and suddenly said, 'Listen, Vadim, we've had a discussion, and we have agreed to nominate you Minister of Interior. Come to the Politburo on Thursday.' Frankly, I was stunned."

During his two years' tour of duty as head of the Interior Ministry, Bakatin faced a nation in transition amid social upheaval, mounting lawlessness, and increasingly independent-minded republics. The ministry itself suffered from a reputation of corruption and had serious internal morale problems. Throughout this period, the bad blood between the MVD and KGB far exceeded the historical rivalry between the two government agencies. Forced to cooperate in joint and overlapping undertakings, they found themselves at odds over tactics and responsibilities. Kryuchkov's confidential reports to Gorbachev and other top officials consistently emphasized, first, that, in contrast to MVD reports, the country was on the brink of anarchy, and drastic countermeasures were essential; and second, that Bakatin was acting irresponsibly, used ineffective tactics, and was generally unsuited for the position he held.

Bakatin, frustrated by lack of control over the republics' agencies, told

*Izvestia* (August 5, 1990) that he had signed a treaty with the Interior Ministry of Estonia, giving to that republican ministry de facto independent status and power to act on its own. This unilateral action provided ammunition to his antagonists—mainly Kryuchkov, who was able to accuse Bakatin of acting outside the Soviet constitution, showing disregard for collective responsibility, and combining administrative arrogance with erratic personality characteristics.

Having, in effect, accepted Estonia—prematurely!—as an independent nation, if only within his own sphere of competence, created major difficulties for Bakatin. His operating as if dealings between Estonia's MVD and the Soviet MVD were equivalent to those between sovereign states provoked anger among Soviet politicians. Calls for Bakatin's resignation grew louder and louder. At the same time, and in the same *Izvestia* interview, he defined what he then saw as the appropriate turfs for "his" MVD and the then-competitive KGB. He outlined an "optimum model" of the two agencies' functions when he said, "I am in favor of the KGB dealing only with its own affairs: intelligence and counterintelligence. Everything that happened before—dissidents, and that sort of thing—is gone now. And, internal crime—racketeering, bribery, terrorism—ought to be under the MVD. To sum it up: everything external, under the KGB; everything domestic, under us." Only a year later, Bakatin would *be* KGB; the "us" would be reversed!

The traditional rivalry between the KGB and the MVD was sharpened by fundamental differences in the personality and outlook of Bakatin and KGB chief Kryuchkov. Bakatin weakened his standing with Gorbachev when he refused to ban mass demonstrations in Moscow on November 7. In a power play that foreshadowed the coup attempt of August 1991, the Kryuchkov camp launched a campaign against Bakatin that culminated in attacks made in the Supreme Soviet on November 16 and 17, 1990. Specifically, members accused Bakatin of creating administrative chaos within the Ministry of Interior, of undercutting its effectiveness in fighting crime, and of illegally negotiating with separatist MVD organizations, as in Estonia.

Bakatin at first planned to answer his critics in a speech to the Supreme Soviet, but then limited himself to a letter, published November 5. The letter was addressed to the parliament's Speaker, Anatoly I. Lukyanov, who later emerged as a more or less discreet supporter of the August conspiracy. Bakatin protested that "paralysis of power" in law enforcement was not due to the MVD, but to outdated "legal and executive mechanisms." He observed that "assumption of power in the republics and at the local level" by political forces at odds with "central authorities" had become "a natural, normal matter." Bakatin concluded, "Authorities in our country show contempt for the law. Under these conditions, the militia, which cannot oppose the authorities, is powerless."

As if in reply, Kryuchkov called upon a group of deputies on November 29, warning that the country's crisis was "deepening in all aspects" but had "not yet reached its lowest point." He cautioned the parliamentarians: "If each of us does not do everything in his power to avert the disintegration of the Union, history will not forgive us." Within days, Gorbachev yielded to Kryuchkov and the anti-Bakatin forces. As part of a sweeping top-level government shake-up—a triumph for the antireform coalition—Bakatin was ousted on December 4, 1990. He was replaced by Boris K. Pugo, who until 1984 had directed the KGB in Latvia.

Had Kryuchkov actually conspired against Bakatin? Was it as simple, and as crude, as all that? Apparently. And Kryuchkov had allies in this campaign. Bakatin told an interviewer on the Russian TV Network (September 19, 1991) that he had fueled Kryuchkov's antagonism when Gorbachev "spotted difference in information furnished by the Interior Ministry and that supplied by the KGB." Bakatin added, "I believe that, on some internal matters, the Interior Ministry provided more reliable information than the KGB." Beyond that, Bakatin felt he had proven too insistent on "my own opinion," had been stubborn and "not very obedient" toward the Communist Party's Central Committee: "The leadership of the Committee, and Kryuchkov in particular, made it their business to spread information about me, so designed that one arrived at the conclusion that I had to be judged superfluous. That is why I was removed."

After that, and until the August coup, Bakatin was "out of the loop" of major Kremlin politics. His activities were limited to paperwork at Gorbachev's Presidential Council. His duties were undemanding, to say the least. He dutifully arrived each morning at eight o'clock. After that, as he later put it, "I looked for work for myself." All that changed drastically when he took command of the KGB and, for four months, worked from the top down to break its entrenched power monopoly.

When his tour of duty was up, what had Bakatin accomplished? Bakatin evaluated his task in a series of interviews both during and after his tenure as KGB chief. His original intention of dismantling the KGB's giant "monopoly"—a staff of 490,000 people—was quickly achieved. But this reduction in size was due to an administrative parceling-out of several segments of the agency. By far the largest move, in sheer man-power and equipment, was the separation of the 240,000 Border Guards from under the KGB central command. Security guard services and the Alpha commando unit were also removed from KGB control. These separations were generally accepted as desirable or logical; even veteran personnel tended to go along with the idea that purely military units did not belong within an agency whose duties were—or were supposed to be—investigative and information-gathering in nature.

Even men at odds with Bakatin, such as Kryuchkov's former deputy, Leonid Shebarshin, agreed that separation of foreign intelligence functions (the former First Chief Directorate) resulted in a more clear-cut administrative pattern. However, Shebarshin was among those who felt that separation of the KGB's vast communications setup—its monitoring, coding, and decoding apparatus—had been ill-considered and hasty. By the very nature of its operations, and under whatever label, this setup (the former Eighth Chief Directorate) had to retain direct links to the Foreign Intelligence Service and the Foreign Ministry.

Bakatin came to the conclusion that the KGB's information gathering and analyzing skills had been vastly oversold and overrated. When examining the agency's daily reports, he found that they did not provide greater insight than, for example, broadcasts of Radio Liberty or the content of a major Moscow newspaper. One reason the KGB was hide-bound was that it operated under some five thousand to six thousand rulings passed down over the years by the Soviet Council of Ministers and other ruling bodies. Given such handicaps, just how effective Bak-atin's reforms were likely to be—in the long run—remained open to question. In one crucial area, he set out to dismantle the Second Chief Directorate, and to eliminate its surveillance of "dissidents"; but the monitoring of suspected criminals (corrupt officials, drug traffickers, terrorists, and so on) permitted continuation of such controversial prac-tices as telephone and mail intercepts. Bakatin himself was quite firm when he told *Komsomolskaya Pravda* (October 23, 1991) that purposeful domestic counterintelligence would be continued:

"We can't catch spies every day, of course. Still, these things need to be done—but more effectively and professionally, in order to ensure that there is some purpose to the work, rather than just 'listening' to everyone and 'watching' everyone. The KGB's most successful line—combating dissidence, and spreading disinformation—is now a thing of the past. This means that we need to clear away all the organizational rudiments of this kind of work from the KGB system."

Once the Russian Ministry of Security was set up, early in 1992, under militia veteran Victor Barannikov, some of Bakatin's hopes began to sound all too optimistic. Certainly, his administrative grasp could not extend to Barannikov's domain, nor could he be sure that his ideas would be implemented by KGB successor agencies in the newly independent states, from Ukraine to Kazakhstan. At any rate, Bakatin acknowledged, functions of the KGB's Seventh Chief Directorate—selective domestic surveillance—would also not be curtailed. "It will continue," he said.

Where overseas intelligence was concerned, exuberant anti-KGB partisans during Bakatin's Camelot period assumed that the practice of placing agents among embassy personnel would be stopped. Bakatin poured cold water on this idea, calling it a "rather hasty" assumption. He explained, "Intelligence officers must have 'cover stories.' And we will continue to make sure that nobody—neither newspaper editors, ambassadors, nor anyone else—know that they have intelligence or counterintelligence officers working for them. This is possible and necessary." In other words, intelligence agents would continue to be scattered, clandestinely, among embassy employees, correspondents of Russian press services and newspapers, and presumably also among students, visiting businesspersons and academics, and employees of Russian enterprises abroad, including airlines and trade agencies.

Bakatin set out to retire a limited number of what he called "ideological dogmatists" within the KGB ranks, to improve the quality of data collection and analysis, to create a leaner, tighter, more efficiently functioning agency. He was asked by *Literaturnaya Gazeta* (December 18, 1991) how he felt about the majority of the KGB staff, about working with men "who persecuted dissidents," who had "hounded" the distinguished physicist Andrei Sakharov. Bakatin admitted that among current staffers were, indeed, "the same people" who had implemented the harsh policies of his predecessors. "But," he said, "we all come, after all, from the same world, from the same society, from the same system. That goes for everyone of us." With a dig at his questioner, he added, "And in the editorial offices as well, most likely." Bakatin concluded, "So, what shall we do with them? Remove all those people and bring in some new ones? Where will we find them? Who could be their judge? All people, I believe, all of us, undergo changes. At least, we all should change. Not only outwardly, in our skins, as it were, but in our very essence. So the question is not whether these are the same people, but whether they will prove capable of changing or not." The KGB had, indeed, changed under Bakatin. But not as much as he had hoped.

# 6

# Bugs in the U.S. Embassy

The case of the Embassy bugs came to illustrate the tug-of-war between old hands and new hands at the KGB. This incident in which Vadim Bakatin during his last days as director of the KGB—or, as it briefly became, the Inter-Republican Security Service (ISS)—handed the U.S. Ambassador blueprints to the Embassy bugging was regarded as treason by his antagonists. More than that: KGB conservatives and their allies used the incident to indict the Gorbachev elite as traitors to the fading Soviet state and the newly emerging Russian nation.

Bakatin presented the gesture as a logical outgrowth of the end of spy mania, of mutual suspicions, and as a means of wiping out distrust. And that, precisely, was what his critics found highly objectionable, even actionable. Bakatin remained bitter; the Soviet media, he felt, never provided a balanced picture of the Embassy case, and he accused even such supposed liberal papers as *Izvestia* of failing to print the full story.

Mutual bugging of embassies, and even surreptitious entry of embassy premises, had been established espionage method for much of the Cold War period. But the practice reached new heights with the American decision to vacate its outdated premises, Spaso House, a sprawling mansion on Moscow's Tchaikovsky Street, and to build a new eight-story office complex that would meet the needs of twenty-first-century diplomacy. Construction, begun in 1976, was in the hands of Russian personnel. When U.S. security specialists made a survey of the building in 1982, they found it riddled with hidden listening devices.

The bugging system turned out to be so extensive, sophisticated, and pervasive that the State Department considered tearing down the building, rather than going to the expense of removing the ubiquitous monitoring devices. Construction was stopped in 1985, and all sensitive Embassy activities remained at the old quarters. That was the situation when U.S. Ambassador Robert S. Strauss called on Bakatin during his last few days in office for what he assumed to be a final courtesy visit. The two men had met before, beginning on October 17, 1991, and had established a precedent-breaking relationship between KGB Chairman and U.S. Ambassador.

During this meeting—and much to Strauss's surprise—Bakatin handed him what were, in effect, precise clues to detect the KGB bugging devices. Strauss told the National Press Club in Washington (December 13, 1991) that Bakatin had gone "to his safe, and reached in and pulled out of his safe a big file like this, maybe six or eight inches thick, and with it a suitcase" filled with electronic equipment. Bakatin then said, "I don't know how long I am going to be here, but I want to deliver something to you. I think it's something that will be helpful. It ought to be done. Mr. Ambassador, these are the plans that disclose how the bugging of your Embassy took place, and these are the instruments that were used, and I want to give them to you, and I want them turned over to your Government, no strings attached." The "no strings attached" term may have indicated that Bakatin expected nothing in return, that this was a one-way gesture of goodwill.

Ambassador Strauss—aware of the mutual residue of doubt between the two countries, as well as the capacity of KGB old hands to withhold crucial material even from their agency's director—replied, "Mr. Bakatin, if I were to try to use that building, people would believe that you'd given me three-fourths of them, and kept one-fourth back." *Izvestia* reported (December 16, 1991) that Bakatin also told Strauss he hoped the material "will help you save some money and, possibly, enable you to use the Embassy building in the future." The same day, Tass quoted the KGB's Public Relations Office as providing the following background information:

"In 1969, the USSR leadership made the decision to install special equipment for collecting information in the new complex of U.S. Embassy buildings, something which was done in the course of the erection of these buildings in the 1976–82 period. Subsequently, in connection with the discovery of these devices, and the U.S. Government's protests, fitting the buildings with special equipment was halted, and the cables for linking the introduced devices with recording equipment were removed, which rendered the entire system of collecting information inoperable.

"Until recently, however, the competent USSR bodies had denied the fact that special devices had been installed. The distrust that existed between our countries for many years was conducive to the adoption by the U.S. Congress of legislative decisions banning the commissioning of the new buildings of the embassies of the United States in Moscow and of the USSR in Washington. The U.S. Congress was forced to allocate appropriations of up to $300 million for rebuilding the virtually ready complex.

"The qualitatively new level of relations between the two countries, based on mutual trust and openness, that has been established of late, required an appropriate decision. On the initiative of ISS chief V. Bakatin, in the course of negotiations with U.S. Ambassador Strauss, an accord was reached to hand over to the American side exhaustive information about the elements and the places where the special devices were deployed in the new U.S. Embassy building. This accord was agreed to by the USSR and RSFSR presidents, and by the [Soviet] Union and Russian foreign ministries. Such a decision fully rules out the need for huge and nonsensical expenditures by the American side in rebuilding the Embassy building and takes into account that the spirit and prospects for our new relations may be met with understanding by the American people."

It was the text and significance of this statement that, in Bakatin's opinion, was largely ignored by Soviet media. In particular, he felt that the press presented his action as a purely personal, idiosyncratic, and high-handed gesture. The text refers to the fact that he had discussed the disclosure beforehand with Gorbachev and Yeltsin, and had acted only after he had their approval as well as the agreement of the Soviet and Russian foreign ministers. When Bakatin left his post at the end of December, Moscow gossip suggested that he had been fired for irresponsible and possibly treacherous action. The anti-Bakatin forces were on the move, once again.

Following dissolution of the Soviet Union, the new President Boris Yeltsin established on December 19 a Russian Ministry of Security and Interior, which temporarily joined the KGB agencies with the Interior Ministry. This merger eliminated Bakatin's position. His critics regarded this as a dismissal and as punishment for his supposedly ill-advised action with regard to the U.S. Embassy. Major Alexander Tsopov, chairman of the Moscow Municipal Subcommission to Combat Crime, told a news conference that the diagram of Embassy listening devices included a "list of major data that constitute state secrets." As quoted by

Tass (December 23, 1991), Tsopov maintained that Bakatin's actions fell under Article 64 of the Russian Criminal Code, which dealt with "high treason in the form of betraying data that constitute state secrets."

The press soon noted that the public prosecutor was not taking any action against Bakatin, that he had gone on two weeks' leave. Moscow was filled with rumors about his possible fate. *Pravda* (December 28, 1991) carried the dual headline "ON THE TRAIL OF A SENSATION: IS BAKATIN SUBJECT TO THE LAW?" The paper observed: "A state secret from which, incidentally, the 'Top Secret' stamp has not been removed to this day, has been divulged to a foreign state. And, what's more, this was not done by a spy, but by the leader of the Soviet special service, Vadim Bakatin." *Pravda* noted that rumors about Bakatin's "possible arrest" were "stubbornly circulating in Moscow." The paper answered its own question of whether he was "subject to the law": "Of course he is, because the *corpus delicti* is there—divulging documents that constitute a state secret. In legal terms, this act qualifies as treason. As for the question of whether there was evil intent, that must be answered by an investigation. However, no one is carrying out any investigation. The Russian Prosecutor's Office is silent, as if nothing had happened." Reflecting sentiments among KGB staffers, *Pravda* added: "Many security officers are wondering what would happen if any employee of these bodies handed over secrets to the U.S. Ambassador. Would he keep his insignia on his uniform? And would he remain free?"

Two weeks later, *Rossiskaya Gazeta* (January 14, 1992) reported that KGB staffers remained upset about Bakatin's "gift" to Strauss; it had, the paper said, "plunged professionals into a state of shock." The plot thickened further when the file "on Bakatin" arrived in the office of Victor Barannikov, who eventually became one of Bakatin's successors as head of Russia's Ministry of Security (inheritor of the KGB's internal operations). *Rossiskaya Gazeta* ascertained that Barannikov's deputy, Anatoly Oleynikov, had "run a check on the possible divulgence of a state secret," but that "no divulgence of a state secret was perceived."

This finding appeared to nullify efforts by a group of disgruntled KGB old hands who had organized a "Public Committee to Ensure State Security," which accused Bakatin of having betrayed his own intelligence service by giving crucial data to Strauss: "In this shameless way, an end has been put to one of the most complex operational-technical undertakings of the state security organs, which required enormous work on the part of many of our best KGB scientists, specialists and operatives, and the expenditure of a large amount of material and financial resources." The committee called for a parliamentary hearing, for criminal proceedings on charges of breaking the military oath and of treason, and for collection of "operational information" on the guilty individuals. According to this appeal, not only Bakatin but Gorbachev, Yeltsin, and the foreign ministers were to have been categorized as among the "guilty individuals."

When Bakatin himself talked to *Izvestia* (January 2, 1992), the paper's interviewer referred to the "storm of indignation among state security personnel and unrest among non-professionals" about his dealings with Ambassador Strauss. Bakatin replied that the press generally, and even "your democratic paper, *Izvestia*," had acted "improperly" in picking bits and pieces from his agency's statement on the case and then commenting only on these fragments. Bakatin recalled that the KGB had been "caught red-handed" installing the listening devices in the U.S. Embassy. He said that this supposed secret—denied officially for years—was actually "known to the whole world." And he continued:

"The storm of indignation of which you speak, is very simply explained. Well-informed KGB circles know, and I have never hidden this, that Bakatin is leaving. This is the most convenient and safest time and gives them the best opportunity to hoodwink people in order to get even with Bakatin. This is a storm in a teacup. It is not a question of formal rights. It is naive to compare the rights of a rank-and-file staffer with the rights of the chairman of the KGB, who can cancel any instruction and declassify any internal departmental ruling. How is damage to be measured in politics? The point is that the KGB's departmental interests cannot, as they did for many years, determine foreign policy, stand above state and society, and limit policy to confrontation and distrust."

Bakatin next told the periodical *Argumenti i Fakty* (January 1992) that the "passions" surrounding the Embassy case were being "whipped up by, and are most advantageous to, forces inside the former KGB that do not want to give up the ideology of 'Chekism' in its dogmatic form." By giving information on the listening devices to Strauss, Bakatin said, he had "considered the opinion of experts directly connected with the 'equipment' of the new Embassy building." These experts, he insisted, were aware that U.S. technicians had used sophisticated instruments to locate "all, or almost all, of our contrivances long ago—'novelties' that dated from the mid-seventies, and not from the 1990s." He said that, "as far back as ten years ago, the system had become completely ineffective," and it was false to allege he had "turned over samples of bugging devices."

The periodical's editors, commenting on the interview, noted that there had been U.S. reluctance to assume Bakatin had "turned over absolutely all of the documentation—not because he did not want to, but simply because he was not given everything, as his action was viewed as treason against the Motherland." The editors reported that, when informed of Bakatin's intention to hand over the data, the two KGB technical subunits responsible for wiring the U.S. Embassy were so furious that they "almost started a strike."

An authentic-sounding criticism was voiced by an unidentified official of the USSR Ministry of Defense Central Intelligence Directorate, who told the Russian-language edition of *Moscow News* (*Moskovskiye Novosti*, December 29, 1991) that Bakatin's action had "damaged the country's security." The officer, employed by one of the ministry's scientific and technical divisions, emphasized that the KGB had not simply planted such routine listening devices as microphones at the U.S. Embassy, but had also installed equipment designed for "tracking the Embassy's electronic devices and monitoring out-going information, while at the same time enabling our agents to work within the Embassy."

The Defense Ministry technician said that, while the building was under construction, "some of the reinforcing rods inside the construction panels were equipped to carry out not just their basic functions but also intelligence functions." He added, "Naturally, when they found out about this, the Americans started investigating. This was done partly by means of high-frequency radiation and partly through ultrasound tomography." The military technician noted that U.S. investigators were able to assemble on a computer screen an overall picture needing further study and analysis. But when investigators spotted something on the screen that looked suspicious, they had to ask themselves, "Is this a piece of intelligence equipment, or a weld, or a flaw in the framework?" The military intelligence officer then explained the ramifications of Bakatin's gesture:

"We have now handed over the blueprint. The problem is not that the Americans will find our devices. Bakatin is right when he says that the devices are old and the Americans now have far more sophisticated equipment. The problem is, having received a precise blueprint, and knowing what it is they can see on a computer and what electronic image a given instrument creates, they can develop means to discover such equipment in other places where they suspect that Soviet intelligence has been at work. Furthermore, having removed such instruments from the panels and walls, they will develop technology capable of finding a given device. As a result, the U.S. special security services will obtain knowledge about our technology in gathering information and will significantly reduce our potential for obtaining intelligence information."

Under cloak of anonymity, the military official was harsh in his judgment of top Soviet leaders who had agreed to the gesture of giving the blueprints to Ambassador Strauss. Asked to explain why Gorbachev, Yeltsin, and the foreign ministers could have sanctioned such a step, he replied with one word: "Incompetence."

Eduard Shevardnadze, interviewed by the weekly *Literaturnaya Gazeta* (January 22, 1992), confirmed that Bakatin had consulted with him, as Soviet Foreign Minister, before turning over the Embassy material to Ambassador Strauss. The interviewer reminded Shevardnadze that there was a "wild scandal" in Moscow, because "huge state secrets" were supposed to have been surrendered. Shevardnadze sneered at this: "What secrets!" He recalled that, when the United States protested the bugging of its newly built Embassy building, he asked the then–KGB Chairman Victor Chebrikov whether the charges were true. Shevardnadze reported their conversation as follows:

"Victor Mikhailovich, I beg of you—after all, we are colleagues, we work together—tell me, for my personal information: Is there anything to this or not? If there is nothing there, I will act more boldly; and if there is, well, we will look for a way out."

Chebrikov denied everything: "No. Categorically, no!" Earlier, Shevardnadze remembered, Chebrikov had checked with the top leadership about the possibility of installing secret listening devices, but "it was decided not to do anything like that. And then—then, the Americans discovered it all!" The interviewer called it "a terrifying story," adding, "You sit next to a person, you work together, you become friends, one might say, and he lies to you—without batting an eye."

Shevardnadze agreed that Chebrikov's behavior was, presumably, the expression of a "conspirators' ethic," involving some supposedly "higher" interest that had to be "concealed from the top leaders." He said that he regarded such manipulators as "the shadow power," and concluded, "I think Bakatin took the right step."

Crowded out by Bakatin's detractors was the supportive opinion of Vladimir Kuzin, chairman of the Russian Supreme Court's Subcommission on Human Rights, who concluded that Bakatin's unprecedented action had actually strengthened legality. In Kuzin's view, the KGB's installation of listening devices in the U.S. Embassy had infringed on the territory of a sovereign state, and it was therefore a violation of international law; by his action, Bakatin had—de facto and de jure—restored the laws violated by the KGB. But Vadim Bakatin, battle weary, may have never heard Chairman Kuzin's soothing voice above the noisy clutter of criticism.

# 7

# The Maxwell Enigma

The *Moscow News* in its issue of December 29, 1991, headlined this question: "WAS MAXWELL A KGB AGENT?" The article dealt with the mysterious death of the ebullient, controversial British billionaire publisher and international entrepreneur Robert Maxwell, who drowned on November 5 near his yacht, the *Lady Ghislaine*, in waters near the Spanish island of Gran Canaria. Subsequent investigations revealed that Maxwell personally, and his multiple enterprises as well, were deeply in debt. To the already much-discussed question of whether Maxwell had died by accident, had been killed, or had committed suicide, the Moscow paper added the provocative question of whether he had been an agent of the KGB.

Thoughtful examination of Maxwell's extraordinarily colorful career can only lead to the conclusion that he was not a KGB agent—at least not in the strict sense of that term—but that he apparently acted on several occasions as if he might be an "agent of influence" for the Soviet secret service. An agent of influence can or could be just about anyone who serves as a conduit to achieving one of the numerous ends of an intelligence service. Among the categories of targets that could have fitted Maxwell's manifold activities and ambitions were political influence, shifts in public consciousness, and, in the broadest meaning of the term, "opinion-making."

Once again, in a most general sense, the KGB and Maxwell were made for each other. The key to this potential relationship was Maxwell's personality, with the very characteristics that marked both his fabulous success and his dramatic downfall. On the international economic scene of the 1980s, particularly in the United States, entrepreneurs tended to self-destruct—mainly because of overexpansion, based in overoptimism, on a feverish search for success that seemed to know no bounds. These characteristics applied to Robert Maxwell to an extraordinary degree, because "boundless" described him in so many ways: boundless energy, boundless enthusiasm, boundless optimism.

Born in Czechoslovakia, having served in the British Army during World War II, Robert Maxwell astounded the commercial world with the relatively rapid success of his publishing enterprises. At the core of these enterprises was Maxwell's scholarly publishing enterprise, Pergamon Press, which made a unique impact with the publication of English translations of Russian academic journals. At the outset, this was a highly unusual and, at first glance, potentially unprofitable enterprise. To begin with, Russian scholarship after World War II was not on the cutting edge of academic advances. Then too, the task of translating technical and scholarly treatises is an expensive and highly specialized undertaking. And finally, the profitable marketing of scholarly journals is, of itself, an enterprise requiring considerable expertise and funding; it is usually undertaken by long-established, well-financed major publishing enterprises. Where did Maxwell get the money to do all this? He did not get it from the KGB. But his company gained very favorable conditions from such Soviet agencies as the Copyright Agency of the USSR (VAAP). And one of his French affiliates appears to have received direct payments from Moscow.

*Moscow News*, trying to get to the bottom of the Maxwell mystery, interviewed a former KGB agent in Great Britain, Mikhail P. Lyubimov. He had served in the London Residence of the Soviet secret service for four years, but was expelled by England in 1964 after he was caught trying to recruit a British cypher operator. After his return to Moscow, he participated in debriefing the exiled British KGB agent Kim Philby; with Philby's help, Lyubimov wrote a classified treatise, "Special Traits of the British National Character and Their Use in Operational Work." Although Lyubimov's knowledge of Maxwell's career did not go back far enough to cover his early years, he stated that the Soviet copyright agency VAAP, "was manned by the KGB Fifth (Ideological) Department at all levels, up to deputy chairman." He said that, "knowing the KGB's love for window dressing," its staff may have listed Maxwell as one of its "agents of influence" and regarded "their relations with him as 'active projects,' much to the [Fifth] Department's credit."

A lengthy account of the Maxwell enigma—"Robert Maxwell: A KGB Favorite?"—appeared in the Moscow weekly *Literaturnaya Gazeta* (April

1, 1992), which picked up speculation concerning Maxwell's possible contact with the KGB's predecessor agency as far back as October 1945, in Berlin, after the end of World War II. Various other media accounts have created the impression that Maxwell—with his sense of bravado and adventurism—may well have sought to establish some kind of early contact with the KGB, but that the agency (a) didn't exactly know what to do with him, (b) couldn't figure out what this Czech-speaking giant of a man in a British Army uniform was all about, (c) thought he could very well be a British decoy, a potential double agent, or an *agent provocateur* (he was, or had been, a captain in British Military Intelligence), or (d) simply had its hands too full just sorting out the avalanche of loyalties, disloyalties, and confusions of post-Nazi Germany to be concerned with the potential usefulness of a fast-talking soldier of dual nationality.

In the book *Maxwell: The Outsider*, one of Robert Maxwell's biographers, Tom Bower, has sought to unravel the publisher's KGB connections. Bower was told by Detlev Raymond—who had worked for Maxwell in New York—that, in Allied-occupied Berlin just after the war, Maxwell's relations with the Russians and the KGB were "not simply social." Raymond asserted that, "either willingly or unwillingly, Maxwell compromised himself with the Russians." He cited a "KGB claim" that Maxwell "signed a document which promised to assist the security agency if required." Bower added this caution: "Since everyone involved in the incident is dead, the circumstances are unclear but the existence of a document seems certain, although it was soon forgotten by both sides."

Almost ten years after the war, when the time came to negotiate on behalf on Pergamon Press, Maxwell's reception in Moscow was exceedingly cordial. Bower wrote that in 1954, in the midst of the Cold War, few Western publishers "would have dared" to deal with the Russians, while the rest would not have considered it worth their while. Bower observed that "Maxwell, who grew up physically closer to the Soviet Union than most publishers in the West, was pragmatic and understanding about the Communist system. He understood the Russian way of life and could speak the language, both literally and metaphorically." That the Russians took to Maxwell at this point in time, and were generous in dealing with him, probably had nothing to do with whatever had happened, or did not happen, between Maxwell and the KGB back in Berlin in 1946. But officers at the Soviet state publishing house, Mezhdunarodnaya Kniga, did have orders to let him have scholarly translation and publication rights on his own terms. Bower quoted the publishing house's lawyer, Yuri Gradov, as saying, "My superiors wanted a source of propaganda in the West to prove that the Russians were not idiotic bears." The project was successful. Foreign publication of scholarly Russian periodicals did, in fact, add an air of international prestige to Russian science; publication of the journals represented a public relations breakthrough on an academic as well as political level. Still, while Maxwell was handed all this material on a silver platter, the project was a prestigious but money-losing proposition. Once the Russians launched their Sputnik satellite into space, worldwide interest in Soviet science boomed, as did the sale of their own technical journals.

According to Mikhail Lyubimov, the former KGB chief in London, Soviet intelligence became "really interested" in Maxwell when he was elected a Member of Parliament (MP) by the British Labour Party. He served from 1964 to 1970. Lyubimov did not specify what direction this KGB interest took. But Bower gives an account that suggests an effort to utilize Maxwell—who by then was, after all, a Czech-born British MP—to soften the impact of the Soviet Union's invasion of Czechoslovakia in 1968. Bower, citing anonymous Soviet intelligence officers, reported that a particularly well-qualified agent was instructed by KGB Colonel Alexander Y. Koinkov on May 15, 1968, to instigate a "spontaneous" encounter with Maxwell. According to this account, Koinkov recalled the pledge of potential help to Soviet intelligence that had allegedly been signed by Maxwell in Berlin after the war. The agent arranged a casual meeting with Maxwell on an Aeroflot flight from Moscow to Minsk on May 28, and a second encounter at breakfast the following morning in the Minsk Intourist Hotel. Later the two men had dinner, at which time the agent supposedly announced that he was "a colonel of the KGB" and told Maxwell, "When you return to Moscow, you will receive a phone call. We would like you to meet chairman Andropov." Yuri Andropov was then head of the KGB.

Perhaps Maxwell's speech in the British House of Commons on August 26, 1986, expressed his own sentiments but perhaps it also pleased his friends in Moscow. At any rate, he reminded his listeners that he had been born in Czechoslovakia and remembered well "the betrayal that I, though very young, and the whole nation of Czechoslovakia, felt at being let down by Great Britain and France at Munich." In effect, he spoke out against governmental reprisals against the Soviet Union, although he suggested that individuals might want to cancel commercial contracts. It seemed, Bower recalls, "at that time a mature and reasoned argument," but it also showed that Maxwell "had become an agent of influence."

Looking back on the Andropov meeting—if it did take place that way—one wonders why the elaborate "spontaneous encounter" preparations should have been made, when all it needed was a phone call to Maxwell's hotel room. But then, maybe that's what *did* happen—a simple phone call—and Maxwell got to see Andropov, just as he met other top Soviet leaders including Nikita Khrushchev and Leonid Brezhnev. (A photograph of Brezhnev and Maxwell appeared in *Pravda*.) Maxwell enjoyed meeting the high, mighty, and notorious, not excluding Erich Honecker, the East German Communist leader, whose autobiography Maxwell published in 1981.

Lyubimov came to the conclusion that Maxwell exploited "the vanity of Brezhnev and his immediate entourage," while "many political careers were boosted" through the publisher's English-language editions of their works. The standard pattern of these personality-boosters were either flattering biographies or collections of speeches. Under a contract between the Soviet copyright agency VAAP and Pergamon Press, Inc. (PPI) that was signed in Moscow and dated March 4, 1975, Maxwell published seven books by Soviet leaders; of these, five were by Brezhnev, one by Andropov, and one by Konstantin Chernenko, Brezhnev's short-lived successor. A later contract, dated April 14, 1978, concerned publication of Brezhnev's book *Peace Is the People's Priceless Treasure*. Maxwell also published works by such now-vanished Moscow figures as Boris Ponomarev and Viktor Grishin.

As documents from the archives of the Central Committee of the Soviet Communist Party are made public, subsidies to overseas recipients have become known. Among accounts publicized in 1991 was a document showing that the party owed the sum of 500,000 rubles (at that time equivalent to $500,000) to the Pergamon Press subsidiary in Paris. Natalia Gevorkyan, who conducted the interview with Lyubimov for *Moscow News*, reported that in 1981 the Central Committee had "passed a secret resolution concerning the French branch of Pergamon Press Ltd., which was the recipient of funds covering the publisher's expenses on Soviet leaders' English-language editions."

*Moscow News* may have taken a particular interest in the exploits of Robert Maxwell because the weekly was disillusioned in dealing with him commercially. While he was still alive, the paper ran a highly critical article, "Robert Maxwell—Drive to the East" (November 18–25, 1990), which took a dim view of the publisher's activities in the Soviet Union and Eastern Europe generally. In an agreement with *Moscow News*, Maxwell acquired the rights to the weekly's English-language edition and promised hard currency through equipment and advertising revenues. The paper confessed that it had "made a bad choice of partners" and reported that Maxwell soon "broke the terms of our contract and abruptly ended our cooperation." Unsurprisingly, *Moscow News* concluded that Maxwell owed his success to his "aggressive style and his goal to get the attention of the country's top leaders." The paper noted that he was involved in the publication of *Jashe Naslediye* (*Our Heritage*), the magazine of the Soviet Cultural Foundation, along with writings by Raisa Gorbacheva, the President's wife. *Moscow News* recorded that by then Maxwell had met three times with Mikhail Gorbachev, and added that the most recent meeting was two weeks earlier, "where they met with the Chairman of the KGB"—of course, none other than Vladimir Kryuchkov.

At that time, the KGB was at the height of its precoup public relations campaign. Previously, one of the most successful Soviet propaganda projects had been a magazine called *Sputnik*, which in size and editorial concept resembled the *Reader's Digest* and was published in several languages. What would seem more natural to the KGB Public Relations Center than to publish its *own* magazine, in digest form, containing highlights from the achievements of the secret service? And of course it could be called *USSR KGB Digest* (*Cbornik KGB SSSR*). Well, just such a magazine was launched in May 1990, and several other KGB publications presented the "new image" of the KGB in 1991. Promptly, Robert Maxwell offered to publish an English-language version of one or several of these magazines. But neither the old KGB nor Maxwell lived to see their joint project materialize.

Such terms as "agent of influence" and "asset" should not be used lightly when intelligence operations and personal integrities are concerned. An eager KGB operator may write a bragging memorandum that winds up in the agency's permanent files. Or an individual, because of vanity or naiveté, may have more or less casual contact with a foreign agent. There are similarities between the Maxwell enigma and the role played over many decades by the U.S. industrialist Armand Hammer (b.1898–d.1990). Hammer created a mystique for himself as a Soviet confidant, because he had met Lenin and thus had entry to Soviet leaders who saw this early encounter as a symbolic liaison. Hammer came to know most of the top Soviet leaders during his lifetime, and usually returned to the United States with praise for their roles and intentions.

Conversely, as he also knew many high-level U.S. leaders, he may at times have been asked to convey, informally, American ideas or to bring back his personal impressions of Kremlin intentions. In their book *The KGB against the "Main Enemy,"* Herbert Romerstein and Stanislav Levchenko list Hammer first in their section on influence operations. They defined "influence operations" as designed to cause an individual "to take an action beneficial to the Soviet Union." In the case of Armand Hammer—a man who enjoyed publicity—a mixture of motives may have been at work in his dealings with Soviet politicians, among those motives being the hope or illusion of making history.

If Hammer thought he was using his own influence rather than being manipulated in the manner of an agent of influence, he shared this attitude with others. As a matter of course, journalists were obvious targets of the KGB. Two controversial cases surfaced after the August coup attempt. One was the accusation that Dusko Doder, *Washington Post* bureau chief in Moscow from 1981 to 1985, had indirectly received $1,000 from the KGB and, as the *New York Times* put it (December 21, 1992), "may have been co-opted by Soviet agents." *Time* magazine (December 28) devoted two pages to the case and reported that a temporary Soviet defector, Colonel Vitaly Yurchenko, had implicated Doder, who had produced "scoop after scoop" on events inside the Kremlin leadership. The magazine wrote that "the FBI believed that Doder had an unusually close relationship with the KGB." *Time* asked, "Did the KGB co-opt Doder? Or was it the other way around?" Doder himself described the allegation as "sheer nonsense"; and the *Washington Post*, after investigating the issue, concluded "there was no evidence that Doder had done anything improper or had a connection to the KGB."

Another case involved the allegation that I. F. Stone (b.1907–d.1989), publisher of a political newsletter called *I. F. Stone's Weekly*, had from 1940 to 1968 been supported by KGB contacts in Washington. Herbert Romerstein reported in *Human Events* (June 5, 1992) that he was told by a former leading KGB officer that Stone had collaborated with him but had eventually become disenchanted by certain Soviet policies—notably the invasion of Czechoslovakia. The identity of the KGB officer was not revealed, although it may be assumed (despite a later denial) that he was Oleg Kalugin, onetime KGB station chief in Washington.

In both cases, the sources were murky. Not everyone having lunch with an assumed KGB officer in Moscow, or with a high-ranking Russian diplomat in Washington, need become enmeshed in the agency's active network. The *New York Times* noted in an editorial that, in "KGB jargon," an agent of influence can be "an unpaid foreign helper—or it can be a name boastfully listed by a local station chief to impress superiors in Moscow." The *Times* added, "Nobody should be surprised that someone like Izzy Stone, or any journalist who lunched with Soviet diplomats, might be mentioned in oral or written reports by KGB operatives." Back in Moscow, for instance, Kalugin had repeatedly and unsurprisingly boasted that his contacts in the U.S. capital included high White House officials and members of the U.S. Congress.

What the Doder and Stone cases illustrated was the risk involved in trusting the memories of KGB agents, or, for that matter, the actual files of the KGB. When the archives of the East German Staatssicherheits-dienst—or "Stasi," for short—were opened to individual inquirers, accusations and counteraccusations created an atmosphere of political turbulence. In Russia, leaks that prominent clergymen had contacts with the KGB could be credited to a calculated antichurch campaign on the part of KGB officers—a campaign designed to reveal clerical hypocrisy.

The ease with which some KGB officers may have taken credit for recruiting influential people, and the damage that undocumented or possibly falsified records can do, dramatize the need for caution in dealing with this elusive human category: the agent of influence.

# 8

# Traitor into Hero

All within one year, Major General Oleg D. Kalugin first became an official outcast from Soviet society, was stripped of rank and pension, and was denounced as a traitor—and then was acknowledged to have been fully justified in his criticisms of the KGB, reinstated, and named to be the agency's reorganization consultant. After thirty-two years of serving in top KGB posts at home and abroad, General Kalugin had shocked the Soviet public in mid-1990 with a series of accusations against the secret police apparatus. And his charges turned out to be dramatically prophetic.

Kalugin did not call for dissolution of the KGB. He professed devotion to its essential functions, as well as to the principles of perestroyka as originally advanced by President Gorbachev. But Kalugin maintained that Gorbachev (who had, it should be remembered, appointed Kryuchkov KGB chief) needed the KGB's support to remain in power. Oleg Kalugin made his initial charges on June 16, 1990, at a meeting of the Democratic Platform, then a major reform group within the Communist Party of the USSR. His statement, which bore the title "The Undisguised KGB," outlined Kalugin's own series of frustrated attempts to achieve reforms within the KGB. He mentioned specifically that he had interceded for a scientist who had been falsely accused of being a CIA agent and who was subsequently framed for alleged currency violations. Kalugin said that, when he was transferred to Leningrad, he had been shocked by the corruption and cover-ups within the city's top administration there. These and other experiences added to Kalugin's frustration over the KGB's resistance to genuine internal reform, in contrast to its public window dressing.

Kalugin recalled that he had appealed, successively, to Yuri Andropov, then KGB chief and one of Gorbachev's predecessors; to the Central Committee of the Communist Party; and finally to Gorbachev himself. In his letter to Gorbachev, Kalugin said, he had insisted perestroyka was incompatible with the existence of a KGB that had "penetrated every pore of our life," that "interferes in all affairs of state and public life—the economy, culture, sciences, sports, and religion." He received no reply.

In the letter to Gorbachev—written in 1987—Kalugin had noted that the Soviet Union continued to show "a pathological liking for maintaining secrecy." He told the Democratic Platform that, since then, the KGB had managed to develop "a new image of sorts." Still, he insisted, this image was largely a matter of "cosmetics," of "applying rouge to the flabby face of the old Stalin–Brezhnev visage." And he added, "The old foundations, methods and practices remain. They include the recruitment of agents in the ranks of political opponents and organizations, infiltration of its agents, the discrediting of activists in popular movements, the neutralization of organizations as a whole, as well as their ultimate destruction."

Kalugin said that the KGB had run out of old targets and slogans but had retained its full strength within all spheres of Soviet life: "They are capable of putting their power to use—their agents, the apparatus of assistants available in all spheres and echelons of our society, from academy members to militiamen, from the Holy Synod of the Russian Orthodox Church to athletes, from military commanders to musicians and literary critics."

General Kalugin conceded that his remarks were likely to have strong repercussions. He recalled that he had spoken to a Deputy KGB Chairman—a man in his sixties—who had only recently been appointed chief of USSR counterintelligence. Kalugin had told his old colleague that, disappointed with lack of response to his efforts to reform the KGB internally, he was about to go public with his accusations. To which the officer had replied, with a polite and engaging smile, "Oleg, aren't you afraid they will think you need to have your head examined?"

The KGB's official reaction—disseminated on June 22 by Tass, the official Soviet news agency—was brief, oblique, and non-specific. It said that Kalugin's views had been reported in press and radio, as well as in "foreign media." Presumably hinting at negative rather than positive characteristics, the release noted that "Kalugin's character is well known to us." This critique-by-innuendo continued: "The statements he has taken the liberty of making, containing crude distortions and attacks on the work of the present state security bodies, logically stem from his actions and conduct during his work for the KGB."

The same release—issued by the KGB's Public Relations Center—added that "the KGB resolutely rejects Kalugin's assertions and expresses indignation at the fact that he has insulted the professional integrity and personal dignity of those who work for the KGB of the USSR." Kalugin was then accused of following "a path of 'sensationalist' public statements" in order to support political ambitions, coupled with a "clear attempt to mislead public opinion." The release ended with the observation that the KGB would make "an all-round appraisal of Kalugin's statements."

The following day (June 23), Kalugin was interviewed on the Moscow television program *Before and After Midnight*. The interviewer Vladimir Molchanov asked quite bluntly, "Oleg Danilovich, your speech has caused a sensation everywhere. Aren't you putting yourself and your relatives at risk by appearing on this program?" Kalugin admitted that his "former organization" was capable of "various dirty tricks," but said he was "psychologically prepared for any turn of events." He added that emotional support from colleagues still working in the KGB had given him "great and unexpected joy." Still the interviewer insisted on asking whether Kulagin's former bosses would not try to "punish you in some way."

The answer came a week later. "At the request of the KGB of the USSR," President Gorbachev issued a decree stripping Kalugin of all state awards and decorations, "for actions discrediting the honor and dignity of a state security officer." At the same time the USSR Council of Ministers, under the chairmanship of Nicholas Ryzhkov, deprived Kalugin of his rank as Major General (retired). His state pension was discontinued. KGB Chairman Kryuchkov stripped him of his honorary security officer badge and other KGB decorations.

Kalugin had been awarded three Badge of Honor orders in 1964, the Order of Red Star in 1967, and the Order of Red Banner in 1977. His own cautious comments on these decorations suggested that they might have been awarded in recognition of specific espionage-intelligence operations or other national security undertakings. Within the KGB, Kalugin had received departmental medals "For Impeccable Service" in all the three grades in which these medals were awarded to service officers.

The night before the announcement of his downgrading, Kalugin had received a telephone call from the KGB. He was asked to come to KGB headquarters. But Kalugin replied that the current leadership had defamed him, and that he would not come to see them of his own free will. As a result, he heard of being stripped of his rank and awards on a Saturday night news bulletin of the British Broadcasting Corporation (BBC), while staying for a weekend at his dacha (country house).

Public efforts to downgrade Kalugin's image continued in a *Pravda* interview ("Everyone Chooses His Own Fate," June 28, 1990) with unidentified officials of the KGB's Public Relations Center: "Kalugin was always distinguished by a desire to acquire influential connections. Those who knew him more closely could not fail to notice his taste for the Bohemian life style and his habit of throwing parties, using his official position." The agency officials noted that his knowledge of foreign languages made Kulagin a valuable officer, but added, "His weaknesses on a professional and purely human level became particularly noticeable after his appointment as head of Foreign Counterintelligence Administration. It was at that time that—in addition to his characteristic pushiness, which even won people over—his ambition, disregard of other's opinions, rancor and tendency to flaunt his connections, began to be increasingly manifested."

The officials said that Kalugin was removed from his counterintelligence post when "a very valuable source, who worked in the CIA, was lost as a result of his incompetent, arrogant actions." Finally, the interview claimed, his work in Leningrad was also unsatisfactory and—despite his making the threat "You will regret this!"—he was "transferred to the reserve."

Asked about these accusations by an editor of the magazine *Sobesednik* (July 1990), Kalugin replied ironically that the KGB officials' remark about "important connections" might have referred to his acquaintances with former U.S. National Security Adviser Zbigniew Brzezinski and former U.S. Senator William Fulbright. As for the performance of the KGB's counterintelligence service, Kalugin recalled that this service had been created "from scratch" by himself and one other general, who had also fallen from favor. Kalugin said that, while he was in charge, "the apparatus of our assistants abroad increased by a factor of three" (meaning, perhaps, that the number of his clandestine agents had tripled during this period). This, he said, happened in 1978, just when he was awarded the Order of Red Banner for exceptional performance.

He replied to the accusation that the KGB lost an agent within the CIA because of Kalugin's incompetence and arrogance, saying, "We had nobody to lose." He insisted that "until January 2, 1980, for as long as I headed the administration, we received various secret documents, but we did not have 'our man' on the staff of the CIA. Right now, they are simply telling lies."

Kalugin was bitter about what he described as increasingly careless control over KGB officers since his own departure from the Foreign Counterintelligence Administration. He said that, during his term, "only one highly-placed KGB officer defected from us to the West." Since 1980, however, about fifteen people had defected and, he added, "virtually our entire agent network has been lost." Exasperated, he exclaimed, "What kind of success is it, if these flights go on! The last KGB officer crossed over to the West in April 1990."

Faced with the accusation that he was attracted to a dissolute "Bohemian way of life," Kalugin wrily admitted that he had "many friends who are actors and artists," and "we do go to restaurants sometimes."

From then on, the Kalugin case proceeded on four levels:

1. The Soviet government began criminal proceedings against Kalugin, accusing him of revealing "state secrets."

2. Kalugin went to court against Gorbachev, Ryzhkov, and Kryuchkov, charging that their actions in stripping him of his rank, decorations, and pension were illegal.

3. Kalugin widened his criticism of KGB operations, at home and abroad, with further interviews in domestic and foreign media.

4. Kalugin successfully ran for election to the Congress of People's Deputies from the Krasnodar region.

Kalugin's observations continued to be remarkably prophetic, as when he warned of conspiratorial trends among antireform forces generally and of reactionary traditions inside the KGB. But he also emphasized that KGB officers came from many walks of life and tended to respond to professional conflicts in highly individual terms. He felt strongly that the "new KGB man"—officers under forty years of age—were impatient with rigid top officials who had learned the secret police trade during the ruthless preperestroyka decades.

Repeatedly, Kalugin insisted that the KGB had to be depoliticized, that its close links with the Communist Party should be broken, that traditional secret police tolerance of high-level corruption had to be eradicated. Kalugin maintained, and other ex-KGB officers confirmed, that blowing the whistle on top Soviet leaders had long been taboo; that dossiers existed on just about everyone of relative prominence or subject to controversy—except for members of the *nomenklatura*, the Soviet elite.

In making these points, Kalugin recalled that, when he was transferred to Leningrad (St. Petersburg)—the city of his birth—after two decades of either serving abroad or directing foreign operations, he quickly encountered the nomenklatura taboo. He told *Moscow News* (July 1–8, 1990) that his former experience came in "quite handy" when he remembered that "the KGB is not authorized to keep compromising material about officials of sufficiently high level." The Leningrad KGB kept a file on a local party functionary, Lev N. Zaykov; but as soon as Zaykov rose to the position of first secretary of the regional party committee, the city's KGB had the file removed so that, as Kalugin put it, "Zaykov's name wouldn't even be mentioned there."

Kalugin arrived in Leningrad in 1980 and discovered that the local militia had been infiltrated by corrupt Mafia-type elements. He found "traitors within its ranks," and corruption at "the middle echelon of leadership." Businesspeople from Ukraine and Moldavia obtained timber by bribing the local officials. Local businesspeople were linked with high Communist Party officials, but, Kalugin told *Sobesednik*, "as soon as it came to verifying the testimony against them, a categorical order came from the regional party committee to stop the investigation."

In his interview with *Moscow News*, Kalugin accused the KGB of having misled the Kremlin leadership about the situation in Czechoslovakia on the eve of the Soviet invasion in 1968. He said the KGB had "whipped up fear among the country's leadership, alleging that Czechoslovakia would fall victim to NATO aggression or a coup, unless certain actions were undertaken quickly." Kalugin's personal contacts, or spy network, within the U.S. government provided him with more authentic information. He told other interviewers that he obtained "absolutely reliable documents from American intelligence, the Pentagon, and the State Department, confirming that neither the CIA nor any other American [government] department had anything to do with the events in Czechoslovakia."

Functioning as the KGB Resident, or senior intelligence officer, in Washington at the time, Kalugin was aware that U.S. officials were, in fact, "taken aback by the scale of events" in Prague, and he so "informed my leadership of this, before the invasion." But he later found out that his reports had run counter to top-level KGB opinions and plans. As a result, his dispatches were bottled up, never passed on to Kremlin policymakers; and all this valuable information "was wasted." As Soviet tanks rolled into Czechoslovakia, Kalugin recalled, he shared with Anatoly Dobrynin, then Soviet Ambassador in Washington, feelings of shock, horror, and despair.

In Kalugin's succession of disillusionments, being publicly stripped of his rank and position must have rated high—the more so, as it was done by his onetime idol, Mikhail Gorbachev. Restoration of his status came quickly following the collapse of the August coup and the downfall of Kryuchkov. On September 1, 1991, Gorbachev signed a decree that reinstated Oleg Kalugin to the rank of Major General, including all privileges and pensions. But how did Kalugin feel about this double-turn-around? An interviewer on Moscow's *Vremya* TV news program (September 14, 1991) reminded Kalugin—rather provocatively—that both his downgrading and reinstatement were simply the "willful decisions of the same person." The interviewer asked, "Perhaps you should not agree to his favors, but should, instead, obtain a legal ruling?"

Kalugin agreed. "Yes," he said, "the decision was illegal." But he allowed that there had been extenuating circumstances. Gorbachev had been misled by Kryuchkov, who had presented the President with "disinformation." Even worse, Kalugin added, the KGB Chairman had "engaged in this practice for several years, putting the country's leadership in a very awkward position." The Kremlin arrived at many an "illegal decision," he said, "because it relied on information from Kryuchkov and the KGB, which systematically dished up tendentious and often simply slanderous information on figures of the democratic movement, including me, presenting them as enemies of our system."

Within a week, Oleg D. Kalugin was asked by the newly appointed KGB Chairman, Vadim Bakatin, to act as his consultant on reorganization plans. Would Kalugin join his old colleagues and return to the KGB's staff? No, Kalugin said; he thought he might be more effective if he remained independent. Within a year, Major General Kalugin's public image had switched from traitor to hero.

When the Soviet Union broke up, Bakatin left the KGB, and Russia's Ministry of Security and its Foreign Intelligence Service were established, Kalugin found himself once again on the side of the security services' critics. They had, he felt, returned to their old habits, practices, and attitudes. Briefly there were rumors that Kalugin would join a private corporation—maybe even run the Moscow office of a U.S. security consulting company. Kalugin told Interfax (February 7, 1992) that he had indeed received many commercial offers, but preferred "being a pensioner" and would concentrate on serving as the elected deputy of the Krasnodar region. Against the background of rapidly changing events, yesterday's traitor was running the risk of becoming yesterday's hero.

# 9

# Missing Archives: Beyond Wallenberg

During the KGB's immediate postcoup period under the direction of Vadim Bakatin, Western scholars and other inquirers hoped that secret police files would be opened sufficiently wide to solve several long-standing mysteries. Foremost among these was the Soviet seizure, in Hungary, of the young Swedish diplomat Raoul Wallenberg at the end of World War II. Wallenberg's daring and ingenuity had saved thousands of Jews from death at Nazi German hands. He soon occupied an unrivaled position in the history of twentieth-century humanitarianism.

Why, then, did Soviet authorities zero in on this outstanding humanitarian, hold him prisoner, and for decades hide his fate? After all, the crude seizure of this citizen of Sweden—a neutral country—who was engaged in a courageous, large-scale life-saving enterprise that was directed at the Allies' common enemy, could do nothing but damage the image of the Soviet state in international diplomacy and public opinion. As it turned out, the unresolved case of Wallenberg continued to absorb world media attention for well over four decades.

Raoul Gustaf Wallenberg, born into a prominent Lutheran family on August 4, 1912, studied architecture in the United States and later became a foreign trade executive in Central Europe. In the spring of 1944, as Hungary sought to negotiate peace with the Allies, the Nazi regime sent troops into the country and started to deport Hungarian Jews to death camps. Five neutral countries—including Sweden—began to issue protective passports, so-called *Schutzpässe*, to some of the Jews. The U.S. War Refugee Board provided funds to protect additional numbers of endangered individuals, and a Swedish group selected Raoul Wallenberg to organize a last-minute rescue campaign. Acting through the

Swedish Embassy, he was eminently successful in this undertaking, using a variety of means to outmaneuver the Nazi authorities. Finally, when Red Army troops entered the country, Wallenberg thought to coordinate his activities with them.

On January 17, 1945, Wallenberg gained permission to visit the Red Army command. Under Soviet secret police guard, he passed through Russian lines, was then arrested, and, within days, sent to Moscow's notorious Lubyanka Prison. Wallenberg was held in Cell No. 123, interrogated at length, and then transferred to Moscow's even more notorious Lefortovo Prison. Soviet authorities belatedly alleged that Wallenberg died of a heart attack on July 17, 1947, while in KGB custody. Yet, reports that he was still alive during later years continued to come from ex-prisoners, and Moscow's replies remained erratically evasive.

During the Bakatin interregnum it seemed that KGB files might at last be assembled to offer documents that would not only provide convincing facts on Wallenberg's fate, but would also offer insight into the Kremlin's motivations for his arrest and imprisonment. One uncovered prison logbook showed entries—with names originally inked out but then restored by the KGB under Bakatin—containing the names of Wallenberg and his driver Vilmos Langenfelder. The logs listed dates of interrogations, most frequently by an agent named Kopelyansky. The last entry for Wallenberg was on March 11, 1947, and for Langenfelder on July 23, 1947.

In 1989, in response to repeated Swedish inquiries, the KGB returned some of Wallenberg's personal belongings to his relatives. Among the memorabilia were money the police had seized at the time of his arrest, Wallenberg's personal notebook, as well as documents dealing with his confinement at the Lubyanka Prison. *Komsomolskaya Pravda* (September 28, 1991) quoted a KGB public relations spokesman as reporting that one of the agency's archivists had accidentally discovered Wallenberg's belongings in the basement of one of the KGB buildings, at 2 Lubyanskaya Square. The oddly chatty and intimate account of the discovery described the place as "a little corner room, its barred window facing the inner courtyard, and water pipes running along the ceiling," looking "more like a storage room for unclaimed evidence or obsolete clerical stuff than an archive."

The archivist told the newspaper that he had been sorting through piles of material when he happened to come across the Wallenberg memorabilia: "I had to replace the wooden shelves with new metal ones. I was looking through one file after another, and suddenly one of them yielded a package, the size of a school notebook, some three or four centimetres thick. It was a brown paper parcel, rather worn. The flap, previously glued, had come undone. Imagine my surprise when I shook out of the packet a gold powder-compact, made to look like a cigarette-case, money, notebooks, and documents in the name of Raoul Wallenberg. The name of the Swedish diplomat was already familiar to me, because I had been getting inquiries about him. I reported the find to my bosses. This is, basically, the whole story. I am very happy, of course, that we have managed to find at least some trace of this man."

The paper also quoted Major General Nikolai Stolyarov, deputy KGB chief, as saying that his agency had given "five documents" to "the Swedish side," although these had made "only indirect reference to the name of the detained diplomat." He added, "Not a single one of them disproves the fact of his death in the Lubyanka Prison in 1947. But the search is going on, and if we find any new documents we will hand them over to all interested parties." Major General Stolyarov also made a comment that threw some light on past and present KGB attitudes toward Wallenberg: "Whoever Raoul Wallenberg turns out to be—the agent of one, two or even three intelligence services—the many thousands of lives he saved have made his name immortal forever."

This speculation—that Wallenberg may have served one or several intelligence services—reflects the paranoid mentality that governed Soviet behavior under Joseph Stalin from the closing days of World War II until Stalin's death in 1953. The Stalinist mind-set could not view a man of Wallenberg's position and activity as anything but that of an intelligence agent in action—possibly serving U.S., Swedish, and perhaps British intelligence agencies simultaneously. And with a man of this stature occupying the limelight in Hungary—a country that Stalin intended to turn into a satellite Communist state as quickly as possible—such an "agent" presented a serious potential threat. What could be more effective than to seize him, interrogate him, and perhaps even turn him into a brainwashed witness to "American imperialist subversion" in one of the show trials that were soon to descend on Eastern Europe's capitals? Oleg Gordievsky, who headed the KGB Residency in London until his defection in 1985, has suggested that Moscow tried repeatedly—but without success—to persuade Wallenberg to become a Soviet agent.

The Wallenberg case must be seen within the psychohistorical framework of Eastern Europe in the years just before Stalin's death. At first, Moscow denied knowing anything about the Swede's disappearance.

Deputy Foreign Minister Andrei Vishinsky advised the Swedish government in 1947 that Wallenberg was "not on Soviet territory and is unknown to Soviet authorities." The effort to turn Raoul Wallenberg into a nonperson—to throw a cloud of unknowing around his persona—can be reconstructed from documents that eventually emerged from interlocking files of the KGB, the Soviet Foreign Ministry, and the Communist Party's Central Committee.

Both the KGB and the Foreign Ministry gave copies of circumstantial documents to Swedish Ambassador Carl Otto Oerjan Berner in the fall of 1991. According to the Foreign Ministry's incoming correspondence log, Victor S. Abakumov—head of Stalin's Ministry of State Security (MGB, forerunner of the KGB)—sent a letter "Concerning the Wallenberg Case" to Foreign Minister Vyacheslav M. Molotov. The letter was dated July 17, 1947—the very day Wallenberg was supposed to have died. Abakumov apparently replied to one of the Foreign Ministry's requests concerning Wallenberg, but there is no specific indication that he reported Wallenberg's death; the letter itself was not preserved.

After Stalin's death, an internal inquiry into Wallenberg's fate was undertaken; a draft report on the case was prepared jointly by Molotov for the Foreign Ministry and Ivan A. Serov, then head of the KGB. According to this report, it was Abakumov who had ordered that Wallenberg be taken to Moscow and charged with spying for the Germans against the Soviet Union. (One document found in KGB files noted that a non-Swedish employee of the Swedish Embassy in Budapest had—most likely fraudulently or under pressure—testified that the Embassy had sheltered Nazis.)

As to Wallenberg's ultimate fate, Serov quoted a memorandum written by the Lubyanka's medical director, Dr. A. L. Smoltsov, dated July 17, 1947, and addressed to Abakumov, which said, "I report that the prisoner Wallenberg, with whom you are familiar, suddenly died tonight in his cell, presumably as a result of a myocardial infarction. In view of your instructions about personal attention to Wallenberg, I request instructions on whom to assign to perform the autopsy." A handwritten postscript by Dr. Smoltsov stated, "Reported personally to the Minister. Order to cremate body without autopsy." But in 1991—despite this document, and despite repeated Soviet and Russian assurances that it is, in effect, the last word on Wallenberg's fate—numerous reports on the Swedish diplomat's apparent survival continued to be received by the Raoul Wallenberg Association in Stockholm.

Bakatin gave the Swedish Ambassador five documents on September

4, 1991, noting that "unfortunately these documents do not shed full light on this affair either, but simply confirm the version that has been current until now." Ambassador Berner commented, "I am fairly convinced that we have everything the present head of the KGB knows exists. That does not necessarily mean everything has been given to us." The Tass news agency listed the five documents and their contents as follows:

1. The first document is a report by the head of the 151st Infantry Division's Political Department to the head of the Political Department of the Seventh Guards Army "on the detention of Mr. Wallenberg and his driver on January 14, 1945." The document stated that Wallenberg protected Jews' rights in Budapest during the Second World War.

2. The second document is an extract from a prisoner's registration book. It says that Wallenberg was imprisoned on February 6, 1945.

3. The third document is a letter from Hans Leut, Reconnaissance Company private first class, to the chief of the Vladimir Prison, in which he mentions Wallenberg. The letter was written in 1949, but this was no proof that Wallenberg was alive at that time.

4. The fourth document is an extract from the testimony of Thompson, former consular officer in Budapest, about Wallenberg's activities to protect Jews during the War. [Thompson's identity and position are not clarified.]

5. The last document is a letter from Lunev, senior KGB officer, to a high Foreign Ministry official, Vanchevsky. The letter, written on June 12, 1957, stated that documents on Wallenberg had been destroyed, under orders from the leadership of the Soviet Ministry of State Security, which functioned from 1946 to 1954.

Of these five documents, the very last one is probably the most significant. By publicizing it, the KGB officers who supplied it to Bakatin were following an earlier pattern of placing blame for the Wallenberg case on Abakumov. Stalin had established the Ministry of State Security in 1946, giving his secret police ministerial status and power. Abakumov had previously directed the "Smersh" investigative unit (which derived its name from the slogan *Smert Shpionam*, or "Death to Spies"). The unit was heavily involved in combating real or suspected dissent within the Soviet military and civilian populations. After the war, under Abakumov, Smersh was absorbed into the Ministry of State Security, where it formed its Third Chief Directorate. Within the labyrinth of Kremlin intrigue during and after Stalin's final years, Abakumov was imprisoned by Stalin in 1951, and executed by Stalin's successors in 1954. In February 1957, then–Soviet Foreign Minister Andrei A. Gromyko acknowledged in a statement to the Swedish government that Raoul Wallenberg had, in fact, been imprisoned in the Soviet Union, and had died in prison, as a result of "the criminal activity of Abakumov."

Another interim officeholder whose term was even shorter than that of Bakatin was Soviet Foreign Minister Boris Pankin. On September 5, 1991, Pankin—who had previously been Soviet ambassador in Sweden— met with Wallenberg's half brother Guy von Dardel and pledged his ministry's cooperation in seeking a final clarification of the case. On November 20 just before his ministerial assignment ended, Pankin handed seventy documents to Ambassador Berner—mainly internal Foreign Ministry memoranda. The matter was once again taken up with new Russian Foreign Minister Andrei Kozyrev. During a Brussels meeting of the European Community (EC) in March 1992, Franz Andriessen— the European Commissioner for External Relations—told Kozyrev that the EC hoped to see the Wallenberg case "solved, once and for all." Kozyrev was said to have pledged his cooperation.

The pursuit of the Wallenberg files illustrated the KGB's ambivalence about access to its archives. Once Bakatin was removed from the agency's leadership, and particularly after the main KGB agencies were absorbed by the Russian government, inquiries concerning some material of public interest met with polite reluctance. Under a decree entitled "Concerning the Archives of the USSR Committee for State Security" signed by President Boris Yeltsin on August 24, 1991, the KGB files were transferred to the jurisdiction of "archival organizations of Russia." The KGB had previously set up a committee with the task of developing "selection criteria" and with instructions to "separate documents of historical significance" from those of a contemporary nature—those falling into the category of "operational intelligence."

Under the chairmanship of Rudolf Pikhoya, the Russian government's Committee for Archival Affairs was designated to coordinate public access to archives. Vera Tolz, writing "Access to KGB and CPSU Archives in Russia" in the Radio Free Europe/Radio Liberty *Research Report* (April

17, 1992), noted that those in charge of KGB archives were reported to have been "quick to use the operational intelligence rubric to hide historical documents of a potentially embarrassing nature." She quoted Pikhoya as saying that the KGB had even classified materials on the Wallenberg case as operational intelligence, although, in Pikhoya's view, they could easily have been made public.

What chances were there that some of the questions on KGB activities that had been asked by world public opinion for years would be answered by access to the KGB archives? The *New York Times* (January 7, 1990) published an editorial titled "Mysteries That Matter" in which it listed some "of the most intriguing questions awaiting answers." Among them were: Who killed Jan Masaryk, the Czechoslovak Foreign Minister who mysteriously fell to his death in 1948? Was Otto John, the head of West Germany's secret service, kidnapped in East Berlin; or was he guilty of treason? Was Lee Harvey Oswald, the man who killed President John F. Kennedy, a KGB "asset"? Was the KGB involved in the 1981 assassination attempt on Pope John Paul II?

The list of KGB mysteries runs into the hundreds. But among the more obvious are those about the presence of Soviet agents in the U.S. intelligence community. And to what degree did Soviet nuclear power gain from data obtained by espionage in the United States and elsewhere? Two questions come to mind that have been asked publicly over and over again. Was Alger Hiss—the U.S. State Department officer who stood accused by the House Committee on Un-American Activities— really a Soviet spy? Were Ethel and Julius Rosenberg—executed in 1953 for giving nuclear secrets to the USSR—in fact guilty as charged? On this final question, the KGB did offer an answer of sorts, during the Bakatin period. In reply to reporters of the *New York Post* (November 25, 1991), the USSR KGB's spokesman Alexander N. Karbainov commented, "I have no material about them. No files. Nothing about the alleged nuclear spying." This was, of course, not an answer that dealt with the role of the Rosenbergs. Files might exist, but were not made available to Karbainov; files might have been destroyed; Soviet military intelligence—the GRU—might very well have been in charge of nuclear espionage, and, accordingly, no files on "alleged nuclear spying" needed to exist in the KGB archives. After all, the archivist of the Security Ministry told Interfax (June 11, 1992) that the KGB's operational files on the world-famous writer Alexander Solzhenitsyn had been destroyed in 1990 as being without "historical or operational significance."

On the controversial case of Alger Hiss, the Russian military historian

General Dimitri A. Volkogonov—head of a research group on declassifying KGB material—answered an inquiry from Hiss himself on October 14, 1992: "Mr. A. Hiss had never and nowhere been recruited as an agent of the intelligence services of the USSR. Not a single document, and a great amount of materials have been studied, substantiates the allegation." Did this clear Alger Hiss? His defenders said yes, and his detractors said no. On December 16, General Volkogonov tried to clarify matters when he protested, "I was not properly understood. The Ministry of Defense also has an intelligence service, which is totally different, and many documents have been destroyed. I only looked through what the KGB had. All I said was that I saw no evidence." In essence, then, Volkogonov's reply did not go beyond Karbainov's on the Rosenbergs: he simply had found nothing in the files. In fact, Volkogonov explained, "What I saw gives no basis to claim a full clarification. There is no guarantee that it was not destroyed, that it was not in other channels." His research had clearly been restricted to a limited number of KGB files. "But," Volkogonov explained, "I did spend two days swallowing dust."

What, then, about Lee Harvey Oswald? Would the KGB have kept a file detailing his role as an agent assigned to assassinate President Kennedy? It seems—to say the very least—unlikely. Energetic U.S. television reporters were actually given a glimpse at the outside of a "real" file on Oswald. The KGB had him under surveillance during his stay in the Soviet Union, where he had asked for asylum. Vladimir Y. Semichastny, KGB Chairman at the time of the Kennedy assassination, told the German weekly *Der Spiegel* (June 6, 1992) that Oswald had threatened suicide if not permitted to stay in the Soviet Union. Asked how the KGB decided that Oswald was "not an American spy," Semichastny replied, "One could hardly assume that the Americans would use such a stupid man as one of their agents." The Soviet agency decided that Oswald "could be of no use," either to the CIA or the KGB. Oswald was sent to Minsk, and the Byelorussian KGB kept an eye on his activities, but somewhat casually. Semichastny said, "We didn't have enough people to accompany him into restaurants, to go dancing, or meet women." Eventually, Oswald asked to return to the United States. And according to the former KGB chief, the Russians were glad to be rid of him.

An interview with a German weekly does not exactly amount to the publication of KGB archives. As for the many questions that might still be answered from declassified Lubyanka files, it would seem best that our expectations be kept low. One U.S. firm, Crown Publishers, made an arrangement with the Russian Foreign Intelligence Service (FIS) for publication of a series of books based on the KGB files. Topics were to include the Cuban missile crisis, Soviet penetration of British intelligence and key establishments, the Berlin operations of the KGB, the case of Leon Trotsky, and a history of Soviet intelligence as a whole.

Yuri Kobaladze—in charge of FIS media relations—told the National Press Club in Washington that the books represented "the quite natural process of making public a number of documents that no longer have any operational value but are of historic interest." According to Itar-Tass (June 24, 1992), Kobaladze said, "Our service takes very thorough measures to preserve the integrity and confidentiality of its enormous archives." One of the co-authors of the books, Oleg Tsarev, emphasized that the Russian Foreign Intelligence Service "will itself be carrying out the selection of materials, in collaboration with the co-authors," and FIS would "guarantee that they are comprehensive and reliable for publication."

No doubt, even such carefully screened materials will be of value to historians. When the Russian Parliament, dominated by a Communist-Nationalist majority, adjourned its session on July 23, 1993, it had voted to seal crucial KGB files for another twenty years. Meanwhile, most of the crucial questions concerning the KGB's archives will undoubtedly remain classified as operational intelligence, and remain firmly unanswered.

# Part III

## Rapid Rebirth

# 10

# Boris Yeltsin's KGB

Even before the Soviet Union was dissolved, Boris Yeltsin arranged for the creation of an independent Russian KGB; after the dissolution of the USSR, President Yeltsin's KGB took over most of the functions of the old KGB apparatus. This arrangement baffled some observers who recalled that Yeltsin himself had earlier been the target of some KGB activities. And yet, like other leaders of ex-Soviet republics or states, he felt the need for a secret service—as long as he could be fairly sure of its loyalty to his administration.

Like others who had advanced within the Communist Party system, Yeltsin apparently regarded the KGB as a necessary evil that could be eminently useful. He mentioned in his memoirs that, early in his career, he made sure that his relations with the KGB in Sverdlovsk Province were businesslike and cordial. Writing in his autobiography *Against the Grain*, Yeltsin recalled that, in the late 1970s when he was first secretary of the Communist Party of the province, "I developed reasonably good relations with the provincial directorate of the KGB." He added that he visited the office of the director "frequently" to ask "for information about the work of the KGB, studied the way it functioned, and acquainted myself with every one of its branches." And while he realized that "certain matters" were kept secret from him, Yeltsin felt that he "got to know the KGB's system pretty thoroughly."

Yeltsin maintained that his inside knowledge of KGB practices prompted him, in 1989, to oppose the direct appointment of Vladimir Kryuchkov to the Communist Party's innermost circle, its Politburo; by tradition, Kryuchkov should have passed through a period of "candidate member" before becoming a full member of the Politburo. In his memoirs, Yeltsin attributed this haste to Gorbachev's need for KGB support. "The winds of change," Yeltsin wrote, had "not touched either the KGB, the army, the Ministry of Internal Affairs, which controls the police and a large contingent of special troops." As he put it, "these organizations have always been the bulwark of state power." His comments are of particular significance, considering the role the KGB's successor agencies and the Interior Ministry later played during Russia's Yeltsin administration.

Boris Yeltsin's relations to the KGB reflected his changing political fate during the Gorbachev regime—which included his ouster from the post equivalent to mayor of the city of Moscow; a period of demeaning downgrading among the Soviet leadership; followed by his dramatic election to the Presidency of Russia; and finally—after the abortive coup of August 1991—his emergence as the outstanding personality among the post-Soviet leadership. As a matter of course, the KGB reported to Gorbachev on opposition movements and leaders—and that most certainly included Yeltsin. Whether or not Gorbachev specifically requested such reports is not a matter of record, but should be doubted. Also in doubt is whether Gorbachev was in any way responsible for a series of political and public relations dirty tricks directed against Yeltsin during the Russian presidential campaign.

On the other hand, a substantial amount of KGB-type "disinformation" on Yeltsin was publicly circulated during the period of Yeltsin's virtual political exile from the center of Kremlin power. Rumors about his emotional instability, his drinking habits, and his generally volatile personality made the rounds in Moscow and abroad, including the United States. This type of gossip contributed to an evaluation in Washington that underestimated Yeltsin's qualities as a statesman, comparing him unfavorably to Gorbachev.

During his first visit to the United States in 1989, a one-week goodwill tour, Yeltsin visited nine states and eleven cities. His lecture fees, totaling $100,000, were set aside to purchase syringes for an anti-AIDS campaign. Upon his return to Moscow, Yeltsin discovered *Pravda* was reprinting an article from the Italian newspaper *La Repubblica* that was alleged to be an account of his boisterous, drunken behavior during the U.S. tour, complete with a description of a huge shopping binge. *Repubblica*, whose enterprising Moscow correspondents could usually call on well-connected sources, had clearly provided a highly biased account. What, exactly, had been the source of this disinformation? And who had furnished Moscow television with a bit of tape that showed Yeltsin drowsy with fatigue, his speech slightly slurred, during a meeting at Johns Hopkins University in Baltimore? In his memoirs, he wondered just how this videotape—slowed down at crucial points—was acquired, "although one can easily guess where and by whom." If he suspected the KGB, he didn't say so.

Another incident that has remained in the unsolved-mysteries category occurred shortly afterward. Yeltsin recalled that he traveled to the village of Uspenskoye, outside Moscow, to visit an old friend from his Sverdlovsk days. He wrote that "not far from his house I dismissed the driver, as I almost always do, in order to walk the last few hundred yards." As Yeltsin began to cross a bridge, another car pulled up, and suddenly, as he put it, "I was in the river." He barely managed to swim ashore, and staggered to the nearest police station.

What had actually happened? Had someone tried to drown Yeltsin? Did someone want to give the impression that, drunk perhaps, he had fallen off the bridge? His reaction to the incident throws some light on relations between Yeltsin and Bakatin, whom he replaced as KGB chief early in 1992. Yeltsin recalled with chagrin that Bakatin, then Minister of Interior, told the Supreme Soviet "no attempt had been made on my [Yeltsin's] life" because, if Yeltsin had really been knocked off the bridge, he would have been severely injured, as the bridge was fifty feet above the water. In fact, Yeltsin maintained, the bridge was only fifteen feet from the water, so that Bakatin had "misled his listeners over facts that can easily be checked." Next, the busy Moscow rumor mill produced the version that Yeltsin had visited his mistress who, in a fit of anger, had emptied a bucket of water over his head.

Russian public opinion took all these stories and incidents pretty much in stride; in fact, Yeltsin's popularity appeared to be strengthened by the rather heavy-handed attempts to undermine his image. He won the Russian presidential race with an overwhelming majority, and proceeded to govern the vast republic with a good deal of skill and steadiness. His political realism came into play when he prepared for the organization of a separate Russian KGB. Yeltsin told the Russian parliament as early as September 19, 1990, that he had discussed the matter with Kryuchkov, who had "consented in principle to support the creation of a Russian KGB."

When Yeltsin presented the definitive proposal to the Russian parliament on December 15, he emphasized that other republics had their own KGB; as he put it, "The Ukraine has its own security agency. Russia must have one, too." *Moscow News* (No. 2, 1991) commented on this development under the headline "RUSSIA'S KGB—WILL CONTROL BE GIVEN TO YELTSIN?" On May 6, 1991, Yeltsin and Kryuchkov signed an agreement establishing a KGB of the Russian Soviet Federated Socialist Republic (RSFSR), but carefully circumscribing the relationship of the central KGB with its Russian counterpart. The delicate deal threw Yeltsin and Kryuchkov into a pragmatic partnership that left demarcation lines of responsibilities deliberately vague. But it nevertheless established the foundation for the relatively seamless continuation of the KGB after the dissolution of the Soviet Union—including, eventually, control of overseas intelligence and over the army of Border Guards.

Yeltsin and Kryuchkov agreed on the appointment of a twenty-year veteran of KGB service, Major General Victor V. Ivanenko to direct the Russian KGB, which would occupy offices in the Lubyanka building and absorb about half the staff of the total Soviet KGB apparatus. Ivanenko was forty-four years old at the time of his appointment and had spent all of his career within the secret service. Virtually on the eve of the August coup attempt, Ivanenko told the newspaper *Trud* (August 3, 1991) that one of the main tasks of the Russian KGB was to combat "those who advocate the overthrow of the current state system."

Ivanenko initially managed to ride out the postcoup storm that shook the KGB, led to the imprisonment of Kryuchkov, and put Bakatin in temporary control of the agency. Of Bakatin's appointment, Yeltsin had said that it was acceptable, being "half Gorbachev's and half Russia's." As for Ivanenko it could be said that he symbolized the Yeltsin–Kryuchkov compromise, and he sought to live up to the postcoup changes in Moscow's political atmosphere. Ivanenko told *Pravda* (November 6, 1991) that, "no matter how unpopular it sounds, no independent state can exist without an intelligence service." He added that there was no sense in acting ostrichlike, "or sneering at the mere mention of the word 'intelligence service.' " He said it was necessary to "stop attempts to penetrate state secrets, particularly if this happens through the subversion of those who are privy to secrets."

As Bakatin's influence faded and the KGB was divided up, the position of Russia's KGB increased. On November 26, 1991, Yeltsin signed a decree that reestablished the Russian service under the name Federal Security Agency (*Agentstvo Federalnoy Besopasnosti*, or FSA). Three days later, Ivanenko held a press conference at his Lubyanka office. He reiterated the standard public relations theme that his agency would combat organized crime, terrorism, narcotics traffic, contraband, and corruption, but would also actively engage in "counterintelligence." He said that twenty thousand staff members would be employed at the agency's central office, and another twenty-two thousand throughout Russian territories, most of the staff being former KGB officers.

Within weeks, the Soviet Union as such was dissolved; Gorbachev reluctantly yielded his Kremlin office to Yeltsin; and the KGB successor agencies passed through yet another period of reorganizational turmoil. Yet, in effect, what had been the USSR KGB simply became the Russian KGB. And as the agency had, throughout its existence, been largely a Russian-operated apparatus, much that happened amounted to a round-about reintegration.

With Kryuchkov in prison, Gorbachev out in the political cold, and Yeltsin apparently in full control, reintegration of the KGB might have been a relatively smooth undertaking. But the project ran into a long-standing rivalry and contradiction: relations between the KGB and the Interior Ministry. The two agencies had overlapping responsibilities, were supposed to cooperate closely with each other, but were divided by an elitist attitude on the part of the KGB and a defensive ("We have to do all the dirty work!") mentality on the part of the much larger Interior Ministry and its far-flung militia. Still, what could seem easier and more logical than to do away with rivalries and duplications, and combine the two agencies into a single law-enforcement body? As it turned out, a great deal.

On December 19, 1991, Yeltsin issued a decree that combined the two services into one Russian Ministry of Security and Internal Affairs. And he thereby kicked straight into a politico-bureaucratic hornets' nest! The decree had the effect of abolishing both the USSR KGB and the newly established Russian KGB, and merging them into the Interior Ministry. Immediately, a barrage of attacks on this merger began—some clearly caused by bureaucratic concern about submerging the KGB identity within a gigantic Interior Ministry apparatus; others caused by more substantial objections to the creation of yet another dangerously mo-nopolistic, superpolice machinery.

One of the most intriguing arguments was that, by their very sepa-ration, the two rival agencies had managed to keep an eye on each other. Another argument—a frequently expressed fear—was that the merger was recreating one of the monsters of early Soviet history: the People's Commissariat of Internal Affairs, or NKVD. Public discussion of the merger was so vocal that, two days after the decree was published, *Izvestia* wrote it had created "diametrically opposed views." The paper commented, "The full range of assessments has been expressed—from complete rejoicing at the strengthening of Russia's legal protection system, to horror because Yeltsin is creating rigid dictatorial structures and the merger of the militia and the KGB means a return to that unforgettable monster, the NKVD [which combined most secret and overt police functions during part of Stalin's regime in the mid-1930s]."

Other critics compared the merger with the advancement of the NKVD to the ministerial level under Lavrenti Beria in 1946, when it became the Ministry of Internal Affairs (MVD). Beria enlarged the MVD into an all-powerful apparatus that eventually absorbed all actual or potential rival agencies. Critics of the merger decree accused Yeltsin of a move that was unconstitutional and that, as far as the country's democratic development was concerned, represented a dangerously regressive step. Moscow Radio Rossii (January 2, 1992) even quoted KGB insiders as suggesting that the merger had been manipulated by supporters of the August coup, stating that "those who unswervingly carried out the decrees of the organizers of the August putsch are taking an active part in determining the future of the Ministry of Security and Internal Affairs."

During the relatively short period of this decree's existence, a public discussion took place that had both historic, contemporary, and future significance. Sergei Filatov, first deputy chairman of the Russian parliament, worried—as it turned out, correctly—that the decree forecast the end of a separate status for other former KGB bodies, such as "government communications, the President's Guards, the guard of the Supreme Soviet chairman, the guard of the state power buildings," which had been turned into "individual structures" but were now endangered by "one more monster that includes everything." Filatov, too, compared the planned ministry to the old NKVD.

Yeltsin was also challenged by the Russian Constitutional Court—the national equivalent to the U.S. Supreme Court—which quickly asserted its independent judgment. It resolved during a meeting on December 26, 1991, that it did not intend to share "the sad fate of the USSR Constitutional Supervisory Committee and, acting as the supreme court body, will take steps to protect the constitutional regime in the country, and to prevent dictatorship and arbitrary rulings, wherever they may originate." The Court's chairman, Valery Zorkin, told reporters after the meeting that the resolution specifically referred to the KGB–Interior Ministry merger decree, which bore the official title "On the Formation of the RSFSR Ministry of Security and Internal Affairs."

The Moscow media were desperately trying to figure out just who had drafted the controversial merger decree, what political forces had sought to force the Russian parliament and public to accept it, and why its backers had so crucially misjudged legal and popular reaction to the project. From the mass of speculation, a few elements of obvious political logic emerged. To begin with, the initiative had mainly come from the Interior Ministry, then headed by Victor Barannikov, who, in fact, briefly headed the combined phantom ministry. While certain KGB hard-liners might have desired the establishment of an old-line monopoly agency, the number of KGB resignations or threats of resignations suggested that most staffers did not like becoming lost within a massive "foreign" bureaucracy. One office being eliminated by the merger was that of Vadim Bakatin, whose bureau had by that time shrunk to a central clearinghouse known as the Inter-Republican Security Service. When Bakatin had directed the Interior Ministry, his leadership was attacked by such career hard-liners as Barannikov for allegedly being amateurish and lacking in administrative cohesion. At the time of his appointment as KGB chief, Bakatin had clearly been Gorbachev's choice, with Yeltsin (remember the bridge incident?) in temporary agreement. On December 21, 1991, Tass quoted Bakatin as warning that the combined ministry provided "the potential possibility of turning into an uncontrollable body" even though there might be a gain in efficiency.

In the end, and after less than a month, Yeltsin called off the merger. But, in an odd constellation of events, the Constitutional Court won the legal battle while Barannikov still retained and ultimately strengthened his powers. Following a series of parliamentary hearings, the Constitutional Court ruled on January 14, 1992, that the merger decree ran counter to "the separation of legislative, executive and court powers established by the Russian Federation" and "counter to the delineation of competences established in the RSFSR Constitution between the highest bodies of state power and administration." Three days later, Yeltsin canceled the decree; that very day, he appointed Barannikov director of the KGB's successor agency, which later became the Russian Ministry of Security.

Victor Pavlovich Barannikov thus emerged as one of the most powerful personalities in Yeltsin's Russia. Insiders quickly asserted that he retained direct lines of communications to the Interior Ministry through his second in command, Victor Yerin, who had succeeded him as head of the ministry. As *Izvestia* put it (January 22, 1992), Barannikov and his former first deputy, who were believed to have been "the originators of the idea of merging the KGB and the militia, will now run these organizations, but separately." One thing was sure, the Bakatin interlude within the KGB—by whatever name—had definitely come to an end. Bakatin had denounced the KGB as being "monopolistic." Well, Barannikov obviously favored centralization, and he soon began to pull the pieces together that Bakatin had sought to separate permanently.

Alexander Rahr, the renowned biographical specialist of Radio Liberty's research division in Munich, dealt with Barannikov's career and position in a detailed analysis, "The KGB Survives under Yeltsin's Wing" in the Radio Free Europe/Radio Liberty *Research Report* (March 27, 1992). Rahr recalled that for three years the KGB had been Yeltsin's "greatest enemy, continually trying to compromise him as he fought his way to the top," but that Yeltsin nevertheless seemed to have "co-opted it to protect his own position and that of the new state and government institutions." The appointment of Barannikov illustrated this point vividly. Bahr noted that Barannikov had "not projected the image of a reformist politician, but "stopped the dismantling of the KGB which had started under Bakatin, emphasizing the need to keep experienced Chekists for the sake of preserving professionalism in the new agency."

According to the Radio Liberty authority, Barannikov was born on October 20, 1940, at Fedosevka. He began his career as a fitter in a mechanical enterprise, where he worked from 1957 to 1958. In 1961 he became an instructor in the Komsomol, the Communist youth organization. His law enforcement career began in 1963 when Barannikov became a police station commissioner with the Administration of Internal Affairs of the City of Chelyabinsk. From then on, he rose on the ladder of police work—as operational commissioner in the Internal Affairs Administration's Criminal Investigation Office from 1964 to 1969; and then, first as acting section chief and finally as section chief of the Department of Internal Affairs No. 42 at Chelyabinsk. From 1972 to 1974 he was chief of the Leadership Sector of Stations Inspectors Office. He moved to Kaliningrad; and from 1974 to 1983 he served successively as deputy chief and then chief of the Department of Internal Affairs No. 10 with the Ministry of Internal Affairs.

Beginning in 1983, Barannikov's career in the Internal Affairs Ministry included a series of positions in such Moscow divisions as the Main Administration for Struggle against Theft of Socialist Property. After the emergence of the Gorbachev regime, Barannikov went to the Transcaucasus; and from 1988 to 1990 he served as first deputy minister of internal affairs at Baku, capital of Azerbaijan. In 1990 he returned to Moscow as first deputy minister of internal affairs in the Russian Federation. Bahr noted that Barannikov "started to work for Yeltsin in September 1990" when he was promoted to head the Russian Interior Ministry. After the August 1991 coup, Barannikov temporarily served as USSR Minister of Internal Affairs.

Analysts examining the special relationship between Yeltsin and Barannikov recall Gorbachev's dramatic address to the Supreme Soviet on August 23, 1991, during which he described his isolation during the coup. At one point during his account, Gorbachev was persistently interrupted by Yeltsin, who presented him with a paper that listed the coup's supporters and opponents during a crucial sitting of the Soviet Council of Ministers. The reluctant Gorbachev was eventually forced to read the roster of all his ministers who, with very few exceptions, had turned against him during this meeting. Yeltsin's persistence in urging the President to read the transcript out loud was widely regarded as an aggressive personal gesture, designed to humiliate Gorbachev publicly. And the source of the memorandum—the person who had provided Yeltsin with this embarrassing account—was privately considered to have been none other than Barannikov.

Under Barannikov, the new Russian Ministry of Security—breaking with traditions of secrecy—made surprisingly sensational news the following summer when it announced a major purge of its leading personnel. In the course of what may be called an "apartment scandal," Barannikov fired a large number of high-level officials on a variety of corruption charges. Who were they? What had they done, or failed to do? And why did Barannikov go public with information that undermined the traditional KGB image of relative incorruptibility—relative to, in particular, the corruption charges that had shaken the Interior Ministry for decades, over and over again?

*Izvestia* was told (June 8, 1992) by Boris Bolshakov, deputy chairman of the Russian parliamentary Committee for Defense and Security Questions, that the men had been dismissed "for discrediting their officers' rank and for official abuses." More specifically, they had been found in "gross violations of the procedure for the use of apartments intended for operation work." The official documents carefully avoided the term "corruption." What, then, had they actually done? The security generals had, "in effect, appropriated apartments for personal use by certain top officers." In addition, Bolshakov said, "financial misdemeanors were uncovered in the expenditure of state resources allocated for special operations purposes." And, in still another sentence of bureaucratic circumlocution, he added, "Here, too, the motive of personal self-interest was discovered."

As it turned out, there had, for instance, been some "misallocation" of such items as refrigerators on the part of high-level security officers, and some of the men were covering up for each other. Still and all, were these misdeeds flagrant enough to cause such a major shake-up? Or was the whole undertaking just a purge of leftover "Bakatin men" with whom Barannikov did not feel comfortable? Bolshakov assured his interviewer, "I will tell you frankly: I have no doubts about the legality to dismiss top state security officers. There is no politics, revenge, or recarving of spheres of influence behind it." Earlier, Moscow TV (June 3, 1992) had speculated that the purge reflected "a struggle for power" between "the KGB Old Guard and the Ministry of Internal Affairs Old Guard."

All told, some seventy apartments had been illegally "privatized" by the top security officials. The Ministry's Public Relations Office identified them as "secret rendezvous apartments," from which furnishings had been removed. One assistant to the first deputy minister was reported to have "visited a hideout in person" and "removed a refrigerator, an Uzbek carpet, two lamps and a bedside table." The most prominent official among those found guilty by an internal investigation commission of the Security Ministry was Major General Vladimir Klishin, director of the Ministry's Chief Counterintelligence Directorate. The newspaper *Rossiskaya Gazeta* (June 5, 1992) turned to former Russian KGB chief Ivanenko—who had been fired on May 22—for comment on the purge. He used the occasion to take a swipe at Vadim Bakatin, saying that "Barannikov, unlike Bakatin, is doing a great deal to protect the security organs from falling apart and to make them work." Ivanenko added, "I say that absolutely sincerely. He has taken under his protection the professional section, which should be beneficial to society, and he is trying to create proper conditions for it and protect it against false accusations and indiscriminate criticism." Two of the officials involved in the scandal were staff members of the Foreign Intelligence Service; and Barannikov's office had to notify Yevgeny Primakov, his overseas espionage counterpart, of this particular invasion of the latter's bureaucratic turf. Both sides maintained public silence on this delicate case of cross-agency relations.

An odd sidelight on internal stresses within the Ministry of Security appeared two months later. *Pravda* reported (September 26, 1992) that it had received the copy of a statement sent to the Russian General Prosecutor's Office by one Major V. Plyushchev, whom the paper identified as "head of the first section of the First Department of the Russian Security Ministry's own security services." The document was dated August 25, 1992. Major Plyushchev asked the prosecutor to investigate what he described as a false accusation that had led to his dismissal as section chief. What had this accusation been?

Apparently, Security Minister Barannikov had drawn up an internal memorandum directing his staff's attention to a book by the ebullient chairman of the Russian parliament, Ruslan I. Khasbulatov, entitled *Reforming Reforms*. Barannikov's memo ordered that, on the basis of this book, the Ministry undertake a "thorough" check of a well-known joint stock company that, he had been told, was "funding" various controversial enterprises. The actual accusation against Plyushchev had been that he leaked a copy of the memorandum to the Russian Supreme Soviet in order, as *Pravda* put it, "to discredit" Barannikov. This, Plyushchev wrote, was a lie. But that's not the end of the story.

When protesting that he was innocent of the accusation—stating vigorously that he had simply not given a copy of the memo to the Supreme Soviet—Plyushchev was warned "by his bosses" that "a denial would 'reflect very badly' on the lives of his wife and children." The newspaper added, "What can be said about this? Evidently things are quite bad in the upper echelons of power, if they are resorting to political investigations and blackmail, as in the past, and suspect everyone, including their own staffers, of treachery." *Pravda* also commented, "It is an obvious truism that, until August 1991, opposition organizations were shadowed and dissenters were persecuted in our country. But what is the situation today? To all appearances, little has changed. Only the people being shadowed have changed."

Shortly afterward, the Ministry of Security reminded the Moscow public of its KGB traditions when it arrested two coauthors of an article dealing with the continued production of chemical weapons in Russia. The article, entitled "Poisoned Politics," appeared in *Moskovskiye Novosti* (the weekly that also has an English-language edition, *Moscow News*) on September 20, 1991 (No. 38). The authors were Lev Fedorov, a journalist holding a doctorate in chemical science, and Vil Mirzayanov, a former staff member of the State Union Scientific Research Institute of Organic Chemistry and Technology. Their article reported that, despite assurances by President Yeltsin and other officials, Russia continued to manufacture and test sophisticated types of binary chemical weapons, superior in their combat characteristics to virtually everything currently known in this field. The institute engaged in this research was located in Moscow itself, the authors said; and its experiments represented a danger to the city's ecological safety, as its emission filtration system suffered from imperfect ventilation. The article criticized General Anatoly Kuntsevich, chairman of the Presidential Committee for Chemical and Biological Weapons Convention Problems, who in 1991 had received the Lenin Prize for developing the "world's mightiest" chemical weapons.

The action of the Security Ministry took place one month after the article was published. A group of security agents arrived at Fedorov's home at 7:30 A.M. on October 22, equipped with a search warrant from the Russian Prosecutor General's Office, apparently on the personal authority of the office's director, Valentin Stepankov. Fedorov was taken to the Lefortovo, the former KGB prison that was now the center of the Ministry's Investigation Directorate. He was questioned for several hours but released that same evening. His coauthor Vil Mirzayanov was detained at Lefortovo, apparently because of his earlier official position and the charge that he had revealed "state secrets" in the article coauthored with Fedorov.

The same day, security agents visited the office of the paper that had published the article. As *Izvestia* reported (October 24, 1992), the *Moscow News* editor-in-chief Len Karpinsky was never told what actual secrets had been revealed in the article, nor "who, precisely, had evaluated the degree of secrecy of the information published in the newspaper." *Izvestia* commented that "the concept of state secrets in our country is so vague and flexible that it is never possible to establish when a secret is still a state secret, as it might become a departmental or even a personal secret." After all, the paper observed, the two authors had not acted as spies, "had not gone to foreign intelligence services, but had openly raised this tricky—to put it mildly—question in the press." The *Moscow News* editors came to regard the actions of the Ministry of Security as an attack on freedom of speech and as a warning to scientists who might be inclined to speak too freely about their work. The editors also speculated that even President Yeltsin might have been unaware that Russia held stockpiles of binary chemical weapons, in violation of international agreements.

On November 3, Vil Mirzayanov was released from custody. Apparently, the Prosecutor General's Office had decided not to proceed with charges against the scientist under Article 75 of the Russian Criminal

Code, directed against "Disclosing State Secrets." If such accusations were to have been found valid, Mirzayanov could have been sentenced to two to five years in prison. He gave a detailed account of his imprisonment to the magazine *Kuranty* (January 23, 1993), in which he suggested that the KGB had the dual intention of intimidating him "and other experts in the field of chemical weapons, but also of covering someone's tracks and diverting suspicion from the real sources of secret information."

Mirzayanov alleged that "the KGB, leadership of the Ministry of the Chemical Industry, and the generals, all have a material interest in providing themselves with a gravy train cloaked in secrecy." He added that there were "three of our experts" abroad "who are much better informed in the field of chemical weapons than I am," and who are "permanent residents of the United States." He did not provide their names but suggested that they were either sent abroad especially, "meaning that the KGB sent them there for the purpose of spreading disinformation, or [else] that a blind eye was turned to their departure." In either case, he said, "KGB authorization was essential." He went on trial before the Moscow city court on January 6, 1994.

Considering President Yeltsin's personal stake in Barannikov's position, it came as a shock to the Russian public when, on July 27, 1993, he dismissed his close associate from the post of Minister of Security. The publicized charges against Barannikov were two-fold: (a) personal involvement in corruption within the ministry, and (b) failure to exercise effective leadership over Russian Border Guards at the border between Tajikistan and Afghanistan.

Moscow gossip asserted that Yeltsin's dismissal of Barannikov had personal reasons as well. The story making the rounds alleged that Barannikov had forwarded confidential secret service files, documenting corruption on the part of Yeltsin's appointees and high-level officials, to Vice President Rutskoi. Rutskoi was, in fact, head of a commission of the Russian Security Council specifically concerned with anti-crime and anti-corruption activity, an assignment received by presidential decree. The appointment was reported by the President's office on October 8, 1992. Consequently, while advising Rutskoi of corruption among Yeltsin's entourage may have been technically correct, it was politically and personally an act of treasonable intrigue.

On September 21, 1993, Yeltsin dissolved Russia's increasingly antagonistic parliament. In turn, a militantly defiant parliament declared Rutskoi Acting President. Rutskoi named Barannikov Minister of Security for his shadow regime. Barannikov thereby aligned himself with Rutskoi against Yeltsin, just as, previously, he had helped Yeltsin to oust Gorbachev. When Rutskoi called for an armed uprising to overthrow Yeltsin, and violent riots broke out on October 2, Barannikov led a brigade of insurgents in an unsuccessful siege of Moscow's Ostankino television center. Two days later, after a fierce battle, troops loyal to Yeltsin stormed the parliament building. Rutskoi and key associates were arrested. As a result, Barannikov found himself in a cell at Lefortovo, the notorious KGB prison administered by the Ministry of Security. On October 6, Yeltsin denounced the uprising as an "armed mutiny," designed to establish "a bloodthirsty Communist-Fascist regime."

Barannikov's successor, Lieutenant-General Nikolai M. Galushkov, was a KGB veteran of thirty years' standing. Born in 1937 in the Ukraine, Galushkov obtained a law degree from Tomsk University in 1959. He worked in the office of the Public Prosecutor in the Kuzbass region until 1963, at which time he joined the Communist Party. Galushkov became a KGB staff member in 1963, functioning in the Kemerovo district. He obtained the top position in the state security apparatus of the Ukraine when he became Chairman of the Ukrainian KGB on May 25, 1987; he was reappointed to the post on July 20, 1990. He also served as a Soviet People's Deputy and as a member of the Supreme Soviet of the Ukrainian Soviet Socialist Republic. When the KGB was officially dissolved, Galushkov became Acting Chairman of the Ukrainian National Security Service.

Yeltsin's appointment of Galushkov as head of the Russian Ministry of Security, succeeding Barannikov, became effective on July 28, 1993. The selection of a KGB officer of long standing served, once again, to emphasize the continuity of the KGB Establishment.

On December 21, 1993, Yeltsin replaced the Ministry of Security with the Federal Counterintelligence Service, charging that the ministry had hampered "implementation of political and economic reforms." Informally, it was assumed that the agency had failed to anticipate the strong showing of the ultra-nationalist so-called Liberal Democratic Party, headed by Vladimir V. Zhirinovsky, at the Russian parliamentary elections of December 17, and that pro-Zhirinovsky sentiments were influential within the KGB successor agency. Yeltsin retained Galushkov as director of the renamed secret police.

# 11

# Whose Codes? Whose Ciphers?

During the much-publicized "breakup" of the KGB's monopoly, one of the agency's major divisions—its Eighth Chief (Communications) Directorate—was officially separated from the Lubyanka central control, Colonel Vladimir Rubanov, then head of the KGB's Analysis Division, complained to *Komsomolskaya Pravda* (September 20, 1991) that the communications apparatus had "swallowed up around a quarter of the entire KGB budget." Yet, like so many other "separated" divisions, the communications section was, before long, reintegrated into the KGB—albeit into its later incarnation: the Russian Ministry of Security. In the interim, it obtained a new name, that of the Federal Agency of Government Communications and Information (FAGCI).

Much like the U.S. National Security Agency (NSA), which is its closest equivalent, the communications arm of the Russian Ministry of Security is as little known as its activities are far-flung, highly technical, and sophisticated. In a detailed account on the agency, Alexander Golubev reported in *Rossiskaya Gazeta* (March 5, 1992) that the communications service supervised hundreds of automatic monitoring stations, commanded sixteen thousand troops of its own, operated a series of satellites in space, and managed a highly sophisticated computer system as well as a unique apparatus for encoding and decoding secret information.

It is to be assumed as a matter of course that it is within this agency's functions to intercept open as well as encrypted messages flowing between foreign governments and their agencies, as well as between government officials who may be communicating over wireless or tapped telephone lines. A weakening of the agency's qualities would, one must assume, affect virtually every major figure and organization within Russia, from the President to the Foreign Ministry, from missions abroad to their home bases, including individual agents reporting to the Russian Foreign Intelligence Service.

Although separation of the communications services from the central KGB was initially popular, critics—within the Foreign Ministry, for example—quietly expressed doubts about the haste with which this step had been taken. Yet, even at that point, the separation was largely formal; or to put it more bluntly, it was largely window dressing. Interagency liaison continued to operate pretty much as before, regardless of the changed nameplates outside of buildings and office doors. One of the major points of controversy between Washington and Moscow was the continued maintenance of a powerful monitoring station in Cuba; this Russian electronic listening post on the American continent, reaffirmed in a Havana protocol on November 2, 1992, outlasted all disagreements between Moscow and Havana and provided Cuba with one of its few strong bargaining points in negotiations with the new Russian regime. Moscow had lost other valuable listening posts, notably in East Germany.

Golubev pointed out that, among other tasks, the communications agency "ensured the communications of the President, the Parliament, the government, the ministries, and the administration heads" and provided "the technical basis for control of the armed forces, including strategic forces." He added that "the existence of its own cryptographic service enables the FAGCI to protect the secrecy of government communications from foreign technical intelligence services." Golubev alleged that "the coders' crypto-schemes now in use make it possible to assert that it will take approximately eighty years to decipher a secret report," and he wrote, "If we speak of scientific developments and new technologies, then technical counterintelligence and intelligence are probably one of those rare fields in which we are at present in no way inferior to the acknowledged Western leaders—the United States and Britain." Golubev concluded that, regarding the communications agency's "rivalry with foreign technical intelligence services, I am sure that the need for such activity will not drop away quickly, despite the warming of the international climate."

When the Russian government decided to bring the communications agency "home" into the former KGB apparatus transformed into its Ministry of Security, some critics wondered whether this move might weaken the integrity of the communications service. The argument was bolstered by persistent reports that Kryuchkov and his predecessors had consistently slanted reports going to top Soviet leaders—be they Brezhnev or Gorbachev—to strengthen their own position and advance their personal viewpoints.

An outsider might well assume that the communications agency itself, as a mere conveyor of data, could remain relatively free from political influence—that, in fact, distortion, slanting, and disinformation could easily be inserted along the winding bureaucratic road from receiving station to analysts and ultimate report. Conversely, and to cite a striking historic example, no matter how much correct intelligence data may be conveyed, leaders may still ignore or misjudge it: Joseph Stalin had reports, from his Western Allies as well as from his own intelligence services, that Nazi Germany was about to attack the Soviet Union during World War II; yet he ignored this massive information, apparently for emotional reasons.

*Komsomolskaya Pravda* recalled (May 1, 1992) that Soviet society had been "entirely unaware" of the KGB Eighth Chief (Communications) Directorate during its "more than 50-year history." The forever alert and conspiracy-minded founder of the Soviet state, Vladimir I. Lenin, scribbled a note to his associates in 1922 in which he said, "There are reports of a British invention in radio-telegraphy, which would allow telegrams to be sent in secret. If this invention could be bought, the military applications of radio-telephony and radio-telegraphy would be of even greater importance." *Komsomolskaya Pravda* questioned a leading Russian authority on cryptography, Vadim B. Kravchenko, on this point. Kravchenko recalled that, a year before Lenin's short memorandum, "a special service was set up which was the forerunner of the KGB's Government Communications Directorate," but that "serious scientific and industrial activity in this area" did not begin until 1931.

Kravchenko added that, during World War II, Soviet leaders from Stalin on down were able to use "secure information transmission systems," but that "strict mathematics only invaded the art of cryptography in the thirties." Kravchenko insisted that the essentials of these developments—the algorithms—were "entirely ours," although "we used foreign equipment," such as captured German apparatus. The KGB employed convict labor during these scientific developments, and Kravchenko wisecracked, "The convicts were uniquely skilled with their hands." At the outset, he observed, "our equipment weighed tons and tons, and required kilowatts of power, yet it had to be installed on planes, ships, satellites, and in the trunks of leaders' limousines."

Looking toward the communications problems of some of the ex-Soviet republics, Kravchenko said, "It is hard to install our equipment in a completed building. If things are arranged properly, it should be included in the work from the very outset." That method was used, of course, when the KGB installed monitoring devices throughout the newly built U.S. Embassy in Moscow. Kravchenko cautioned, "Now, for instance, the new authorities in the sovereign states are busy housing their departments. This will be harder than they think!"

Kravchenko was quite candid concerning communications secrecy between Russia and other ex-Soviet states. He noted that, as long as there existed a single communications system, "the former republics' autonomy in the information sphere is a sham, and they are beginning to realize it." He added, "If it were not for political niceties, from the viewpoint of Russian security, we would have to isolate the capitals of the former Union republics, as special communications centers that have fallen into the hands of foreigners." In the future, the leaders of the new republics may have to go abroad for new secure communications equipment; shortage of hard currency, and foreign export restrictions, are likely to make this difficult. Will such regions as Kazakhstan, Georgia, and even Lithuania come to Moscow for secure communications equipment? The question is loaded with intrigue and irony.

A straw in the wind of future complications appeared in 1992, when on June 3 the embassies of Estonia, Latvia, and Lithuania were cut off from the communications systems that had traditionally linked them with Russian officials. Baltfax, the news service of the three Baltic states, recalled that the embassies "had been using the government communications facilities ever since the offices of the republics had been established in Moscow." The communications systems affected were identified as the ATC-2 and HF (direct link) services. The three Baltic embassies were rather brusquely advised that they had been disconnected because "such types of services are not provided to representatives of foreign states in Moscow." The government of Lithuania had, in fact, requested such disconnection on its own, but Latvia and Estonia had not. Shortly afterward, on July 2, Baltfax quoted the Latvian Embassy in Moscow as denying that it had installed eavesdropping equipment in its offices. The newspaper *Baltiiskoya Vremya* had asserted earlier that the Latvian security service was "intercepting telephone conversations from an especially equipped room."

After the coup attempt of August 1991, Moscow was rife with rumors that the KGB was drastically curtailing its telephone-tapping activities. *Komsomolskaya Pravda* (September 12, 1991) noted that Moscovites were reporting their phones had been "turned off" so listening devices could be removed. Apparently, however, such obvious mechanical actions were not necessary. The paper asked a representative from the KGB computer center to explain how such "bug removal" actually worked. He said that telephone conversations can be tapped when appropriate machinery deletes from a specific section of the telephone cable the "electromagnetic background to the conversation." Or, he said, the intercept can take place "directly, via an automatic telephone station which decodes it, and, if necessary, records it." He explained further, "With the existence of powerful, rapid computers, the automatic functioning of a bugging system for a large number of telephone subscribers is simultaneously possible. The frequencies of code words or voices are fed into the computer beforehand. If they appear on the air, recording automatically begins."

The paper added what has long been known even among laypeople interested in the field: that "to penetrate other people's secrets, it is by no means necessary to 'eavesdrop' only on telephones, especially if a scrambling device is used." As the paper also pointed out, "It is possible to use laser apparatus which can, for instance, with the aid of a beam of a specific wavelength, detect vibrations in window panes during conversations in a building and, after decoding, produce a tape recording of the conversation. The windows of several embassies in Moscow are angled in such a way as to be protected against such apparatus, which [must then be] directed at the window from an angle. ([And thus,] according to the physical law of refraction, a beam cannot return to the point from where it was sent.)"

A communications leak that specifically affected the Russian Foreign Ministry—and possibly involved a code violation—created a brief diplomatic scandal in mid-1992.

According to Interfax (August 11, 1992), texts of an exchange of letters between Russia's UN delegate Yuri Vorontsov and U.S. Secretary of State James Baker were published in the weekly *DEN*. The letters dealt with the possible participation of Russia in sanctions against segments of Yugoslavia (presumably Serbia) in order to counteract mass killings, "ethnic cleansing," and other acts of violence in the area. The Moscow publication *Diplomatic Panorama* reported that Foreign Minister Andrei Kozyrev had ordered a strict investigation of the leak; according to its sources, "publication of full texts of secret documents by the press might help foreign secret services break the codes used by Russian diplomats in their correspondence."

A potentially very significant discussion on the future use of secret communications in business affairs started within official as well as unofficial Russian circles. The end of the Cold War had begun to shift emphasis toward worldwide economic competition—between nations as well as between corporations. The degree to which national interests might be affected by economic shifts, and the possible use of "industrial espionage," gained considerable prominence. In earlier years, U.S. monitors had observed that Moscow routinely intercepted conversations among U.S. grain traders and between U.S. government agencies and grain merchants; because of this information, Soviet negotiators could anticipate the availability and pricing of grain. Other negotiations, both political and economic, had also benefited from advance knowledge—clandestinely obtained—by any and all participants.

Over the years, former intelligence officials had established themselves worldwide in commercial fields in which they had gained special expertise, ranging from arms trading to financial transactions. Could and should Russian intelligence services spy on foreign economic enterprises and then transfer their findings to state or private interests? Similar questions were being raised in other countries, including the United States. Just before his new appointment as director of the U.S. Central Intelligence Agency, R. James Woolsey told senators during a confirmation hearing in February 1993 that the issue had become "the hottest current topic in intelligence policy."

On July 1, 1992, the Moscow TV program *Vesti* reported on a meeting of staff members of the Federal Agency of Government Communications and Information. The meeting was chaired by the agency's director general, academician A. Starovoytov. His background was publicly described merely as his having directed one of Russia's "major closed science-and-production associations." Starovoytov emphasized that the communications agency's operations should, if at all possible, function "on an inter-state scale." Analysts suggested that this would assure a certain amount of Russian hegemony over the structure, security, and ultimate value of communications on the part of the non-Russian states of the former USSR. According to the *Vesti* account, the meeting also discussed "the possibility of providing major commercial and entrepreneurial enterprises with confidential information."

The topic of industrial espionage was discussed more extensively at an international conference, "Business and Security," which took place in Moscow on October 22, 1992. According to the Itar-Tass news agency, the meeting was attended by former "superspies" from major Western countries, as well as by lawyers, business persons, law enforcement officers, and journalists from Russia and other ex-Soviet republics. The report said that most of the participants had retired earlier from the agencies they had served, but implied that some remained in active service. It stated that "more than sixty leading officials and high-ranking representatives of the CIA, the FBI, the National Security Agency, the U.S. military intelligence and the police" were among those present, together with specialists from Canada, Latin America, and several Scandinavian countries.

The news service noted that participants had come to Moscow "in order to establish business contacts here," and that they were also meeting with private Russian investigative and guard services, as well as with officers of the Russian Foreign Intelligence Service and the Ministry of Security. The participants heard more than twenty presentations by experts from Russia and the United States. The news report added that the meeting devoted special attention to "problems of economic security." Panels were divided into three sections: (1) legislation in the sphere of security of entrepreneurship; (2) security within companies, and private security services; and (3) dishonest competition, and industrial espionage concerning confidential information and business procedures.

A potential for insidious "conflicts of interest" exists when intelligence agents and ex-agents mix with business people. In the chaotic post-Communist world of commerce and finance, the distinction between "free market" activities and criminal activities is often difficult to discern. Astonishing amounts of raw materials have been flowing out of the former Soviet Union, at cut-rate prices, and often with only a partial return on the hard currency paid for them. The same goes for armaments of many types. Meanwhile, the import of foreign luxury cars, and of other extravagances, by Russian and non-Russian "Mafia" types illustrates the disequilibrium within the country's economy.

Against this background, the presence of freelancing ex-KGB specialists (often with residual contacts within their old agencies) has created a unique labor market. Its potential was explored by Peter E. Sakkas, president of Global Computerized Countertrade Interexchange, in a paper titled "Espionage and Sabotage in the Computer World," published in the *International Journal of Intelligence and Counterintelligence* (Summer 1991). Sakkas noted that former KGB and East German (Stasi) computer experts became available to an array of potential employers ranging from Mideastern potentates to drug cartels. The experience they had in breaking into computer networks, extracting information, planting false information, and sabotaging vast linkups of computers was part of their stock-in-trade.

Sakkas stated that computer "espionage—military, industrial, or political—usually involves the stealing of confidential information or data, leaving no telltale trace." He cited as examples the theft of "geological data from oil or mining companies; the design and performance specification for a new product; as well as proprietary computer software pertinent to a business enterprise's competitive edge; data relating to financial transactions, capital flow, budget allocations, research and development priorities; or expansion/contraction plans, sales and promotion strategies."

According to Sakkas, personnel changes in the former KGB agencies, in the Soviet Union and Eastern Europe, provided "a global talent pool" of experts who were "quite capable of perpetrating high-level computer espionage and sabotage." Among Russian members of this talent pool, Sakkas listed former staff members of the "Osnaz" group, which, he stated, "operated under the control of the KGB." He surmised that such agents had offered their services to "unprincipled commercial enterprises for industrial espionage, computer sabotage, and key-man assassination." He added that "the less ideologically inhibited among them may offer their services to criminal syndicates such as the Cali Cartel [narcotics], the Asian Triads, and the Unione Corse."

The Russian Ministry of Security showed itself to be well aware of these trends. Covertly and overtly, its agents prevented intelligence specialists from leaving the country, and there has been a tendency to make such skilled—and potentially damaging—individuals wanted at home, either in other government agencies or in the newly developed enterprises. Russian security units have intercepted technicians on their way to North Korea, where their expertise might have been utilized in the development of nuclear devices. Still, the churning within Russian society, and within the societies of the other ex-Soviet republics, has created an explosive restlessness among former KGB communications specialists—whether they felt unwanted, unneeded, underpaid, or simply in search of a new life.

# 12

# Baltic Turmoil

Relations between Russia and the Baltic states—Lithuania, Latvia, and Estonia—are inevitably stamped by one historic event: annexation of the three nations by the Soviet Union in 1940, as part of a special Hitler–Stalin agreement. As a result, and as soon as the Gorbachev era began, strong nationalist movements gained strength in all three republics, aiming at complete independence. This trend was resisted by Moscow, which feared that successful Baltic independence movements would inevitably set precedents for other Soviet republics. Gorbachev publicly sought, at the very least, to slow down the independence movements. The Moscow leadership was particularly chagrined to observe that nationalist sentiments were gaining strength even within the Baltic Communist parties. Through a mixture of threats and promises, Moscow sought to dilute the independence movements—while the KGB, first under Victor Chebrikov and later under Kryuchkov, used various means to discredit, undermine, and sabotage the nationalist movements. Soviet armed forces and the Interior Ministry's Special Security Unit, or OMON, were also involved in these activities.

The transition period was most volatile and bloody in Lithuania, with a population of 3.6 million. Yegor Ligachev, the orthodox Communist member of the early Gorbachev administration, recounted Politburo discussions of the Lithuanian crisis in a manner that was bitingly critical of Alexander Yakovlev, Gorbachev's close confidant. Ligachev's criticism foreshadowed even more vitriolic attacks on Yakovlev in Kryuchkov's postcoup memoirs. Both men accused Yakovlev, by implication, of acting in a manner that was misleading to the point of treachery. Ligachev, in recollections published in *Sovetskaya Rossiya* (April 11, 1991), wrote that Yakovlev returned from a mission to Lithuania in 1988 with assurances that "nothing special is happening there; nothing in particular; only the usual perestroyka processes." This appraisal, Ligachev recalled, clashed with a KGB analysis that had warned of a dangerous "destabilization of the situation in Lithuania," including a nationalistic "split" in the local Communist Party. Ligachev called KGB chief Chebrikov, quoted Yakovlev's assurances, and got this reply, "What do you mean, nothing in particular is happening? The situation is alarming and unsettled, and the consolidation of nationalist forces has begun."

Two tragic incidents continued to throw a dark shadow on Russo-Lithuanian relations. In both of them, the role of the KGB remained controversial. During the early morning hours of January 13, 1991, the television center at Vilnius, Lithuania's capital, was attacked, presumably because of its independence-oriented programs. During the attack and subsequent clashes, fourteen people died and about eight hundred were injured. The news agency Tass reported a year later, on January 10, 1992, that the Lithuanian Prosecutor General had accused the Soviet Communist Party, the KGB, and the Soviet Army of conspiring "in their bid to overthrow the government in Lithuania."

A second incident occurred at the border town of Medininkai on July 31, 1991, where several Lithuanian customs and border officials were killed or wounded. The independent Soviet military organization "Shield" alleged on August 8 that the killings had been "masterminded" by the KGB, with the Interior Ministry's OMON units playing a "supportive role." The KGB's Public Relations Center in Moscow denounced these accusations, claiming they "[are] totally unfounded, do not correspond with reality and are provocative," and adding that the KGB "resolutely condemns the criminal action." Still, that one of the KGB's special "antiterrorist" Alpha units, possibly in disguise, was involved in the attack on the TV station was a general assumption that could not be silenced. Certainly, the very existence of such a Lithuanian frontier station dramatized the country's independent status, and was therefore a thorn in the side of militant defenders of an undivided Soviet Union.

The initials KGB—symbolizing Moscow's wide-ranging control—remained potent on Lithuania's political scene even after the country's independence. Personal accusations of earlier KGB involvement became part of a power struggle that was particularly evident between the strongly nationalist "Sajudis" movement and the newly patriotic Communist or ex-Communist leadership. One of the initial targets was the country's first Prime Minister, Kazimiera Prunskiene. Accusations about her alleged collaboration, both early in life and during her premiership, were widely circulated. (One of her defenders was Vadim Bakatin, Moscow's reformist interim KGB chief.) Finally, on September 14, 1992, the Lithuanian Supreme Council's Commission for the Investigation of Activities of the Soviet KGB in Lithuania concluded its survey into these charges as follows: "Kazimiera Prunskiene, deputy of the Supreme Council, consciously cooperated with the KGB." At a press conference the following day, the former Prime Minister replied that, as a student, she had merely written a "scientific report" on one of her trips abroad, "in the standard form for higher educational establishments," and that it had been countersigned by the rector of her university. It was, she said, the kind of report that at the time all people traveling abroad had to make, and was, besides, "a fact I have never concealed." She added that other evidence implying voluntary cooperation with the secret service—notably an alleged receipt with her signature—had been "forged at the time" by the KGB, although she acknowledged that it was "a good forgery." Prunskiene said she would appeal the commission's findings.

Political furor also surrounded the personality of Virgilius J. Cepaitis, a parliamentarian and the founder and chairman of the nation's Independence Party. Documentary evidence alleging his long-standing collaboration with the KGB was clouded by the fact that much archival material had been destroyed or removed, or was of dubious reliability. During the weeks following the collapse of the August coup in Moscow, KGB headquarters in Vilnius remained unguarded for part of the time; they were visited by numerous people whose motives were quite mixed. Among them were the merely curious, those bent on vengeful destruction, and, presumably, KGB agents themselves who had the opportunity to remove crucial files. Even before the coup attempt, substantial Lithuanian KGB archives had been shipped to Russian depositories. The USSR KGB promised to return these files, and a good deal of material—reportedly, fifteen thousand documents—was, in fact, shipped back. But obviously, not all of it. As late as February 12, 1993, Russian Security Minister Victor Barannikov met with a Lithuanian delegation to discuss the return of additional archival material.

Public accusations against Cepaitis were therefore the subject of elusive, if passionate, charges and countercharges. A provisional investigatory commission advised the Lithuanian Parliament on October 15, 1991, that it had uncovered documents "testifying to collaboration between some deputies and the KGB." The government resolved that—"taking into account the KGB's criminal anti-government activity in Lithuania"—former members of the USSR KGB and their informers should be banned from leading government posts for a period of five years.

The newspaper *Mazoi Lietuva* (November 14, 1991) quoted an anonymous ex-KGB officer as stating that Cepaitis had been an informer since 1980 and had reported on some forty individuals, including prominent Lithuanians living abroad. Five days later, Cepaitis gave an impassioned interview to Radio Vilnius, saying that such accusations reminded him of the time, "thirty years ago, when the KGB first interrogated me." He said the KGB had then tried to get him to admit that he had "contacts with foreign intelligence services" and had sought to "undermine Soviet authority." He said that "documents, real or fabricated, are now being produced from bottomless pockets, concerning still others of my colleagues." Cepaitis asked the Prosecutor General to find out "where these documents and audio tapes were obtained, to analyze their authenticity and to examine questions of criminal responsibility of the individuals who supplied this material." He concluded by saying, "No, I have not been a KGB agent!"

Yet, on December 10 the investigatory commission concluded that Cepaitis had, in fact, been "consciously collaborating with the KGB" and urged that he resign his official posts. Various media reports, including an account in the daily *Respublika*, alleged that Cepaitis, using the code name "Juozas," had "admitted" collaborating with the KGB as far back as 1963, or at least of having had "contact" with it. Meanwhile, the Independence Party's governing council voted as to whether Cepaitis had, in fact, been a KGB collaborator and should therefore be removed from party membership. Of thirty council members who participated in the vote, only four voted against Cepaitis. On January 18, 1992, an Extraordinary Congress of the Independence Party—voting in closed session—reelected Cepaitis as its chairman.

Officially, the liquidation of the USSR KGB's Lithuanian operations had followed an orderly process. Once Bakatin had taken over in Moscow, the KGB's Lithuanian branch formally ceased operations on August 23, 1991. However, negotiations concerning border control and the transfer of property, arms, and other equipment proved difficult and prolonged. The question of what would happen to KGB staff members who were suddenly unemployed by the political developments was also discussed. Would and could their professional expertise be utilized within a national Lithuanian KGB? Could they switch loyalties? Or were their personalities too tainted by having worked for Moscow? If not utilized, where would they go? Would their future occupations represent a risk to the Lithuanian state? And who would pay their pensions? Seventy-seven percent of the local KGB staffers were, after all, Lithuanians.

Thirty-eight ex-staffers published an open letter in *Respublika* (February 13, 1992), threatening that, "if we, former KGB officers who now have other jobs giving us bread, are fired from government offices, we shall have to retaliate," presumably by disclosing government secrets. The men were protesting a pending law that would ban former KGB collaborators from positions in such areas as police, customs, border control, law enforcement, and education.

The Lithuanian political scene underwent a drastic shift on November 15, 1992, when Sajudis leader Vytautas Landsbergis, who had declared the country's independence in 1990, suffered a startling electoral defeat. Voters gave a parliamentary majority to Algirdas Brazauskas, who had led the Lithuanian Communist Party in its split with Moscow, and who now headed the newly formed Democratic Labor Party. The identity and status of a national successor agency to the KGB—the Lithuanian State Security Service—was quickly clarified. The new agency's Director-General Jurgis Jurgelis stated, according to the news agency Baltfax (December 30, 1992), that his agency would "strictly observe the law, and would fight all efforts to undermine Lithuania's sovereignty, territorial integrity, its constitutional system and authorities." He pledged that the State Security Service would "not serve any party or politician," and that among its major targets would be the KGB itself. He did not specify whether this target would be the remnants of the KGB within Lithuania, or Russia's new Foreign Intelligence Service—which, technically and practically, had come to regard the onetime Soviet republic as a foreign nation.

Neighboring Latvia found itself in a very different position from Lithuania, whose majority population was clearly made up of ethnic Lithuanians. But of Latvia's 2.7 million inhabitants, slightly more than half were ethnic Latvians, while Russians made up a substantial and influential minority. In addition, economic and cultural links to Russia had historically been strong. Thus, fear of Russian domination—direct or indirect, past or future—played a major role in relations between Moscow and Riga, Latvia's capital. Fear of continued Russian KGB activity, deepened by the drawn-out presence of Russian troops on Latvian soil, strongly influenced the nation's political attitudes. In consequence, the

Latvian Ministry of Defense issued a report covered in several media (January 20, 1993), stating that more than twenty Russian intelligence services were still operating on Latvian territory. The document charged that Russian intelligence engaged in "recruiting agents and placing them in government, in the ministries of defense and internal affairs, and in other state structures." The report did not specify which KGB successor agencies were alleged to be involved in such activities.

Latvia's antagonism against the KGB had been strong enough to create considerable ambivalence toward the creation of a national secret service. The news agency Baltfax reported (January 29, 1992) that a Security Service of the Latvian Republic had, after all, been set up; the report specified that the agency would be limited to three departments: one, to guard the Latvian Parliament; another, to protect foreign embassies and diplomats' residences; and a third one, engaged in "fighting terrorism and organized crime." Yet, additional and more substantial intelligence activities appeared to have been assigned to the Department of Information of the Ministry of Internal Affairs.

Initially, during the Bakatin period of the Moscow KGB, a transition of intelligence activities from the Moscow center to the Riga government appeared to be going relatively smoothly. Latvia's Prime Minister Ivars Godmanis conferred with Bakatin in Moscow on September 27, 1991. Godmanis also met Barannikov, who at that time was Soviet Interior Minister. They signed an agreement that formally ratified the liquidation of the KGB in Latvia. Transition proved complex, however, particularly where it involved valuable properties, caches of arms, and sophisticated communications equipment. The facilities involved were valued at many hundreds of millions of rubles. Publicly unacknowledged was the likelihood that the KGB's communications directorate had used Latvian and other Baltic territories as bases for the monitoring of a variety of Western European nations, including those of Finland and the Scandinavian countries—bases that the KGB and its successor agencies were loathe to give up, and would seek to retain at all cost, under whatever innocent-sounding cover.

Prior to the August coup attempt and Latvia's national independence, the role of the KGB in Latvia had been less controversial than in Lithuania. Latvia had sought to obtain its independence in successive stages, technically within the framework of the Soviet constitution; as a result, there had been less open friction beween Moscow and Riga than between Moscow and Vilnius. Nevertheless, the KGB was clearly engaged in monitoring, recording, and—where possible—undermining Latvian movements toward separatism, strengthened autonomy, and eventual full independence. The agency also used its standard argument that it was counteracting Western intelligence activities.

Back in 1988, the local Latvian KGB chief Stanislav Zukul, quoted by Tass (November 10), followed his agency's public relations theme of stating that "society is entitled to know what we are doing, and this will help to avoid any lawlessness and arbitrary judgment of our activities." Zukul quickly warned that "the methods and forms of work conducted by the secret services of our adversaries are becoming ever more sophisticated." Implying that Latvian independence sentiment was subversively supported from abroad, he added that "the incidence of acts of ideological and political sabotage is not decreasing." He became even more specific when he said that the KGB was engaged in combating "reactionary Latvian emigré organizations seeking to foment unhealthy nationalist sentiment in the republic, in order to exploit it for dismantling the Soviet political and economic system."

KGB activities were the topic of a Supreme Soviet session in Riga on July 16, 1990, which considered setting up a commission for "determining the status" of the agency in the country. One delegate, Einars Repse, noted that recent actions confirmed the popular supposition "the KGB in Latvia, in fact, fulfills, blindly and obediently, Moscow's instructions." Repse noted that, generally, "fear of the KGB persists, as a sense of the inevitability of its omnipotence, and of its existence everywhere." Small wonder, then, when Latvian independence became a reality a year later and the KGB was officially dissolved, that suspicions of its covert continuance remained very much alive. Eventually, in 1992, Juris Vectiraus was named Chairman of Latvia's Security Service.

Fear of Russia's newly formed and retargeted Foreign Intelligence Service reflected not only what had become an inbred distrust of Russian power and intention, but also distrust of shifts within the Moscow power structure. As Moscow reformists came under fire at home, and as Russian nationalism gained in popular appeal, Latvia reacted with deep concern to a mixture of apparent threats from a militant segment of its own ethnic Russian minority, the continued presence of Russian troops (including Border Guards) on its soil, potential frontier disputes, and the possible utilization of newly sophisticated KGB techniques to thwart Latvia's political, economic, and cultural independence. The country's Foreign Minister, Georg Andreyev, put these points succinctly when he told the daily *Die Presse* in Vienna, Austria (February 23, 1993), "From a legal viewpoint, we are an independent state today, but in practice we are still an occupied and colonialized country."

In neighboring Estonia, with a population of 1.6 million, liquidation of the KGB and transfer of its resources appeared originally smooth. Ethnically and linguistically linked to Finland, the nation was about 60 percent ethnic Estonian; of the remaining 40 percent, many were ethnic Russians. The transitional Bakatin administration in Moscow made a series of agreements with the new government in Tallinn, Estonia's capital, that seemed to provide a practical blueprint for the transfer of power and facilities.

Right after the abortive coup in Moscow, the Estonian KGB chief Reinar Sillar told the news agency Baltfax (August 27, 1991) that his organization had "suspended all activities" except for maintenance of the government's top-priority telephone hot line and of the communications department's deciphering service. Sillar quickly added that the Estonian government would certainly not "receive the lists of KGB servicemen," as "none of the secret services ever provides such data." At the same time, Mayor Hrdo Aasmae of Tallinn, chairman of a newly created Commission on the Liquidation of the KGB in Estonia, pledged that his commission's main task would be to "preserve the KGB archives." As it turned out, personnel identity and archives availability would become long-term topics of friction and objects of administrative maneuvering.

By September 3, 1991, Bakatin met with Estonian Prime Minister Edgar Savisaar at the Lubyanka offices in Moscow, where they signed a "Protocol on the Mutual Commitments of the Estonian Republic Government, the USSR KGB, and the Estonian KGB." The document covered topics such as the safekeeping of former KGB buildings, properties, and facilities. It committed the KGB to maintain intercity government communications and to "transfer criminal cases currently being processed to the republic's Prosecutor's Office."

The Estonian government, in turn, guaranteed to observe "the rights and freedoms of KGB staff and families" and even to create a commission that would look after their reemployment and job placement. The document also dealt with the role of the Border Guards and the security of Estonia's borders generally. Bakatin and Savisaar met again the following month to settle details on movable property, real estate, special arms, and, once again, the disposal of archives and "other documents." Tass, reporting the agreement on October 10, quoted a section that banned "use of the Estonian KGB's secret agent network to the detriment of the Estonian Republic."

The document rather surprisingly committed the Soviet KGB to transfer documents on the "activities of its secret agents, including information about assistance by citizens, to Estonian KGB bodies." It added the proviso, however, that such disclosures would only be made after the Estonian government "provides sufficient legal guarantees and secrecy of the content [of such personnel documents], as well as security of the individuals mentioned in them."

Just how tightly such secrecy could be maintained, particularly in a society as small as that of Estonia, remained an open question. And while the government might officially seek to hide the lists of KGB personnel, others openly sought to uncover them by indirect means. Thus, the weekly *Eesti Ekspress* offered one million rubles to anyone providing "a list of full- or part-time KGB employees." It promised to keep the identity of such a reward-winning informer secret, presumably to guard against reprisals. The paper said the informer could choose "means, time and place to hand over the information." The Tass news agency, reporting on the promised award (February 18, 1991), observed that "the source of financing for this action was, however, not mentioned."

A brief furor arose when the chimneys of the KGB headquarters on the capital city's Pagari Street began to emit an unusual amount of smoke, so much so that neighbors complained about an all-permeating, acrid smell. KGB chief Sillar sought to reassure listeners of Radio Tallinn (August 27, 1991) that the KGB's files on 29,500 "criminal cases" were safe, and that their "preservation is guaranteed." When he was asked whether the smell of burning did not indicate that key documents were being destroyed, Sillar answered, "We have not destroyed any documents from the archives." But, he added, "as far as the burning smell is concerned, naturally, we must consider the psychological state of our staff—we are all human beings, we all have nerves, and, of course, it is very hard for us at the moment."

The KGB chief insisted that papers being burned were simply private letters, adding that "we will, of course, destroy personal correspondence and not leave it for strangers to find." He used the occasion to repeat— "as leader of the special service and as a man"—that "we will never, ever, no matter what the circumstances, make known the identities of those individuals who, at various times, have rendered assistance to the

KGB in its activity." Still, he added, "As far as specific security workers are concerned, if any of them have committed any crimes, they will be held accountable, according to law."

Inevitably, the transition was marred by delays and frictions. The transfer of forty-two border posts from Russian to Estonian control created a series of major and minor problems. Not unexpectedly, the Estonian Border Defense Department encountered difficulties in quickly manning and equipping units to safeguard the country's maritime territory, rivers, and lakes; and it envisaged a patrol fleet equipped with small cannons, deep-water bombs, and machine guns. Well-equipped smugglers and so-called Mafia networks of internationally connected criminals challenged the nation's security during the post-KGB period, and beyond; among their products in transit through Estonia were Central Asian drugs and counterfeit U.S. dollars.

At the outset, both Tallinn and Moscow had apparently assumed that Estonia would relatively quickly set up its own national KGB, taking over where the Mosow-controlled agency had left off. Tallinn's Mayor Aasmae, head of the KGB liquidating commission, told Baltfax as early as November 10, 1991, that he foresaw the "speedy creation" of a national secret service. He noted that there were some fifteen thousand illegal residents in Estonia, and that "locating those people should be the first priority of the Estonian secret service." He acknowledged that the USSR KGB had sent his commission between fourteen thousand and fifteen thousand files on criminal cases, and that he expected another seven thousand files from KGB storage facilities in Ulyanovsk, with an additional twenty-five hundred from Moscow, St. Petersburg, and Archangel. The manner in which the KGB had scattered archives throughout Russia indicated its ability to disperse and—if desired—conceal archival material.

As the forces of nationalism began to show increasing strength both in Russia and Estonia, some points of friction became sharper. The issue of a possible revision of the Russo-Estonian border was raised on both sides. In Moscow on February 27, 1993, Foreign Minister Andrei Kozyrev urged Estonian authorities not to yield to pressure from extreme-nationalist "decolonization" groups, which, he said, sought to "expel from Estonia hundreds of thousands of people who lived there for decades, and even some who were born on Estonian territories." He was, of course, referring to members of Estonia's substantial ethnic Russian minority.

Estonia's own Minister of Justice Kaido Kama told the newspaper *Paevaleht* (March 5, 1993) that he opposed a draft law designed to exile former KGB agents who were not Estonian citizens, as well as Estonians who had collaborated with the KGB. Such a law regarding these individuals automatically as guilty of "espionage and high treason" would be premature, Kama said, as long as the status of the KGB itself—prior to establishment of the Estonian Republic—had not been legally defined. Kama proposed conditions for the rehabilitation of former KGB agents: "They must have an opportunity to appeal to a state institution, such as the State Court, for an evaluation of their guilt and to obtain guarantees that former colleagues could not blackmail them." If such procedures were established, he said, many individuals might be able to "rid themselves of the burden of their past," while the state would obtain badly needed information.

While this dispute made it clear that the concept of keeping the identity of KGB workers secret had turned out to be, at the very least, porous, the agency's own capacity for survival also attracted renewed attention. In fact, the Estonian government at its highest level was concerned about these contradictory trends. Interior Minister Lagle Parek told the news agency Interfax (February 20, 1993) that a network of former KGB agents continued to exist in the country. Therefore, Parek added, "the danger and possibility of blackmailing even the top leadership of the country will always remain a risk." He presumably felt that certain high-level officials who earlier—if only fleetingly—had contact with the KGB could be put under pressure by individuals who knew about such past transgressions, even if these had been insubstantial.

Minister Parek acknowledged that, under the law, former KGB members could not hold government positions or serve on the police force. Nevertheless, he said, they remained "potentially dangerous" to the state and needed to be under "covert surveillance." He concluded, "A country such as Estonia cannot afford to lose interest in former KGB officers, particularly highranking ones." Parek, obviously referring to the ethnic Russian population, urged non-Estonians to "have enough sense" not to cooperate with Russian secret services.

Mayor Aasmae told the Estonian Parliament on February 26, 1993, that the KGB was functioning within Russian Army units still stationed in Estonia. His Liquidation Commission, Aasmae said, had no power to deal with such "KGB special units," including those attached to the Border Guards. He expressed frustration about the limited number of documents received from the Russian KGB—a situation that was concealing the past activities of a number of key individuals. Aasmae said that his commission's only way of obtaining personal information was a totally inadequate "oath of conscience," which he angrily described

as having been "put together in an absolutely incompetent manner."
He revealed that "no individual engaged in serious collaboration with
the KGB has, so far, owned up to it."

Interior Minister Parek and Justice Minister Kama were apparently of
one mind when it came to the performance of the Estonian KGB's successor, the Estonian Special Service, which had been organized rather
hastily after the KGB's collapse and appeared to have absorbed some of
its predecessor's dubious practices. Kama, chairman of a commission
on government security, told the press on December 18, 1992, that his
commission had uncovered "loss and forgery of important government
documents." These documents were mainly concerned with the Special
Service's so-called Third Bureau, which had previously been asked to
stop what was somewhat euphemistically described as "gathering operational information" or "collecting and analyzing information." Such
elusive, presumably illegal activities might have included just about
anything from telephone tapping to the interception of mail, covert
surveillance, up to and including forcible interrogations. It is even con-
ceivable that an ambitious Third Bureau had extended its surveillance
to members of the Estonian Parliament or other officials.

In the end, the government decided to do away with the Special
Service altogether and, at the same time, remove Police Department
control over the Defense Police. The *Baltic Observer* (January 5, 1993)
said the move was designed to "overcome the controversy" between
"the two secret services." Instead, the government created an independent Department for Defense Police. The agency was assigned the protection of high domestic and foreign officials; likewise, procedures were
established for guarding the airport and seaport. According to the news
agency ELTA, the new department would also be charged with safeguarding "state security, territorial integrity, and the constitutional regime, as well as engage in counterintelligence." In other words, the
Department of Defense Police was to operate in the manner of a comprehensive intelligence service.

At the same time, the government was organizing a task force to
"investigate the circumstances related to the liquidation of the KGB."
The Aasmae commission had come to the astonishing conclusion that
"the copy of the agreement between the government of the Estonian
SSR [Soviet Socialist Republic] and the USSR, with regard to the dissolution of the Estonian KGB, had been forged." Behind these moves
could be sensed a renewed fear and distrust of Russia and, specifically,
of the Russian KGB's successor agencies. When Interior Minister Parek

not so subtly warned Estonia's ethnic Russians not to collaborate with Russian intelligence agencies, he certainly assumed that such agencies were, in fact, operating within his country.

Well, then, was the Russian Foreign Intelligence Service active within the Baltic states, was it considering such operations, or was it making concrete preparations for doing so? Yevgeny Primakov, head of the Service, was asked about this when he signed a collaboration agreement between his agency and the Belarusian KGB. According to the ELTA news service (September 9, 1992), Primakov replied that, if Western "special services" were "allowed to operate" in the Baltic countries, Russia would "resort to retaliatory measures." As an experienced diplomat, Primakov had skilfully qualified his answer to turn it into a provocative question. Considering the Baltic states' stark memories of events during and after the 1940 annexations, the ominous reply by the head of Russia's Foreign Intelligence Service could not fail to sharpen the alertness of the Lithuanian State Security Service, the Department of Information of Latvia's Ministry of Internal Affairs, and Estonia's Department of Defense Police.

# 13

# Bonds That Separate

More than fifty million people inhabit Ukraine, Russia's Slavic neighbor, ally, and antagonist. Economically strong because of its grain production, yet lacking energy resources, Ukraine found itself in a love/hate relationship with the Moscow leadership when the Soviet Union fell apart. Russia, Ukraine, and Belarus (formerly, Byelorussia) formed the core of the Commonwealth of Independent States (CIS) that emerged from the ashes of the USSR. And while Moscow went through a series of violent political crises, the Ukrainian government at Kiev initially underwent a relatively smooth transition.

At the center of Kiev's transition stood a leader who himself had undergone an apparently seamless transformation, from Communist Party chief to strong Ukrainian nationalist: the republic's President, Leonid M. Kravchuk. Spokespersons on both sides of the Russo-Ukrainian frontier emphasized that the two countries shared too much and were much too interdependent to go their separate ways or—Heaven forbid!—become antagonists, enemies.

Yet, major points of conflict existed, ranging from the status of the Black Sea Fleet and the Crimea to the price of Russian oil. About one-fifth of Ukraine's population were ethnic Russians, and millions of Ukrainians lived in Russia. Above all, for seven decades Moscow told Ukraine what to do—economically, culturally, in virtually every walk of life. At Moscow's KGB center, Ukrainian nationalism was regarded as virtual treason, as anti-Soviet agitation. On September 25, following the August coup attempt in Moscow, the former Ukrainian KGB chief Nikolai Galushkov was appointed temporary head of the new Ukrainian National Security Service (NSS). On October 8, Kravchuk—then chairman of the Ukrainian Supreme Soviet—introduced a new head of the NSS, Yevgeny Marchuk. Kravchuk used the occasion to note that Ukraine's "sociopolitical and economic situation" had become "more complicated" and that any "further worsening" should be avoided: "The time of guests and experiments has gone, and the period for resolute action has come."

Marchuk himself was quoted by Moscow's Radio Rossii (April 19, 1992) as assuring a press conference that his agency "differs greatly" from its KGB predecessor. First of all, he said, his service did not serve an "ideological consumer of information," as the KGB had served the Communist Party. Furthermore, he explained, the Ukrainian NSS had been placed "on a legal footing," some staff members' suitability had been "reassessed," and certain sections of the agency had been disbanded. Other NSS staff members assured the press that, with Ukraine having achieved independence, the nation had abandoned its "siege mentality, so that its policies and actions" were now "based on the principle of nonaggression." For this reason, the Ukrainian service found it possible "to coordinate operations with foreign counterparts"—presumably, and foremost, Russia's intelligence services. The NSS spokespersons denied reports that Ukraine had signed an agreement during a conference at Alma-Ata, Kazakhstan, that would have pledged "its own intelligence agency to coordinate work with the appropriate agencies of the other CIS states."

The Ukrainian secret service agents added that NSS operations within the country would be "aimed at upholding constitutional order and Ukraine's territorial integrity; all attempts to impinge upon the principles at the heart of Ukrainian statehood will be handled with determination." They specifically added that this warning concerned those "who support the idea of an independent Crimea." The NSS had expelled "several CIS generals" from Ukraine "for trying to cast doubt on the legality of swearing an oath of loyalty to Ukraine." It could be assumed that most of these generals were ethnic Russians. Radio Kiev had reported earlier (March 21, 1992) that, when the security staff at the city of Odessa swore allegiance to Ukraine, "representatives of more than twenty nationalities swore to firmly stand in defense of the interests of the young state." The news service Ukrinform reported (April 9, 1992) that more than two-thirds of the officers and all the service personnel of the Black Sea Fleet's "Intelligence Directorate" had sworn allegiance to Ukraine; those who did not take this oath were "sent for further service to the former USSR republics" of which they were citizens.

Marchuk used the press conference in April 1992 to emphasize that, in comparison with other republics, Ukraine was socially and politically stable. He noted that there had been "no armed clashes between warring sides or bloodshed or combat operations" on the new nation's territories. Therefore, he said, the main task of the Security Service was "to preserve stability in society, civil peace and inter-ethnic concord." The press was told that the NSS chief counterintelligence department had "stopped several attempts of Ukrainian citizens who sought to cooperate with foreign secret services." It had also "prevented a number of deals between Ukrainian and foreign firms that could inflict great damage on the Republic." In one instance, the service "prevented illegal transfer operations amounting to 80 billion rubles through new bank structures."

Both the Russian and the Ukrainian KGB successor agencies kept emphasizing lack of antagonism between the two nations and sought to discourage speculation that the two services might—at least potentially—be pitted against each other. On March 3, 1992, the Russian Ministry of Security and Ukraine's NSS signed what they termed "a package of protocols." As reported the same day by Moscow's Ostankino TV news service, the heads of the two services "provided guarantees that they do not view one another as potential adversaries." The report said that the two agencies would "direct joint efforts towards a fight against the drug trade and terrorism" and would seek to develop "a form of cooperation" in the investigation of economic and ecological "emergency situations."

This reference inevitably recalled the fact that it was on Ukrainian territory, at Chernobyl, that the major Soviet nuclear energy accident, the explosion at the local atomic energy station's Number Four Reactor, had taken place on April 26, 1986—resulting in ecological and medical damages beyond accurate measure. The two security services pledged that they would jointly undertake "to ensure the protection of nuclear installations and the security of the civil maritime fleets." Russian Security Minister Victor Barannikov commented, "We have turned from simply making declarations to giving an effect to our potentialities in practice." Asked whether the new protocols included joint protection and security of military nuclear installations on Ukrainian territory, Ukraine NSS Chairman Marchuk replied, "At present, protocols have been signed concerning nuclear power-engineering installations. But we have a cooperation agreement between the [Russian] Security Ministry and the Ukrainian Security Service, which provides for cooperation over a very wide range, ensuring the security of military nuclear installations."

Marchuk's cautious comments illustrated the delicate role the security services might have to play in the projected transfer and destruction of nuclear devices situated on Ukrainian territory. While pledged to turn Ukraine into a non-nuclear zone, the Kiev government apparently sought to use the continued presence of atomic weapons on its territory as a politicoeconomic factor. Generally, historical hostilities and distrust, mingled with a somewhat irritating economic interdependence, created an air of strictly limited cooperation between the security services of Kiev and Moscow.

From the start, the fact that the Kiev government meant to maintain a strong intelligence service was never in doubt. Much like a commercial corporation, the NSS issued a report on six months of its activities on May 1, 1992. The account began with the statement that the agency had "taken under control and neutralized 120 foreign military spies." The Kiev agency's public relations office stated that these spies had come to Ukraine "among the flow of tourists and businessmen from the West." In addition, the agency said, it had arrested twenty-nine "corrupt high officials and some leaders of the criminal armed units who participated in the division of areas of influence in the Crimea."

Providing further statistics, as quoted by the Postfactum press service, the NSS said it had sent 220 confidential reports to President Kravchuk, some 150 reports to the Supreme Soviet, and 167 to the Cabinet of Ministers. The report continued, "The Security Service analysts informed the republic's high officials and organs of supreme state power about the course of events in the Crimea, the Dniester region [of bordering Moldova,] and areas adjacent to Ukraine, on attempts to provoke violations of the Ukrainian territorial integrity, on the export and embezzlement of armaments, on the organization of the Armed Forces, on matters relating to economic, socio-political and other spheres, as well as on the functioning of the currency and financial system."

The Security Service also reported that, during the six-month period, it arrested six criminals who had used firearms to shoot at the homes of deputies in the Sumy, Chernigov, and Kirovograd regions. It was instrumental in arresting 102 "Mafiosi," who were subsequently convicted; and it safeguarded thirty clandestine shipments of nuclear shells.

Nevertheless, the agency did not view its activities as "satisfactorily efficient." It blamed what it called its "KGB trail"—the inheritance of a negative reputation that was expected to last for years "within mass consciousness, as well as in the consciousness of the republic's leaders, ministries, departments and organizations." At the same time, the NSS faced rifts within its own ranks, which suggested that KGB personnel holdovers and methods had remained entrenched. For example, the Security Service's staff in the northwestern city of Lvov (with a population of about half a million) came under severe scrutiny.

As early as January 16, 1992, the Lvov newspaper *Za Vilnu Ukrainu* observed that "negative aspects of reform" had "come to manifest themselves." The paper quoted V. Chornovil, chairman of the local Council of People's Deputies, as saying, "We have ground to believe that the former KGB has been doing everything to resist attempts to change its leadership and to bring new people into it. This repressive agency has only formally changed its appearance." The Lvov paper charged that the local NSS command was still following KGB patterns by "appointing to key positions only people who share their views and who until recently opposed the 'so-called democrats.' " The agency was accused of making staff changes "based on personal devotion, subjectiveness and subservience, without taking public opinion into account." In addition, the KGB old-timers were accused of character assassination by seeking to "disseminate carefully fabricated data of a biased nature, with regard to individuals who are supporters of democratic reforms."

More than a year later, the Kiev paper *Molod Ukrainy* reported (February 26, 1993) that a new regional NSS chief, Major General Vasyl Horbatyuk, had taken over in the Lvov area with a dual task: to calm relations between the Security Service and angry local authorities, and to "establish order" within the service itself. Horbatyuk, a deputy chief of the NSS, faced the task of dismissing some forty local security officers—although, the newspaper stated, Horbatyuk himself had "not abandoned old habits" and still wrote his instructions in Russian, rather than in Ukrainian. Among the new candidates for top security positions, according to this account, there were "not only no locals, but not even Ukrainians." The paper accused "the majority of administration" of having "direct ties with the Russian special services"; and it added, "Cadre officers do not even conceal the fact that they are using the information base of the Russian Security Ministry." The Kiev paper indicated that its own report was based on information that "is leaking from within" the agency, prompted by a feeling of "anxiety that has seized the Ukraine's Security Service Administration of the Lvov Oblast."

The struggle between moderates and extreme nationalists both in Russia and in Ukraine could not fail to be reflected in the tasks, the personnel, the conflicts, and the ultimately unavoidable stresses within the Ukrainian National Security Service. The strains of Russophobia and xenophobia fluctuating among the Ukrainian general population could easily be reflected within the Security Service. The service's regional department at Dnepropetrovsk reported (February 5, 1993) that it had caught twenty-six members of "foreign intelligence services" among visitors to the region during the preceding year; some of them, the service charged, "had made attempts to engage in intelligence activity in defense enterprises." Exactly what standards did the regional NSS apply when it categorized these individuals as foreign intelligence agents? Or were the local security officials just particularly eager to demonstrate their zeal?

If Ukraine could point to relative domestic tranquility, neighboring Belarus (formerly, Byelorussia or Belorussia) with its ten million inhabitants might have boasted of even greater stability. The republic's virtually seamless continuity was even expressed in the fact that its KGB chief, Eduard Ivanovich Shirkovsky, survived the crucial 1991 transitions with his position intact. On November 3, 1990, Shirkovsky's appointment was endorsed by the region's Supreme Soviet with a vote of 225 in favor, 5 against, and 8 abstentions. Until that time, the then fifty-eight-year-old KGB veteran had been the agency's deputy chairman; he had the distinction of being the first ethnic Byelorussian to occupy a position of such authority in the republic.

Under Shirkovsky, the Belarus KGB exhibited a remarkably ebullient and aggressive public image. It tended to speak out with great frankness about its own activities and was equally outspoken in warning against security threats facing the republic. A year before the 1991 coup attempt in Moscow, the local KGB told the press that it had uncovered "several attempts by Soviet citizens to hand over to representatives of foreign special services some materials which qualify as state and military secrets." As reported in the Minsk newspaper Zvyazda (August 16, 1990), the KGB's local public relations office made this statement: "At this time, a criminal case against a former member of the military of Belorussia, arrested during an attempt to hand secret materials to a foreign national, is being conducted by the investigation department of the USSR KGB. The operation is being carried out by workers of the republic's KGB, jointly with their colleagues from Moscow. Unfortunately, the case in question shows that, for the sake of personal profit, a person even resorted to inflicting harm on the interest of the state and on the defense capacity of the country."

Shirkovsky, then still regional deputy KGB chief, was quoted in *Pravda* (August 28, 1990) as telling a press conference, "We have not come to justify ourselves but to describe our work." In line with the USSR KGB public relations campaign at that time, Shirkovsky used this first press conference in more than forty years to state that his agency had provided "a large volume of information of a scientific and technical nature" to benefit the nation's economy. He said the KGB had "prevented attempts by individual foreign firms to 'palm off' on the republic equipment of poor quality and obsolete documents, worth a total of about five million rubles in hard currency." This statement echoed the views expressed during this period by Soviet KGB chief Kryuchkov. Shirkovsky added that the KGB had "thinned down" the cost of "blatantly overpriced contracts offered by 'tycoons' to some Belorussian enterprises."

Shirkovsky also said that during the two preceding years the region's KGB had detected "the intelligence activity of a number of foreign special services and uncovered several of their envoys." Since 1988, he said, the agency—with the help of its Border Guards—had arrested 109 people with forged documents, and confiscated "a considerable quantity of firearms and about twenty thousand rounds of munitions."

More than three years later, Shirkovsky was quoted by the Moscow TV Ostankino (January 3, 1993) as reporting that corruption and foreign espionage were still major KGB targets. The television news program reported that the Belarus KGB was working on two hundred cases of corruption, "most of them concerning the highest echelons of power." The agency had detected more than two hundred individuals who were "combining official state jobs with commercial activity." The TV report said that Shirkovsky's KGB was keeping "the export of strategic raw materials" and "various deals with foreign partners" under close scrutiny.

The report also quoted the KGB chief as stating that Belarus "had been virtually flooded with hundreds of spies from the West and from neighboring East European countries, and even from former Soviet re-publics." According to Shirkovsky, "foreign special services have set up an entire espionage network, which regularly briefs interested foreigners on the internal political and economic situation in Belarus." The news program added, "The KGB chairman is also worried by the—in his view—excessive openness in military matters. As confirmation of his misgivings, Shirkovsky cited a specific information leak. The only thing that the Security Committee is, so far, unable to boast of is a single detained spy."

According to the news agency Itar-Tass, Shirkovsky and Yevgeny Primakov, head of the Russian Foreign Intelligence Service, signed an agreement on September 2, 1992, to "refrain from activities on each other's territories and to make joint efforts in collecting economic information abroad." Primakov was quoted as saying that the two secret services would jointly gather "mostly economic information abroad, and will also exchange data, aid each other's investigations, and undertake joint training of personnel." Interfax news service reported (October 26, 1992) that the Russian Ministry of Security, together with the Belarus KGB, had "stopped the illegal activities of a group stealing natural uranium from a secret plant" in Udmurtiya (Russia). The group conspired to smuggle one hundred kilograms of uranium abroad; it consisted of eight Russians, one Belarusian, and three Poles.

On New Year's Eve, the beginning of the year 1993, the KGB leadership took a ceremonial oath of allegiance to the Republic of Belarus. The ceremony was described by the news agency Belinform as having taken place on December 31, at 11 P.M., "under the vault of the State Security Committee," beginning with a report by Shirkovsky. The KGB Chairman pledged the "readiness of the KGB generals and officers, who guard state interests, to take the military oath"; and he was the first to take the national oath.

Opinions of the role and performance of the Belarus KGB are far from uniform. On June 1, 1992, the Postfactum news service reported that the Belarus Supreme Soviet's Commission on National Security Issues had concluded the Belarus KGB "should not be engaged in combating crime and corruption," presumably because other government agencies were already performing these tasks. It confirmed that the KGB should continue guarding government buildings and embassies, as well as communications facilities. The news service added, "Meanwhile, opposition parties issued a statement which describes the KGB as a gangster-type organization and demands that the republican KGB be completely disbanded."

By contrast, KGB chief Shirkovsky told the newspaper *Zvyazda* (August 31, 1992), "If our state wants to fully protect its sovereignty and independence, we should increase the activity of our special services." He warned once again that "the interest of foreign secret services in Belarus has always been high, because of its strategic location, and this interest has increased of late." He repeated the claim that foreign agents sought to obtain secret military, industrial, scientific, and technical information.

Totally different problems faced the KGB of Moldova (formerly, Moldavia), squeezed between Ukraine and Romania. Independence presented the Moldova Republic of less than 4.5 million inhabitants with serious minority and territorial problems. As in so many other cases, the troubles could be traced to the Stalin period. The bulk of the area was annexed from Romania in 1944; a segment of Ukraine, north of the Dniester River, was tacked onto it. Once Moldova declared its independence, a good part of the Ukrainians and Russians living in the Dniester area feared they would be overwhelmed by Romanian-speaking Moldovians. About 13 percent of the population was Russian; another vocal and militant minority—the Turkic-speaking Gagauz—formed part of the remaining 23 percent of non-Romanians in the republic. Thus, when the Moldova security service spoke of guarding the republic's integrity, it had the separatist activities of these minorities firmly in mind.

Even before the republic's independence was finalized, its KGB sought to adjust to the changing balance of political forces. It transferred to Moldova a native of the region, Tudor Butnaru, with the difficult task of allowing for national sentiments as long as they did not extend to demands for true independence. Botnaru told *Pravda* (February 9, 1991) that he could not conceive of "my Moldova" existing outside the Soviet Union. He allowed that there were "hotheads demanding the disbanding of the KGB and the creation of a national security committee or ministry." In his opinion, "only a dilettante could think that way," because of the expenses involved and the fact that "it takes us years and years to train a professional." Nor, in his opinion, could a regional agency "possibly function without tapping into the enormous potential of the entire [Soviet] Union KGB system, without the help of colleagues in other republics, or the KGB's central intelligence data bank."

However, soon after the August 1991 coup attempt in Moscow, Moldova did dissolve its KGB. On September 10 the agency was replaced by a Ministry of National Security under the direction of Valery Plugaru. On November 10, Plugaru signed an agreement of "cooperation and interaction" with Bakatin in Moscow, which nationalized Moldova's KGB buildings, communications facilities, and all its material and financial resources, including arms.

Ethnic strife in the Dniester region as well as in the southern area of Moldova, where about 150,000 Gagauz lived, created problems not only for the newly established Moldovan Ministry of National Security, but also for its counterparts in Russia and Ukraine, as well as for all three governments and their various armed forces. On April 8, 1991, the Supreme Soviet of the "Gagauz Republic" appealed to its counterpart in Moscow to recognize the region as "an integral part of the Russian Federation." On June 30, 1992, Moldova's Minister of National Security Anatol Plugaru told the press service Interfax that "the actions of the separatist forces aimed at splitting Moldova are assuming a more and more threatening and cynical character." He charged that "the leaders of separatism enjoy serious support from certain circles in foreign countries, first and foremost with the pro-imperial, militarist forces of the Russian Federation." He added that these forces were "highly influential and have enormous clout on the government level."

The Minister was asked whether it was true that the National Security Ministry itself was "forming and coordinating the activities of terrorist groups in the Trans-Dniester region?" Plugaru denied that his Ministry ran "any terrorist groups." He added, however, "Undoubtedly, we are conducting certain operations in Moldova's eastern areas, and we are cooperating with the organizations which struggle for the unity and territorial integrity of our country, offering resistance to the pro-Communist regime in control of Trans-Dniester. In fact, our patriots there are waging a guerrilla warfare against the supporters of separatism and their armed bands. We are, naturally, supporting the forces in Trans-Dniester which want Moldova to be a single, indivisible state. Our patriots are arrested, harassed, treated with psychedelic agents [mind-altering drugs] and forced to appear in public with various 'disclosures.' We are aware of this, and I hope that the time will come when the squalid setting of the separatists' provocative activities will be investigated and presented to the world public."

A few days earlier (June 15, 1992), the Dniester press office in Moscow gave Itar-Tass a statement in which one Vladimir Garbuz, a forty-five-year-old Moldovan, testified that the Moldovan National Security Ministry had "masterminded" and approved "terrorist" activities in which he was involved. He was quoted as saying that, "after acts of terrorism were staged against several managers of Slabodzeysky district, we were received by senior executives" of the Ministry. Garbuz continued, "We were invited to a lavish dinner and had a brief rest at a smart hotel. National Security Minister Plugaru put a new task to us—to prepare and carry out a series of new terrorist acts, to destroy several national economic facilities: oil terminals, fuel and lubricants storages and railway bridges, and also to eliminate several staffers from the Dniester Government apparatus."

In his Interfax interview, National Security Minister Plugaru was also asked to what he attributed Russia's "prominent interest" in Moldova, except for a "natural inclination to provide protection to the Russian-speaking population there." Plugaru said that Moldova was of interest to Russia "from the strategic point of view." He recalled that the territory had been headquarters of the Soviet Union's Southwestern Strategic Command. "The geopolitical situation of Moldova," he said, "against the European background, has always been in the focus of attention of all states that sought to actively influence the correlation of forces in the Balkan region and the Middle East."

Just a day earlier (June 29, 1992), Plugaru had told Itar-Tass during a press conference at Moldova's capital of Chisinau (formerly, Kishinev) that eighty percent of the soldiers and military hardware of Russia's Fourteenth Army, stationed in the Dniester region, were "involved in the conflict" and acting in support of the "Dniester rebels." He also said that, a few days earlier, three hundred Russian "officers" had officially left the Russian Army and joined the "Dniester guerrillas." Earlier, a Romanian newspaper had reported that a KGB officer had changed his identity to support the Russians in Dniester in their fight against the Moldovians. The Bucharest paper *Dreptatea* (December 1, 1991) quoted Vadim Shevstsov—identified as Security Minister of the "self-proclaimed Dniester Republic"—as admitting that his real name was Vladimir Antiufeyev. The paper said that he had previously been assigned to the KGB in Latvia, but was "sent by the democratic forces of Russia" to the Dniester region. Shevstsov was quoted as saying that "several experts of the former USSR KGB and of the security forces in former Soviet republics" had also been sent to the region.

Amid various rumors, charges, and countercharges, the Gagauzian head of the Moldovan Department of Interior, Ivan Burgudzhi, was kidnapped. Leading Gagauzian spokespersons said that six men had participated in the kidnapping and that it was "supposed" that they were "employees of special services of the Moldovan National Security Ministry or of a criminal group." The Moldovan National Security Ministry told Interfax (October 13, 1992) that it "denied any possibility of participation" by their staff members "in this action."

The tough-talking Moldovan National Security Minister Anatol Plugaru was removed from his post on July 16, 1992. But his successor Major Vasile Kalmoy appeared equally outspoken. Questioned in the

Moldovan Parliament on March 11, 1993, Kalmoy said that the situation within the republic was so explosive that "a coup cannot be excluded." He added that alleged coup conspirators were "under investigation, in cooperation with Romanian special services." According to the Romanian news service Rompress, Kalmoy said that weapons were widespread among the Moldovan population, various political groups were inciting to revolt, and even deputies were threatening in the press that they would attack the leaders of the republic. He added, somewhat enigmatically, that "many Asians" had recently entered Moldova, and they were "posing a real threat."

While the KGB successor agencies in Ukraine, Belarus, and Moldova faced distinctly different challenges, they shared the dilemma of controlling their new borders. At various times, Border Guard officials of all three republics referred to sections of frontiers as "porous" or "transparent." They blamed the frequent uncontrolled border crossings and smuggling on a lack of guard manpower. *Krasnaya Zvezda*, the Moscow army newspaper, commented (April 28, 1992) that Moldova's eastern borders—directed toward Ukraine and Russia—were subject to vigilant attention; but the paper quoted regional commanders as warning that, to the West, control of the Moldovan-Romanian border was "collapsing before their eyes."

A few months later (July 19, 1992), Kiev TV quoted Ukrainian guard commanders that the number of armed men crossing the border from Moldova was "becoming more and more frequent" and that the number of guards would have to be increased "to prevent weapons and armed formations from being infiltrated into Ukraine." Conversely, and on the same day (July 19, 1992), Ukrinform reported that "armed violators of the state border were increasingly penetrating Moldova from Ukrainian territory." Overall, the ex-KGB agencies were engaged in making a strong case for the continuity and expansion of their activities.

# 14

# Transcaucasus Tragedies

Central control from Dzerzhinsky Square began to disintegrate well before the August coup. The KGB's administrative powers had been weakening for years; its influence throughout the country became diffused and fragmentized. As individual republics asserted their independence, the KGB apparatus was exposed to a variety of strains: it needed to intervene in local conflicts, acknowledge regional self-assertion, defuse ethnic stresses in its ranks, and face the reality that some of its own regional units put national loyalties above central KGB commands.

Accusations against the KGB increased with mounting nationalist sentiments and regional violence. From Lithuania to Uzbekistan, from Latvia to Armenia, the KGB was criticized for real or imagined sins of omission and commission. Where local violence endangered the lives of minority populations, the KGB was variously accused of failing to warn the affected populace of coming trouble, of being ineffective in halting outbreaks of violence, or of actually fomenting conflict for political purposes. The KGB was also accused of starting rumors that caused ethnic conflicts, of backing one ethnic group against another, of intimidating individuals and groups during elections, and of representing central power in resisting regional aspirations.

Where its units interceded in regional armed conflicts, the KGB often shared accusations of ruthlessness or partisanship with the Soviet Army and the Interior Ministry's militia. In this maelstrom of ethnic conflicts reflecting a multitude of social forces in collision, the KGB experienced a backlash from its partly self-created reputation as the all-knowing, all-controlling, all-powerful force in the land. In the Baltic states (Lithuania, Latvia, Estonia), in southern republics (Georgia, Armenia, Azerbaijan), and also in Soviet Central Asia, the KGB had to deal with extreme militancy, as well as nationalist sentiments, within its own local staffs.

Increasingly, the role of individual KGB officers—particularly those of Russian nationality—who were detailed from the center to service in outlying regions became an exercise in stressful isolation. Unable to communicate in the regional language, and often simply bivouacked on a bunkbed inside a KGB building under siege, the officer might spend weeks condemned to humiliating inactivity. If trained in intelligence-gathering (perhaps through the recruiting and interrogation of agents or informers), such an officer would find himself (or herself) in almost total isolation. Even if he had previously served in the area or had at least undergone briefings on sociocultural and political conditions, chances were that unprecedented events had overtaken his earlier ex-periences or training. The fact that an ethnic Russian or other "outsider" might find himself avoided socially, even by his local colleagues, and lacking in competent interpretation services would add to this pattern of ineffectiveness. In purely human terms, these experiences in frustra-tion and fear foreshadowed the dismemberment of the KGB.

In the months prior to the August coup, the KGB suffered serious defeats in Georgia. By the spring of 1991, the republic voted in favor of independence. Its controversial leader Zviad K. Gamsakhurdia cited personal reasons for disliking the secret police, although he eventually chose to convert it to his own service. Gamsakhurdia asserted that, during his years as a militant nationalist, the KGB tried to poison him twice, as far back as 1975. Next, he said, he received an anonymous telephone call on New Year's Day in 1977: he was told that his first celebration of the year would be a bomb concealed in his car. A week later, Gamsakhurdia discovered that the brake cables of his car had been cut. As he lived in a house on a hill in Tbilisi, Georgia's capital, a brake failure might have been severely damaging. A man of dramatic ap-pearance and oratory, Gamsakhurdia has since claimed to have survived additional assassination attempts by what he has come to call "Mafia, Communist Mafia." He has fallen into the habit of frequently, and rather casually, accusing political opponents of being "KGB agents."

Gamsakhurdia, who taught Georgian and Anglo-American literature at Tbilisi University, opposed ethnic self-assertion by such minorities as the Ossetians and Abkhazians among Georgia's 5.5 million inhabitants. Georgian nationalists maintained that these separatist sentiments were encouraged from Moscow to punish Georgia for its single-minded nationalism, and were backed by the KGB. On November 23, 1989, armed Georgians entered the South Ossetian city of Tskhinvali: in two days of fighting, six people were killed and 167 wounded. Militia troops intervened; tensions continued, as did ethnic warfare and deaths.

Georgian nationalist and anti-KGB sentiment came to a climax on the night of September 16, 1990, when about one hundred people stormed the first and second floors of KGB headquarters on Tbilisi's Lesi Ukrainki Street. The Soviet Army newspaper *Krasnaya Zvezda* (September 18, 1990) compared the scene to "a beach house hit by a tidal wave." The paper said the road was covered with "bits of broken glass, smashed tables, burnt portraits of political figures, broken bas-reliefs, and piles of official documents."

The main target of the attack appeared to have been the KGB's local investigation department; some documents were removed from safes. During the next two days, demonstrators gathered outside KGB headquarters and the Interior Ministry building next door, demanding the release of David Gelashvili, a member of the Society of St. Elijah the Righteous, a religionationalist group. Radio Moscow reported on September 18 that Gelashvili had been released from custody.

The Moscow KGB office quickly—on September 19—denounced the event. Archly observing that the Tbilisi crowd had attended an "unauthorized meeting," the statement said the demonstrators had actually "demanded the disbanding of the Georgian KGB." It categorized the action as part of "a frenzied campaign against the state security organs," designed "to reduce, dismember, and even eliminate the KGB." It added that this campaign had been "effectively coordinated with propaganda inspired by certain Western special services and imposed on public opinion by forces the KGB obviously prevents from carrying out their illegal activities."

The term "Western special services" had long been used by Soviet media as a synonym for foreign intelligence agencies—particularly the CIA. Still, the idea that a hot-blooded crowd of Georgian nationalists might need the encouragement of the U.S. Central Intelligence Agency appeared oddly outdated, even then. As released by Tass, the KGB statement concluded that "current increased intelligence work by special services and the growth of organized crime" would suggest the "attacks on the KGB do not serve the cause of stabilizing the situation in our country."

Two months later, Georgia held its first multiparty election. The nationalist coalition known as the Round Table–Free Georgia Bloc obtained two-thirds of the parliamentary seats (155 out of 250). Gamsakhurdia was elected Chairman of Georgia's Supreme Soviet. Shortly afterward (November 29, 1990), the nightly Moscow television newscast *Vremya* reported that the Georgian Supreme Soviet had ordered "removal of the Georgian KGB chairman and his deputies." Quoting the Moscow KGB office, the report said that, "as a result of this illegal action, Georgian KGB activity is practically paralyzed." Citing constitutional violations, the broadcast said, President Gorbachev asked Chairman Gamsakhurdia "to invalidate the illegal decisions adopted."

The Georgian Supreme Court replied that Georgia's own laws superseded any earlier regulations, and that, "by removing a number of [the agency's] members," it was actually "strengthening the republic's KGB leadership." On April 9, 1991, the Supreme Court proclaimed the republic's independence. On May 26, Gamsakhurdia was elected Georgia's President with 87 percent of the votes cast. He quickly proceeded with the regionalization of the KGB. The agency was renamed Sakhemtsipo Ushishvroebis Komiteti (SUK), or National Security Committee. Shortly before the August coup, Gamsakhurdia met with the committee's new leaders. They finalized the unit's break with the USSR KGB and defined its "priority directions."

As reported by Radio Tbilisi (August 8, 1991), the regional security service would play "a major role in exposing and neutralizing hostile actions by imperial forces against Georgia." The announcement reflected Gamsakhurdia's increasing tendency to view any and all—real or imagined—antagonists as traitors to the cause he represented. During the coming months, his erratic (paranoid? megalomaniacal?) tendencies became ever more pronounced. One by one, his former friends and allies became disillusioned, alienated, and ultimately hostile toward the formerly almost undisputed hero of Georgian independence.

Finally, in late August the National Guard—which Gamsakhurdia had created—turned against him. Open warfare broke out on December 22. Gamsakhurdia and his followers retreated to a bunker in Government House, where they resisted attacks for two weeks. Meanwhile, the capital city's major avenue Rustaveli Prospekt was wrecked beyond recognition, by rival gunfire. The KGB building with all its files and valuable equipment was totally destroyed by fire. In January 1992, Gamsakhurdia was forced from office and into exile by a military council formed partly by his former associates. The political image of Georgia changed even more drastically in March, when Eduard A. Shevardnadze—Soviet Foreign Minister during much of the Gorbachev era—returned to his native Georgia as head of the Provisional State Council.

Shevardnadze inherited the violent ethnic conflicts that had come to the surface since Georgia declared its independence, mainly in South Ossetia and, increasingly, in the Abkhazia region. On September 27, 1993, Abkhazian forces captured the provincial capital, Sukhumi. At the same time, Gamsakhurdia loyalists remained an internal threat. In all these situations, the KGB apparatus—which Gamsakhurdia had recreated—played diverse roles under changing names and different leaders. On May 2, 1992, the Georgian State Council abolished the Ministry of Security, the KGB's latest successor. In its place, the Council established an Information and Intelligence Bureau. Irakli Batiashvili, a thirty-year-old philosopher, was named the Bureau's director. In Moscow, *Pravda* (May 14, 1992) reported the appointment with the headline "PHILOSOPHER BECOMES CHEKIST."

Shevardnadze met with former KGB staff members, according to *Rossiskaya Gazeta* (May 26, 1992), and told them that the new agency did not simply amount to a "change of label." He said that the new Bureau should "inform the state leadership, as well as the public, objectively of events taking place inside and outside the [Georgian] state." He assured unemployed KGB staffers that they would be able to obtain positions in other government departments.

On the surface, conditions in neighboring Armenia resembled those of Georgia. Armenia's KGB also developed an increasingly nationalist orientation a good while before the August coup, notably in Armenia's conflict with neighboring Azerbaijan. Among the similarities, both republics projected a distinctive ethnoreligious identity, were keenly conscious of their historic role, and, in contrast to Moscow or Russia generally, were "southern" in geography, climate, and national temperament. And just as in Georgia, the controversial role of Armenia's KGB was violently dramatized when its headquarters were attacked by an angry crowd—this time, on Sunday, April 14, 1990.

The attack on the KGB building in Yerevan, Armenia's capital, grew out of an ecology protest meeting. It began the day before and was originally directed against a chemical plant, the Nairit Scientific Production Association, which had just experienced a dangerous chloroprene leak. The protest, organized by the unofficial Armenian National Movement, brought some 150,000 people to the city's center. Overnight, the character of the demonstration changed focus, protesters assembled outside the KGB building on Yerevan's Nalbandyan Street, and voices among the one thousand demonstrators there called for total disbanding of the Armenian KGB.

According to the KGB's own account of the disturbance, which lasted for two hours, a group of young people began to throw stones at the building's windows and "tried to force their way in." The report added, "Three incendiary charges were thrown from the crowd, causing pockets of fire. Flares were set off. A teenager in the crowd was holding a homemade device, which exploded and tore off his wrist. Militia men took him to a hospital where the young man died. A girl next to him was left in a state of shock."

Kryuchkov, then KGB Chairman, blamed the incident on "extremist elements" and charged that it revealed "the cynicism and hypocrisy of those behind this action who represent themselves as 'champions of democracy and of defenders of the interests of the people.' " Kryuchkov then added, "Unfortunately, of late, threats and illegal actions aimed at certain state security bodies have become more than mere isolated incidents, and if the USSR KGB has shown restraint in its public reactions, then it is only to prevent an escalation of the situation and to avoid giving the extremists an excuse to perpetrate new audacious acts that violate public order."

Behind Kryuchkov's broad denunciation stood the extraordinarily complex and volatile position of Armenia, with a largely Christian population of about 3.3 million, and its neighboring republic Azerbaijan, a largely Moslem region with a population of about 6.7 million. A major point of conflict between the two republics has been the presence within Azerbaijan of the Nagorno-Karabakh Autonomous Region, a mountainous area inhabited largely by Armenians whose primary allegiance has been to Armenia. Since early in 1988, attacks on individuals and communities, ethnic violence, strikes, border incidents, boycotts, forced mass migrations, and other elements of civil unrest and intermittent warfare have characterized Armenian-Azerbaijani relations. Even while still technically under the direction of the USSR KGB, Armenia's KGB increasingly identified itself with Armenian nationalist sentiments, just as Azerbaijan's KGB became identified with Azerbaijani nationalism.

Two days after the attack on KGB headquarters in Yerevan, a leading Armenian KGB officer named Georgi A. Sokisyants admitted on Moscow Radio (April 16, 1990) that "distrust of the KGB" had "its origin in the past, when there were many distortions in the KGB's work." Sokisyants, who had been present during the Yerevan clashes, also said, "Our republic and our people have undergone two years of spiritual suffering, equivalent to physical pain. We understand this well. It was totally clear that, among those assembled outside the KGB building, the vast majority took no part in the attack."

Hostility toward the KGB was once again dramatized when, on July 21, 1993, Marius Yuzbashian, Armenia's KGB chief from 1978–88, was shot to death while walking his dog. He had retained contact with the KGB's successor agency by teaching at Armenia's National Security School.

The distinctly national, Armenian, character of the regional KGB was emphasized six months later by the newly appointed Chairman of the Armenian KGB, Usik S. Arutyunyan. He assured readers of the Yerevan paper *Hayastan* (October 28, 1990) that the secret police "now has a national character," which "is becoming more distinct and obvious." He added, "This reorientation toward the interest of the republic and of our people is due to the major democratic reforms that have taken place, not only in Armenia but in many other regions of the country." Arutyunyan was asked just how the KGB, "under the current complex circumstances," could "successfully meet the requirements of the republic which has declared its independence and sovereignty—and, how is it able to defend its security?" To this he replied as follows:

"In the past, a cruel state centralism did not spare the organs of the KGB. During the consolidation of the state regime, it functioned as a tool to execute the wishes of the center. However, with the republic's gaining of independence, the security organs, too, are establishing their sovereignty. As such, and in conformity with the republic's laws, and under directives of the supreme organs of Armenia, priority is given to the defense of the interests of the republic."

Such a "defense of the republic" did, of course, reflect the conflict with Azerbaijan—which came to dominate Armenia's economic and political scene. As a result, the changes in Moscow had only a limited impact on Armenia. During the Bakatin period, archives and current files of the Armenian KGB were returned to Yerevan from storage in the Russian city of Smolensk. In October 1991, the KGB applied to the Armenian Council of Ministers for permission to let commercial enterprises use its communication lines for a fee. The agency argued that the funds would be used to "strengthen the committee's technical services and help resolve some of the problems in providing social and consumer amenities for personnel."

Whatever the degree of KGB loyalty to the Armenian state may have been during this period, it was nevertheless decided early in 1992 to replace the republic's Committee for State Security (CSS) with a State Directorate for National Security (SDNS). On February 12, 1992, Valery Vagarshakovich Pogosyan, who previously headed the Ministry of Interior, was appointed director of the new agency. In an interview with the newspaper *Hayastan* (March 5, 1992), Pogosyan promptly denied that there had been "merely a cosmetic name change." He recalled the old KGB's loyalty to the Communist Party and pledged his agency's service in "the defense of national security and democracy." If there was an ideology to follow, he said, it was "the ideology of statehood, not that of a specific party or class."

Pogosyan denied that there continued to exist a "political intelligence service" in Armenia. He added that opponents of President Levon Ter-Petrosyan and of the Armenian government "can sleep in peace, provided that none of them infringes on the state's security, honor or dignity." Pogosyan expressed hope for closer cooperation with the security services of neighboring Azerbaijan. "For the time being," he said, "our cooperation is limited to local affairs, such as negotiations pertaining to the exchange of hostages."

Pogosyan's muted optimism reflected the tactics of Levon Ter-Petrosyan. Advocating gradual steps toward the region's independence, Ter-Petrosyan had avoided the extremes of confrontation that characterized the situation in Georgia. Still, the fate of the Armenians inside Azerbaijan—in Nagorno-Karabakh and close to the Armenian border—continued to create grave problems.

In 1990, Soviet President Gorbachev issued a decree outlawing paramilitary formations and empowering the KGB and the Ministry of Interior's militia to disarm them. A year later, the KGB's Second Main Directorate announced that it would apply this directive to the Transcaucasus. *Izvestia*, the Moscow newspaper, gave this information the upbeat heading "AZERBAIJAN–ARMENIA: KGB RECONCILING WARRING SIDES." The report (May 24, 1991) stated that a KGB officer from Moscow would act to coordinate such "control groups" in crucial areas. These groups would consist of one local KGB man, one militia representative, and one local soviet (council) member. Control groups would seek to pacify the regions, establishing a buffer zone; "in parallel with reconciliation," the statement added, "we will also use force."

On August 15, 1991, the Azerbaijani KGB—reflecting nationalist sentiments of its own—objected to Gorbachev's decision to delay implementation of his decree by two months. It accused the Soviet President of, in effect, being soft on the Armenians: "Any decision to extend the deadline for the illegal groups to surrender their arms voluntarily merely delays further implementation of the measures to effectively stabilize the situation in the Transcaucasus." The Azerbaijani KGB noted that "just as before, arms are being seized and acts of banditry and terrorism are still being committed in the Armenian SSR [Soviet Socialist Republic]." The statement added that Azeri (Azerbaijani) KGB officers had "defused hundreds of explosive devices, foiled extremist activities, and captured a number of terrorists, who have been brought to trial." The Chairman of the Azerbaijani KGB, Vagif A. Guseynov, told a Radio Moscow interviewer (August 20, 1991) that "many people did not expect that inter-ethnic conflict would enter our life; they were unprepared for reality on such a scale and in such an aggressive manner."

Implementation of the KGB's "pacification" program soon became a matter of bitter controversy. During the spring and summer of 1991, Armenians in the border areas of Azerbaijan reported that, in sweeping searches for "guerrillas," whole villages had been openly attacked; so-called passport checking operations had resulted in persecution and abuse; and KGB and militia units had, in effect, aided Azerbaijani efforts to rid the areas of Armenian inhabitants. Ter-Petrosyan telephoned KGB Chairman Kryuchkov on May 15, and again on July 7, protesting what he described as excesses by Azerbaijani OMON units against Armenian civilians in the border areas.

Ter-Petrosyan summarized his relations with the KGB in an interview with the Madrid newspaper *Diario* (May 17, 1991). He said that, in dealing with the military forces involved, he spoke only with Kryuchkov directly, "because it is the KGB which coordinates the operations of the Army and the Interior Ministry against Armenians." And he added, "Kryuchkov even admitted to me that atrocities have been committed against the Armenians, but 1,000 paratroopers have arrived in Yerevan. 108 Armenians [in the border areas] have been taken hostage (it cannot be said that they are being detained, because not one of them was a guerrilla), and women and children are being forced to sign documents certifying that their deportation was a voluntary departure."

Asked about the status of the Armenian KGB, Ter-Petrosyan replied candidly: "While it is still formally under Moscow's authority, its staff members—and we have replaced many officers—are loyal to Armenia and working in favor of its interests. But the USSR KGB removed all its records from Armenia (they are now in Smolensk). That paralyzes us, because they contain vital information on our society, our economy, and our past." When Vadim Bakatin replaced Kryuchkov as KGB chief, his office pledged that historic Armenian documents would be made available for research and, as soon as possible, returned to Armenia. The de facto separation of the Armenian KGB was confirmed when, on September 21, 1991, out of 96 percent of the region's adult population, 99.31 percent voted in favor of Armenia's independence.

In neighboring Azerbaijan, volatile events revealed the limits of the KGB's ability to anticipate, analyze, or influence developments. The region displayed an extraordinary degree of separation from events in Moscow, both during and after the August coup. Once the conflict with Armenia started in early 1988, Azerbaijanis grew increasingly radicalized; moderate intellectuals, who hoped that political maturity might lead to their republic's gradual independence, were overtaken by anti-Armenian, anti-Russian, and generally extreme-nationalistic and xenophobic sentiments. This trend, which began with clashes in the disputed Nagorno-Karabakh region, led to fierce clashes between Azerbaijanis (Azeris) and Armenians, and to murderous attacks on Armenian homes, families, and individuals in several Azerbaijani cities, including the capital, the port city of Baku.

KGB critics originally maintained that the secret police had advance information on most of these outbreaks, could have prevented them, and may even have encouraged them—as part of Moscow's calculated "divide-and-control" policy. Conspiracy theories aside, the USSR KGB and its Azerbaijani branch apparently failed to estimate correctly the extent to which the migration of Azerbaijani refugees would influence political events. While persecution by Azeris had forced hundreds of thousands of Armenians to flee their homes in 1988 and 1989, Azeris, in turn, had fled Armenian-controlled areas, with many of them settling in Baku. These angry refugees turned their fury on Baku's Armenian population—originally some 220,000, most of whom abandoned their homes and fled in fear.

Meanwhile, a coalition of independence-seeking groups, calling itself the Popular Front, gained increasing support inside Azerbaijan; its most extreme members ruthlessly hunted down Armenians. Finally, Gorbachev ordered that the KGB, the army, and the Interior Ministry put down the Baku violence by force of arms. This campaign began on January 20, 1990. The next day, Gorbachev spoke of the "tragic character" of events, of "rampages, killings, and the driving of innocent people out of their homes and outside the republic."

A total of seventeen thousand troops were employed; the numbers of dead and wounded were never fully tallied. On-the-scene observers maintained that the armed intervention came too late; that KGB intelligence had been inadequate and slow; that outrages against the city's Armenian residents had, for all practical purposes, run their course by the time KGB, army, and militia forces took action. The local KGB sought to mend fences with the region's population by maintaining a stern anti-Moscow and anti-Armenian stance, insisting on a ruthless pursuit of Armenian guerrillas in the border regions, and cracking down on "economic criminals."

Azerbaijani KGB Chairman Guseynov told a news conference at the agency's Baku Public Relations Center on December 17, 1990, that his service had begun to "combat economic sabotage and to ensure the proper distribution of goods and humanitarian aid sent to the republic." He said the KGB had discovered "persistent failures to unload idle railroad freight cars," totaling 342 twenty-ton containers filled with provisions, shoes, and medicine. Guseynov added that hidden food supplies totaled 115 tons of sugar, 247 tons of powdered sugar, and 20 tons of butter. These KGB efforts, he concluded, were a fresh departure, and his service also planned to "exert pressure on leading officials of economic establishments, many of whose actions impede the efforts at stabilization."

Maintaining the KGB's image in Azerbaijan appeared a particularly difficult task, considering the failure of its Border Guards to prevent a series of damaging assaults on its Azerbaijan–Iran frontier posts. Beginning on December 31, 1989, and lasting for about two weeks, Azeris stormed guard towers, set fire to barracks, tore down fences, demolished security systems, and harassed patrols to the point where Border Guards' families had to be evacuated. Soviet media reported that the riots had caused many millions of rubles in damages. Iran said that as many as twenty thousand Azeris had crossed the frontier.

The border disturbances took place in the Nakhichevan region, separated from Azerbaijan's main territory by Armenia. The local Popular Front movement demanded freer access to the Azeris' ethnic kin the "South Azerbaijanis" of Iran, who were fellow Shiite Moslems and numbered about four million. KGB Lieutenant General Nikolai Britvin—speaking for the Border Guards—said that "the organization of large-scale unlawful actions in the border area" was being used to "draw attention to the situation in the republic." When the combined Soviet troops took over Baku, the KGB temporarily managed to seal the border with Iran.

The KGB's Public Relations Center in Baku sought to bolster the agency's nationalist image by issuing anti-Armenian bulletins. On August 10, 1991—shortly before the August coup—an Armenian Communist Party official, Valery Grigoryan, was shot to death in Nagorno-Karabakh's capital city of Stepanakert. The KGB office asserted that he had been killed by opponents of an Armenian-Azerbaijani truce; Grigoryan had been part of a delegation that met in Baku with Azerbaijan's President Ayaz Mutalibov. The office also reported that, on August 13, Armenian guerrillas had taken thirty-two Interior Ministry troops hostage. On September 8, Mutalibov ran unopposed in Azerbaijan's presidential election. The KGB continued to serve Mutalibov as President, just as it did when he was head of the now-defunct Communist Party of Azerbaijan. Visitors to Mutalibov's office noted that, in his waiting room, a biography of Felix Dzerzhinsky had remained in place, undisturbed.

Events in Moscow, and Russia's growing reluctance to remain involved in regional conflicts, increased the pressure on Mutalibov. On November 16, 1991, the President upgraded the Azerbaijani KGB to a Ministry of National Security, directly responsible to him. However, the opposition accused his regime of failing to halt Armenian violence in Nagorno-Karabakh; and on March 6, 1992, Mutalibov was forced to resign as President of Azerbaijan. He was succeeded by a medical scientist, Yakub Mamedov, who served as Interim President. On May 8, 1992, the ousted President's supporters attempted a coup that would have restored Mutalibov to power, but did not succeed. Interfax (May 8, 1992) reported rumors that Mutalibov's KGB chief Guseynov, now the Minister of National Security, had masterminded the abortive coup. On May 16, Mamedov fired Guseynov (who was later arrested) and replaced him with Sadvettin Akhmedov.

Ex-President Mutalibov fled the country and went into exile in Russia. When he was reported to be a patient in a heart clinic, the new Baku government asked KGB special hospital authorities in Moscow to return the former President to Azerbaijan so that he might be tried for treason. But on December 8, 1991, Radio Baku asserted that Mutalibov was, in fact, staying at the dacha of Victor Barannikov, who was then Interior Minister and later became Russia's Minister of Security. The broadcast quoted Azerbaijan's Interior Minister Iskender Khamidov as saying that Mutalibov was being protected at Barannikov's country residence by his own bodyguards, as well as by a unit of the KGB's Alpha commando group. Khamidov added that seven Azerbaijani police agents were keeping the dacha under surveillance, but that "Azerbaijani law enforcement organs cannot arrest the ex-president, because he rarely leaves the confines of his hideout." The minister also alleged that Barannikov was extending this particular hospitality to Mutalibov for personal reasons, as he feared that "certain facts about crimes" in which Barannikov and Russian Foreign Intelligence chief Yevgeny Primakov had been "involved" might "become public knowledge." This assertion presumably referred to actual or alleged KGB and MVD activities inside Azerbaijan during the Mutalibov regime.

The political scene in Azerbaijan underwent yet another drastic change when, on May 19, 1992, the Popular Front candidate Abulfax Elchibey won a clear-cut election victory. Nevertheless, antagonism toward real or imagined Russian interference in internal Azerbaijani affairs, as well as in the conflict with Armenia, remained a strong political factor. Interior Minister Khamidov addressed a large rally in Baku on March 6, 1993, in which he accused Russian Foreign Intelligence chief Primakov of responsibility for Azerbaijani domestic unrest. Khamidov said that Moscow was trying to force Azerbaijan to join the Commonwealth of Independent States (CIS), which it had steadfastly refused to do: "Russian imperial circles increased their pressure on Azerbaijan when Baku had resolutely rejected an ultimatum of Russia's military circles." Khamidov said that Moscow was trying to create new trouble spots "of instability" within the country. He specifically referred to youth demonstrations that had just taken place in the Gusar District, on March 5 and 6. The official government version of what happened was that the young men had shown anger merely to avoid conscription into the region's army. Khamidov said that "members of the Russian intelligence service, led by one of the main organizers of the carnage in Baku in January 1990, Yevgeny Primakov, took an active part in staging the events in the Gusar District."

Suspicions of a Russian role in Azerbaijani events, designed to at least reestablish Moscow's indirect control, were heightened by developments that occurred during the first half of 1993. The key figure in this dramatic transition was Geydar Aliyev, Azerbaijan's KGB chief in the 1960s and head of its Communist Party from 1969 to 1982. Aliyev was the dominant figure in Azerbaijan when former Soviet KGB chairman and then Soviet head of state, Yuri Andropov, summoned him to join the Communist Party's highest council, the Politburo. He remained in this position until 1987, when he was "retired" by Gorbachev. After three years in political limbo in the Soviet capital, Aliyev returned to

Azerbaijan and quickly achieved leadership in his native province, the Nakhichevan Autonomous Region.

During his years in Nakhichevan, Aliyev showed extraordinary flexibility. He not only achieved an apparently seamless transition from Communist Party loyalty to Azerbaijani nationalist convictions, but he also managed to retain or establish contacts with Russia, Iran and Turkey. On February 4–5, 1993, Richard Miles, the U.S. Ambassador to Azerbaijan, visited Aliyev in order to discuss American assistance. (A month earlier, Aliyev had appealed to President Bill Clinton for humanitarian aid.) Shortly afterwards, Aliyev went to Baku, where he had a four hour visit with President Abulfaz Elchibey. On February 11, Aliyev called on Azerbaijanis to "rally still more closely around" the President, "who was elected by all the people." However, the Moscow paper *Nezavisimaya Gazeta* (February 16, 1993) noted that "People's Front propaganda" had accused Aliyev of "links with the KGB and Moscow."

In the early summer, Elchibey came under severe military-political pressure from an army unit commanded by Colonel Suret Guseinov, a thirty-four-year-old millionaire wool merchant whose troops had found little armed government resistance and were threatening to advance on Baku. On June 18, Elchibey fled from Baku and took refuge in Nakhichevan. Earlier, he had invited Aliyev to Baku to mediate his dispute with Guseinov. But, when Elchibey left the capital, Aliyev claimed presidential power for himself, citing "the inexplicable and unwarranted absence of the President" as his motivation. His status up to that point had been that of Chairman of Parliament, a position which automatically made him Vice President and, in effect, Acting President. On June 24, Parliament voted to strip Elchibey of all authority. Aliyev promptly appointed Colonel Guseinov to the position of Prime Minister, thus removing the most immediate challenge to his own rule. On September 20, he strengthened ties to Moscow, as Azerbaijan joined the Commonwealth of Independent States. At age 70, ex–KGB chief Geydar Aliyev had completed his dramatic comeback.

To the degree that the KGB successor agencies of Georgia, Armenia, and Azerbaijan face common problems, they can be found in the nearly unrestrained nationalism of majorities and minorities in all three countries. In addition, fear of interference and of potential outside domination—from Russia, Iran, or neighboring republics—has provided a strong motivation for intelligence activities, despite anxieties concerning any return to much-condemned KGB traditions and practices.

# 15

# Central Asian Chessboard

When Yevgeny Primakov, head of Russia's Foreign Intelligence Service, visited Alma-Ata the capital of Kazakhstan in April 1992, his primary host was not the republic's KGB chief, but the young nation's President Nursultan Nazarbayev. The top-level meeting illustrated a mutual understanding on a variety of topics: Kazakhstan's importance to Russia, the republic's internal ethnic problems, its vital role within the Commonwealth of Independent States (CIS), President Nazarbayev's status as a strong moderate on the national and international levels—and the crucial role of intelligence services in the future of Eurasian relations. It also reflected Primakov's expertise on Central Asia, an area that fell within his specialty as an "Orientalist." Kazakh Radio Network reported (April 4, 1992) that the two men had discussed the coordination of activities of Russia's and Kazakhstan's state security services. The communiqué released after their meeting emphasized that this projected cooperation should "meet the needs of the democratic reforms which are being implemented, particularly for the purposes of international cooperation." Almost as an afterthought, the communiqué noted that they had also discussed "certain other questions."

The announcement added that Lieutenant General Bulat A. Baykenov, Chairman of Kazakhstan's Committee for National Security (Komitet Natsionalnoy Bezopasnosti, or KNB), also participated in the discussions. The security agency had adopted its new name—actually quite similar to that of the old KGB—only a day before the meeting. The new KNB was identified as "directly subordinate to the President, while operating under parliamentary supervision." Under a law drafted by the region's Supreme Soviet, the KNB would be subject to "prosecutorial oversight," with its expenditures under the control of the Ministry of Finance. Baykenov, born in 1942 and with long experience in secret service activity, had been appointed Kazakhstan's security chief on October 25, 1991.

Baykenov held a press conference on July 9, 1992, in which he noted that the eighth session of the Supreme Court had passed a law on national security agencies generally, which lifted the veil of secrecy from some of their activities. He suggested that this would have "a positive effect on the fulfillment of important tasks." Baykenov reported that the KNB had signed bilateral agreements of mutual assistance not only with Russia, but also with Kyrgyzstan and Belarus, and was planning similar arrangements with other states.

The KNB's chief appealed to the public for help in its "intelligence and counterintelligence service." Baykenov then came to a crucial point in the republic's and his agency's agenda: interethnic frictions. Kazakhstan, with a total population of seventeen million, was actually only 40 percent Kazakh in its ethnic mix, with another 40 percent being ethnic Russians, 5 percent ethnic Germans, and another major segment—10 percent—representing other ethnic groups. In other words, because of a variety of historic events, Kazakhs represented a minority of the population of Kazakhstan.

For decades, the Kazakhs had felt—with some justification—that their country was being treated as a "colony," controlled from Moscow and often directly governed by an on-the-scene Russian administration. This factor, more than any other, apparently created the emotional basis for student riots that shook Alma-Ata on the night of December 17–18, 1986. The immediate cause was the appointment of an ethnic Russian, Genady Kolbin, as first secretary of the Communist Party of Kazakhstan; he replaced a Kazakh, Dinmukhamed Kunnayev. There had long been accusations that the Kunnayev administration—and its predecessors—were rife with bribery, misuse of state property, deeply ingrained nepotism, and other forms of corruption. Some analysts of the riots charged that those who had benefited from these corrupt traditions had instigated the riots, countering Moscow's efforts to oust the "Kunnayev crooks." Nazarbayev replaced Kolbin on June 22, 1989.

While the Alma-Ata youth riots attracted attention throughout the Soviet Union and were reported worldwide, riots that occurred in the town of Novy Uzen in mid-June of 1989 had even more tragic results. In this instance, the targets of rampaging Kazakhs were members of various ethnic groups originally from the Caucasus area. They included

Azerbaijanis, Chechens, and Lezghins. The Kazakhs charged that the "immigrants" had taken scarce jobs and apartments, and demanded that they be "deported." A considerable number of the targeted minority members did, in fact, flee the area. As in other situations of this type, the KGB was accused of having failed to anticipate and guard against the outbreaks, or of actually having encouraged them.

Thus, when KNB chief Baykenov spoke of a need for "public support" in order to assure "stability of interethnic relations in the republic," he was referring quite delicately to dangerous undercurrents in Kazakhstan's society. He emphasized that social stability would not "develop by itself, but is a product of the activity of the President and government of the republic, and of law enforcement bodies." Baykenov charged that there continued to exist "a group of people, striving to provoke a conflict on an interethnic basis." He cited as one example "the illegal dissemination of an anonymous leaflet which aims to sow chaos and discord." In the past, such leaflets had charged that the so-called immigrants had been given preferential treatment in the allotment of housing, or that certain ethnic groups were guilty of sharp commercial practices.

Recalling the ethnic riots that had been plaguing Kazakhstan, Lieutenant General Baykenov said that his agency, together with the Ministry of Internal Affairs, would "do all that is necessary to stop similar actions in the future." He added, "The people of Kazakhstan must and will live in peace and concord, without which there cannot be any changes for the better in the economy, and in the social and domestic conditions."

Other regional secret services had made agreements with Russia's Ministry of Security that would assure them access to Moscow's central data bank and additional KGB resources. It was therefore unusual that Primakov, Russia's FIS director, held direct talks with the President and the security chief of Kazakhstan. After all, Moscow's Foreign Intelligence Service was mainly concerned with distinctly "foreign" matters. Why, then, this visit to Alma-Ata? The answer may be found in Kazakhstan's increasingly important role on the international scene, this being a factor of its geographical position bordering China. The republic took a major step in international economics when it negotiated a $10 billion joint venture with the U.S. oil company Chevron; the deal, called "Tengiz-chevroil," involved the republic's Tengiz oilfields and included construction of a pipeline to the Black Sea.

Kazakhstan's relations with China encompassed a multiplicity of interests and problems, including the presence of one million ethnic Kazakhs on adjacent Chinese territory. Kazakhstan developed close economic relations with China's neighboring Xinjiang-Uighur Autonomous Region (previously, Xinjiang was known as Sinkiang), along a border of some 1,500 kilometers. Telephone service between Alma-Ata and Xinjiang's capital, Urumchi, direct postal service, and fax transmissions were established. A railway connection between the two territories—long in preparation—was completed. President Nazarbayev described this rail connection as "the shortest way from the Asia-Pacific region to Western Europe," but also as a means to "develop economic, trade, cultural and tourist exchanges with Xinjiang." An Alma-Ata–Urumchi air link was also established.

After a Xinjiang delegation visited Alma-Ata, a Kazakhstan delegation that was led by President Nazarbayev toured China in July 1991. He visited Beijing (Peking), but showed particular interest in the southern Chinese province of Guangdong where the special economic zones of Shenzhen and Zhuhai, with their distinctly free-market characteristics, had been functioning for about a decade. Of course, Nazarbayev traveled widely; he toured the United States in July 1990. However, the geopolitical role of Kazakhstan within the framework of future relations between Moscow and Beijing may well have been a major topic of Primakov's talks in Alma-Ata.

One need give no particularly nefarious interpretation to the Moscow–Alma-Ata intelligence discussions on topics relating to China generally and Xinjiang specifically. Even if exclusively economic-technological considerations were on Primakov's mind, the utilization of Kazakhstan's intelligence service on developments inside Xinjiang—possibly in exchange for intelligence briefings of Nazarbayev on the FIS's appraisal of events in Beijing—could be welcomed by both sides. The politicoeconomic evolution of China, in all its long-range aspects, would be of major concern to both Moscow and Alma-Ata, and the use of each other's informants would be mutually beneficial. Beyond this point, Kazakhstan's emergence as a stable power with strong links to such nations as Japan and South Korea may well have been among Primakov's considerations.

In neighboring Uzbekistan, a major Central Asian nation with a largely Islamic population of twenty-one million, the fate of the KGB appeared to follow what had become routine throughout the former Soviet Union. On September 26, 1992, Uzbek President Islam Karimov issued a decree that disbanded the KGB; in its stead, he immediately established a National Security Service (NSS). The former KGB chief, Gulam Aliyev, was appointed director of the "new" agency. A few days earlier, the statue of Soviet secret service founder Felix Dzerzhinsky had been removed, undamaged, from its pedestal outside KGB headquarters at Tashkent, Uzbekistan's capital. The statue was put in storage, to be put on display someday with other sculptures regarded as "no longer politically relevant, but valuable as pieces of art."

Uzbekistan's National Security Service followed in the footsteps of its predecessor, the KGB, in that it sought to avoid publicity; even when Moscow headquarters undertook its major public relations drive, its Uzbek regional office clearly preferred the old obscurity. What was significant about the announcement of the changeover was the emphasis that the NSS would be "subordinated to the Republic's President," Karimov. This move strengthened what had long been a decisive element of Uzbek politics: rule by a dominant, strong-minded, patriarchal figure. Islam Abduganiyevich Karimov—formerly, First Secretary of the Central Committee of Uzbekistan's Communist Party—continued this pattern. He had been President since March 24, 1990.

Karimov's security service, like the KGB before it, faced a variety of difficult tasks. Whenever he was asked about limits on public demonstrations and political activities generally, Karimov could point to neighboring Tajikistan's continuing bloody turmoil. He told the Paris daily *Libération* (September 8, 1992) that Uzbekistan bordered on the north and east of Tajikistan, and that there could not be "a real border" between the two countries: "The Tajik problem is a time bomb which could cause another conflict like [Nagorno] Karabakh here, but a hundred times worse. Especially because the situation is influenced by what is happening in Afghanistan. I know that there are Stingers [missiles] in Tajikistan which have come from there. The border between Tajikistan and Afghanistan no longer exists. Every day groups cross it with weapons and drugs."

Karimov reminded readers of the Paris paper that it was "impossible to redraw the borders of our states without starting a bloodbath. Uzbekistan is inhabited by 800,000 Kazakhs, another 800,000 Tajiks, plus smaller numbers of Kyrgyz and Turkmen. Several million Uzbeks live in the other four republics." What Karimov did not mention in this interview was the presence of still other minorities, including Russians, in Uzbekistan. Riots and other violent incidents involving different ethnic groups have taxed the Uzbek KGB and militia over and over again. *Izvestia* reported (September 12, 1990) that the emigration of skilled physicians and surgeons from Tashkent included Russians, Jews, and Germans; the paper quoted one local doctor as stating that the remaining physicians "cannot cope with the emergency workload, and our team is only 50 percent staffed at the moment."

Uzbekistan's low-profile KGB faced severe criticism for neither anticipating nor preventing large-scale rioting in the Fergana Valley area in early June 1989. The victims were Meskhetian Turks—a minority group that in 1944, on Stalin's orders, had been exiled from their homes in Soviet Georgia. Official statistics on the 1989 riots stated that one hundred people were killed and 1,010 injured; 1,055 cases of arson were registered; and 753 houses, 275 vehicles, and twenty-seven "state installations" were set on fire. More than sixteen thousand Meskhetians were airlifted into Central Russia; in all, thirty-five thousand "citizens of Turkish nationality" were reported to have "voluntarily left Uzbekistan to live in other USSR republics." Georgia—troubled with the violent autonomy claims of Ossetians and Abkhazians—resisted any influx of its former Meskheti residents.

When the Uzbek KGB changed into a National Security Service, the agency's function was described as "aimed at better protection of the republic's territorial integrity, state independence and sovereignty, constitutional rights and civil freedoms." More specifically, the security service was to engage in "intelligence and counter-intelligence," and in "combating organized crime." Historically, organized crime in Uzbekistan could be found on many levels of its society, notably among its power elite. During the early period of the Gorbachev regime, investigating teams from Moscow visited Uzbekistan regularly, unearthing what they described as widespread corruption and prompting a series of arrests and trials. Later on, some of these interrogations and findings were said to have been fraudulent and otherwise illegal. In Tashkent, such findings were often regarded as part of Moscow's efforts to undermine Uzbek independence aspirations. Uzbek KGB officials and, in particular, Interior Ministry personnel were among those accused of bribery, kickback schemes, and falsification of official records, particularly in overreporting the region's crucial cotton production.

With the dissolution of the Soviet Union and the separation of the Uzbek KGB from its Moscow control, such outside intrusions came to an end. Thus, in "combating organized crime," the renamed agency was on its own. Being directly responsible to the republic's President, could the National Security Service be expected to operate with independent vigor? When one uses the term "patriarchal" in describing much of Uzbek society (as well as social patterns in neighboring states), it is essential to keep the importance of family and clan in proper perspective. A culture of kinship, clan loyalties, and a resentment of foreign economic-ethical standards have long been traditional. It is impossible to speak of Uzbek society without naming the region's longtime patriarchal leader Sharif R. Rashidov (b.1917–d.1983), who personified the father figure–politician, who also played the role of poet-novelist, and who, not least of all, was a close Kremlin associate during the years of Leonid Brezhnev's leadership.

Rashidov was ousted from his position shortly before his death, and both Moscow and Tashkent media revealed in great detail that his administration had tolerated rival networks of corrupt Uzbek officials, often organized along family or clan lines. A series of much-publicized trials followed, and some of the convicted officials received the death penalty. Since then, a number of those who were originally accused have either been exonerated, quietly reinstated, or retired. *Izvestia* reported (March 25, 1991) that President Karimov had endorsed a proposal that an "agro-industrial complex" in the Dzhizak district, Rashidov's birthplace, be named after the once-discredited Uzbek leader.

While elsewhere the KGB has been credited with exposing corruption within the Ministry of Interior, in Uzbekistan that ministry's Department to Combat the Misappropriation of Socialist Property—which was established specifically to fight corruption—was implicated in widespread racketeering practices. For Karimov's new KGB, his National Security Service, to combat organized crime effectively, it would have to face the unpopular task of dismantling part of a social fabric that was long established and tightly knit.

When President Karimov spoke of the dangers that neighboring Tajikistan represented to his own country, he was not exaggerating the risk potential faced by the Central Asian republics; ethnic, religious, economic, and foreign pressures existed throughout the area. Tajikistan, with its population of 5.4 million, differed from its neighbors in that its Islamic population was not Turkic but Persian (Iranian) in its ethnic and linguistic roots. Ethnic Tajiks made up about 63 percent of the population; a little less than a quarter of the population were Uzbeks.

After the Moscow events in 1991, the fate of the KGB in Tajikistan was as unique as that of the republic itself. Yet another patriarchal Communist leader, Rakhman N. Nabiyev, was forced to resign on September 7, 1991; but his supporters rallied quickly, and Nabiyev was reelected President in November. His backers were the old Communist establishment. The opposition included a relatively small Democratic Party, demanding a multiparty system; the Islamic Renaissance Party, which called for "an Islamic democracy"; and population groups from remote mountainous areas who felt deep resentment of Nabiyev's regime at Dushanbe, the country's capital.

The chronology of Tajikistan's KGB illustrates the republic's rapidly changing politicomilitary scene. Echoing the central KGB's warning campaign, Vladimir Petkel—then chief of the Tajik KGB—was quoted by Tass (November 20, 1990) as saying that "activities by secret services operating against the USSR have not subsided one bit in recent months." Petkel added that "subversive activities against Tajikistan have been stepped up," and that the withdrawal of Soviet troops from Afghanistan had led to "an outburst of subversive activities in local areas." Petkel also said that foreign intelligence officers had increased their efforts to smuggle "their people" into the country and to enlist informers and agents. He concluded, "There are no grounds for complacency in the present situation in Central Asia. The situation is deteriorating, and confrontation is growing."

Next—again following the Moscow example—Radio Dushanbe could report (December 17, 1990) that the local KGB had created "a new subunit," to be called its "Public Relations Service." The service was designed to "inform the population in greater detail on the activities of the organs of state security," and to establish contact with work collectives, unions of creative workers, deputies, public and scientific organizations, and the mass media. A KGB museum would be open to the public from 11 A.M. to 2 P.M. every second and fourth Saturday of each month.

On June 28, 1991, the Tajik Parliament confirmed the appointment of General Anatoli Stroykin, then fifty-five years old, as the new Tajik KGB chief. He had previously headed the Kazakhstan KGB. There was no mention of his predecessor. As noted above, Petkel had made a number of general references to the machinations of foreign intelligence services. More specific accusations were made by KGB deputy director Anatoli Beloyusov. He told the Tajikta-Tass news agency (August 1, 1991) that the "strengthened influence of the ideas of Islamic fundamentalism" in Tajikistan was "directly linked to increased activities by Pakistani special services."

In view of future events, and whether or not Pakistani intelligence agents were actually involved, Beloyusov's observations offered unusual details. He attributed to a so-called Program M the intention to "de-

stabilize the sociopolitical situation in the USSR's Central Asian republics" and to encourage independence movements. According to Beloyusov, the KGB had "incontrovertible evidence" that Pakistani agents
were creating "an armed Afghan opposition." Specifically, he said,
"schools have been set up in Afghan settlements near the border to give
religious and military instructions to young Tajiks, Uzbeks and Turk-
mens." These men were being trained, he added, to engage in "hostile
activities against the USSR."

Following the August coup attempt, Tajik KGB chief Stroykin went
to Moscow where he met with Bakatin and, on November 11, 1991,
signed an agreement that pledged the KGB services to "cooperation and
interaction in defending the vital interests of the parties and strengthening collective security." Following the general pattern, the Tajik KGB
was dissolved by President Nabiyev on January 2, 1992, and replaced
with a National Security Committee. Stroykin, the agency's chief, was
removed from his post on April 23, and went home to Russia. He was
replaced by a Tajik named Safarali Kenjayev, who had been one of his
deputies. But this was only an interim appointment, and Kenjayev was
soon replaced by Rezo Tursunov—who mysteriously disappeared in
May, after reportedly burning "Top Secret" documents.

The missing KGB chief was replaced by Colonel Alidzhon Solibayev,
who, in turn, was dismissed by Nabiyev on August 4. Itar-Tass reported
(August 4, 1992) that the new Tajik KGB chief Shakhob Sharipov—
identified as "a career security officer"—had previously been chairman
of a rural district council. When the newly appointed KGB chief was
introduced to his staff by one of Nabiyev's ministers, the men refused
to accept Sharipov as their chief. According to Radio Dushanbe (August
4, 1992), they told the minister to "convey their dissatisfaction to the
President." The KGB staffers said the appointment of Sharipov would
"further aggravate the strained situation in the republic." By that time,
President Nabiyev was under severe pressure from the combined opposition; his actions—he had also just fired his defense chief—appeared
to reflect irritation and personal stress.

Radio Dushanbe quoted a statement it had received from three deputy
KGB chairmen who recalled rather bitterly that, "during a four-month
period of this year, four people have been appointed to the position of
chairman of the National Security Committee of the Republic of Tajikistan." They accused President Nabiyev of having made a "serious
mistake" in firing Colonel Solibayev, who had "introduced many needed
reforms" during "this particularly tense situation." They warned that

"this latest action by the President can only aggravate an already serious condition." In addition to the three deputies, the statement was signed by a group of other KGB staff members. Clearly, in addition to his other troubles, President Nabiyev had a KGB mutiny on his hands.

It got worse. On August 20, the KGB's deputy chief Dzhurabek Aminov told the press that Nabiyev had dismissed his security chief out of personal antipathy. Aminov said that "Solibayev was known among his colleagues as a man loyal to democratic reforms and values." Aminov drew the journalists' attention to the fact that the presidential decree of dismissal was issued a day before Solibayev had intended to announce his resignation. The deputy explained, "My chief faced a *fait accompli* and agreed to step down under pressure from the President and his retinue." Itar-Tass, reporting on this development (August 11, 1991), added that "leaders of all opposition political parties and movements, several prominent scientists and men of culture, as well as representatives of the Moslem clergy, expressed solidarity with this demand." It seems fair to say that rarely had a KGB chief enjoyed such popular support.

Fierce fighting, violent street demonstrations, and near-chaos in Tajikistan's economic life continued to reflect the struggle for power. In September, Nabiyev was once again forced from office. In November, his allies regained power; and on December 10, 1992, Nabiyev reentered Dushanbe with the help of tanks, helicopters, and armored vehicles. But, ailing and fatigued by the struggle, he told Parliament, "I am still the President. My people have chosen me, but I am ready to resign if that will bring peace." On April 11, 1993, Itar-Tass quoted a KGB spokesperson as stating that, over the weekend, Nabiyev had "died a natural death."

During the President's exile from the capital, Colonel Solibayev had, in fact, been reinstated as KGB chief. On November 23, 1992, as quoted by Interfax, he told Parliament that published rumors of "tens of thousands" of civilian deaths in the south of the republic, and of the shooting of eight hundred refugees, were inaccurate. Solibayev said that investigations had shown "no mass graves of enemy soldiers." He confirmed that twenty-five thousand refugees—mainly women and children—had fled to a southern area that was under the control of Russian Border Guards. Meanwhile, Solibayev was mourning the death of his courageous deputy Aminov, who had challenged President Nabiyev so dramatically four months earlier. On the night of November 18 at 10:30 P.M., the forty-three year-old KGB officer had been ambushed as he was returning home in his car. The KGB office stated the next day that Aminov "was attacked by unidentified individuals who fired a grenade launcher and submachine guns, in the very center of Dushanbe." The announcement added, "The staff of the Security Service is shocked and outraged by the incident, and protests against attempts of various armed groups to involve the KGB in political fighting. As an executive body of state power and law enforcement, the KGB will enforce law and ensure people's safety and the integrity of sovereign Tajikistan, despite threats and blackmail."

In any case, with the Communist forces back in power and the opposition groups once more on the defensive, yet another security head appeared on the scene. Presumably selected by the retinue of the emotionally and physically exhausted President—who was a man near death—the newest KGB chief Saidamir Zukhurov gave a wide-ranging interview to *Pravda* (February 6, 1993), in which he offered a colorful version of the civil war: "Fundamentalist gunmen in Afghanistan are exchanging two assault rifles for one good-looking girl seized on the Tajik bank of the Panj River. Cars, bicycles, motorcycles, carpets, and gold are also converted into weapons." Zukhurov added that "the area controlled by the Islamists is shrinking like the skin of a wild ass. Nevertheless, the four regions of the Garm mountain range and the Ramit ravine are still inaccessible to the legitimate government. The unique topographic design of the area has enabled some seven hundred to eight hundred gunmen to maintain its defense for three months running."

The KGB chief ended on a cautiously conciliatory note: "Still, all these people are our brothers, our relatives, fellow countrymen, even though they are on the wrong track. And, therefore, we do not want large-scale bloodshed. We are holding talks." It must be recalled that, in reality, some forty thousand people had been reported killed during the preceding nine-month period. In addition, as many as ninety thousand uprooted, desperate refugees had crossed into Afghanistan, hoping to settle on territory largely inhabited by fellow Tajiks; however, adverse living conditions forced thousands to return to Tajikistan.

President Karimov of Uzbekistan had warned about unrest in Tajikistan, but he was also aware of deep ethnic rifts in neighboring Kyrgyzstan (formerly, Kirghizia). Deadly riots in this republic of 4.3 million inhabitants had pitted Uzbeks against Kirghizians. Much of the summer of 1990 was poisoned by these clashes, which might have led to conflict between the two neighboring states like the warfare between Azerbaijan and Armenia. Again, the fault lines of unrest could be found in chessboard demographics that dated back to the structuring of the Soviet Union, which drew internal frontiers that created large ethnic minorities. Kirghizians made up just over 52 percent of the country's population. In addition, there were more than 20 percent Russians, although many of them decided to return to Russia. The Uzbek population—heavily concentrated near the nation's border with Uzbekistan—has been estimated at as high as half a million, or nearly a quarter of the total population. Other minorities included Ukrainians, Germans, and Tatars.

When fighting broke out between Uzbeks and Kirghizians, rumors made the rounds in the country's capital of Bishkek (formerly Frunze, after the Russian military leader Mikhail V. Frunze who was born in Kirghizia) that the KGB had instigated, or at least permitted, the conflict to weaken the region's claims to self-government. In point of fact, neither the KGB nor the Interior Ministry's militia had been effective in halting the disputes that were at the core of the outbreaks. Initially, homeless Kirghizian youngsters had occupied land belonging to Uzbeks, apparently with the intent of becoming permanent squatters. Earlier, threats of violence had succeeded in the capital city, where scarce housing was made available to unruly groups of young men demanding it.

When these tactics were tried on the land belonging to Uzbeks in the Osh district, clashes broke out on June 4, 1990, with a second series of riots on the fourteenth of the month. A month later, the number of deaths was put at 230, with five hundred buildings and one hundred cars burned, and a major part of the harvest in ruins. But all this had not happened overnight. What did the KGB know, and when did it know it? And what, if anything, did the agency do about it? These questions were raised by an Uzbek delegate to the Twenty-eighth Communist Party Congress. USSR KGB director Kryuchkov answered them in a letter to the Tashkent newspaper *Pravda Vostoka*, which published the letter on August 11, 1990.

Kryuchkov admitted that the "tragic events" in Osh had "not come as a surprise" to the central KGB in Moscow, nor to its staff in Kirghizia. The agency had, he wrote, "received warning signals, as early as the beginning of 1990, about increasing tensions between the Kirghiz and Uzbek populations." He added that the KGB had alerted government and Communist Party officials, and had "repeatedly warned in writing concerning the development of negative trends." The KGB chief added that his agency had "offered proposals to normalize the situation, by means of political and preventive measures."

Kryuchkov said that, early in April, the Kirghiz KGB for the Osh district had advised local authorities that "persons of Kirghiz nationality planned to organize an action in the city of Osh, aimed at the forcible seizure of plots of land." The KGB report recommended what it called "precautionary conversations with the initiators of the impending actions." The KGB chief ended his letter with the standard bureaucratic proposal that a "commission" be set up to provide "an objective evaluation of the activities of organs of authority and administration concerning the prevention and suppression of the tragic events that took place."

From a historical viewpoint it would appear that the Osh conflict remained limited, largely because President Karimov of Uzbekistan and the soon-to-be President Askar Akayev of Kyrgyzstan succeeded in cooling tempers on both sides. Akayev had already been a leading figure in the Kirghiz parliament when on October 27, 1990, he was elected President without opposition—which, he admitted, was an embarrassing situation for a candidate advocating free expression of political views. Boris Yeltsin visited Akayev the following July. And Akayev later traveled to Washington, where on October 26, 1991, he said that Kyrgyzstan was the first republic "to draw up and submit to parliament a law on defending the rights and freedoms of ethnic minorities."

On August 20, 1991, President Akayev dismissed the local KGB director Dzhumabek Asankulov (who had held the post since January 1989), with the polite explanation that he was "meeting the KGB general's request to resign on pension." Asankulov had apparently sympathized with the Moscow coup attempt. Akayev named Vice-president German Kuznetsov acting chief of the republic's KGB. Kuznetsov quickly expressed his agreement with the reformist measures envisioned by Vadim Bakatin in Moscow. Kuznetsov told a press conference on August 30 that, under his direction, the region's KGB would engage exclusively in "intelligence, counter-intelligence, antiterrorist activity and, in cooperation with the Interior Ministry, in the struggle against organized crime." A few days earlier, a group of twenty Kirghiz KGB officers had issued a statement denouncing the support that the local Communist Party had given the attempted coup. They described the events in Moscow as an effort to establish "a totalitarian regime," and they therefore "found it no longer possible" to remain party members.

Vice-president Kuznetsov yielded the top KGB position to a more permanent officeholder, Anarbek Bakayev. By November 21, although Bakayev retained this post, his agency was renamed the State Committee for National Security. Bakayev held a press conference on January 30, 1992, in which he reiterated his predecessors' pledges about the KGB's priorities. He added, however, that, in order to defend the state's economic interests, "special services have been set up to protect the credit and general financial system, and to control the removal of valuable materials from the republic." He said the KGB's leadership had been completely replaced, and that 70 percent of its department heads were "newly appointed." Bakayev told the press that, while his agency was operating on an annual budget of ten billion rubles, it was "far from well-equipped," lacking such essential facilities as a fax and video network.

Yevgeny Primakov, the head of Russia's Foreign Intelligence Service, must take a particular interest in Turkmenistan, with its 3.3 million inhabitants, whose southern borders are shared by Iran and Afghanistan. Turkmenistan developed with Iran probably the closest links of any former Soviet republic. Turkmenistan's longtime leader Saparmurad Niyazov personally visited Iran's President Hashemi Rafsanjani. *Izvestia* reported (October 10, 1991) this was the first time in the history of the two neighboring states that "friendly talks were held at a presidential level." Niyazov said that the two countries were planning close cooperation in transportation, border trade, joint construction of dams on border rivers, and the spheres of culture and science.

Niyazov had long expressed distress over the high prices his country had to pay for the 70 percent of food and consumer goods it was forced to import from other ex-Soviet republics—while expected to sell them oil at fixed low prices. Being able to channel its oil through Iran under a joint pipeline-cum-refinery arrangement would enable Turkmenistan to expect payment at close to world price levels. For decades, the republic had been restricted to a one-crop economy—cotton—while its once-rich vegetable and fruit output (the region having been famous for its melons and watermelons) was cut back.

But while Turkmenistan was seeking to revise its domestic economy and develop new contacts abroad (notably in Teheran), its top government was adjusting to the dissolution of the Soviet Union with hardly a ripple. At the very top, Niyazov, named First Secretary of Turkmenistan's Communist Party Central Committee in late 1985, later served as chairman of the republic's Supreme Soviet. *Izvestia* reported (October 30, 1990) that he had been elected President "by an absolute majority of the electorate." After the abortive Moscow coup in 1991, the Communist Party of Turkmenistan evolved into a "Democratic Party," with the patriarchal Niyazov at its head.

Subsequent changes in the Niyazov government closely resembled a game of musical chairs: the KGB was transformed into a Committee of National Security, with Danatar Kopekov as director. In late January 1992, Kopekov was appointed the republic's First Minister of Defense, although the announcement emphasized that this did not mean Turkmenistan was immediately establishing its own army. On May 26 the former first deputy chairman of the Turkmenistan KGB, Saparmurad Seidov, was promoted to Chairman. Niyazov used the occasion to tell the KGB staff that its major duty was to "provide and preserve stability" within the country. He added that Turkmenistan's relations with its traditional neighbors—Turkey, Iran, Afghanistan, and the new CIS states—would be based on "principles of mutual respect and noninterference in each other's internal affairs."

Niyazov's KGB could visualize a variety of challenges, ranging from entrenched, clannishly administered corruption to the illegal growing of opium poppies, as well as local drug addiction and drug trafficking. Unforgotten was the murder, back in 1987, of Khalina Dzhorayevna, a Communist Party official in the city of Chardzhou. According to local press reports, she was murdered because high city officials found her persistent anticorruption investigations personally threatening. The local Interior Ministry—supposedly a traditional KGB investigation target—was directly implicated; according to one charge, the ministry managed to have "crimes concealed from official records, and 250 cases were closed for fraudulent reasons." Tass reported (May 23, 1989) that "more than forty persons were convicted" after a ten-month trial in Ashkhabad. Led by one Ilias Sarkiyev, the crime ring practiced extortion and "other illegal activities," and its members were sentenced to various terms of imprisonment.

Drug-running from Iran and Afghanistan through Turkmenistan's capital city Ashkhabad had remained a KGB target for several years. With a relatively open border toward the two southern nations, a standard traffic pattern had been established. *Pravda* noted earlier (August 22, 1988) that Turkmenistan's fight against "producers, sellers, and consumers of drugs" was "complicated by the fact that consuming drugs is traditional in Turkmenia." Here, too, KGB enforcement would encounter long-established social patterns. The paper added that, "since time immemorial, opium, for example, has been used here as an anaesthetic, and children were even 'treated' with this dangerous potion." The paper also said that the drugs were being brought into Turkmenistan "whole," because "wild, drug-containing crops do not occur here, and local climatic conditions do not make it possible for them to be grown for most of the year." Law-enforcement officials attributed "one break-in in four" to "drug users."

Turkmenistan appeared to have been relatively free of ethnic or other civil disorders, or at least of disorders serious enough to be reported in the rather conservative local media. An exception were limited riots following May Day celebrations in 1989, which began in Ashkhabad's Central Park and led to the destruction of property, the burning of motor vehicles, and attacks on police. The press identified the perpetrators as students "urged on by criminally minded elements." But no particular group of victims was identified, and the destruction did not appear to have ethnic undertones.

All told, the reconstituted KGB operations in the Central Asian states of the former USSR faced one major change in target: from controlling national independence movements in the name of an indivisible USSR, they now had to be alert to ultranationalist, virtually tribal hostilities that were aggravated by such basic elements as overpopulation, ineffective land use, and the need for efficient economic production and distribution. One well-known Uzbek writer, Timur Pulatov, analyzed this situation in the *Moscow News* (August 8–15, 1990) when he noted that "classic Central Asian inter-community conflicts, usually sparked by claims concerning land, water and pasture," were frequent in the nineteenth century and "took the toll of thousands of lives." Pulatov wrote that "new ethnic and territorial demarcations" can only cause "new bloody outbursts." The very idea of any redivision of lands, he concluded, would "only outline areas for new violent conflicts; they will smoulder, and again flair up for years to come, leaving the region psychologically fatigued and in a state of complete economic decline." Therefore, the task of the new KGB in the Central Asian states must be the correct anticipation and defusing of such ethnic clashes—admittedly, a challenge difficult to meet.

# Part IV

## Today and Tomorrow

# 16

# Border Guards in Disarray

Immediately after the coup attempt of August 1991, the regime of Mikhail Gorbachev took steps to reduce the power of the KGB, to break up its monopoly on domestic control and disperse its power centers. Primary among these steps was the separation from the KGB of its military arm: the so-called Border Guards. Throughout the history of the Soviet Union, the role of the Guards has ranged from ever-present to obscure, from irrationally feared to pragmatically accepted. After all, the USSR encompassed a vast Eurasian landmass, bordering on sixteen countries after World War II, and its borders ranged from the Kurile Islands facing Japan to those of Eastern Europe.

Russian historians like to recall that the tradition of the Border Guards can be traced to the rule of Catherine the Great. But it was actually the initiative of Lenin that gave the Guard its contemporary identity and its crucial position as the armed forces of the Soviet secret police—ultimately, the KGB. The most dramatic display of the KGB's power by way of Border Guard force came immediately after Joseph Stalin's death in 1953 when the Guards, following instructions by secret police chief Lavrenti Beria, moved tanks and other heavy equipment into central Moscow—allegedly to guard against unrest, but in effect providing inescapable evidence of Beria's personal power, even over rival men within the Kremlin leadership.

The actual number of Border Guard troops has fluctuated, and estimates as well as supposedly authoritative statistics cannot be regarded as definitive. During the early Gorbachev years, estimates ranged up to 450,000. After the August coup attempt, official announcements asserted that the number of troops was less than half this total. Even allowing for attritions of various types (including resignations and desertions), this figure seemed too low at the time; later, as the tasks of the Border Guards became more diffuse—and, indeed, confused and confusing—substantially larger contingents must have been necessary to provide the Border Guards with the number of troops required for their far-flung tasks.

The term "Border Guards," as such, has always conveyed an air of pure defense—of "safeguarding the motherland," to use a frequently preferred term. In reality, the Border Guards were self-sustained and fully equipped as a military organization, commanding their own air force (air patrols), naval forces (sea patrols), land forces (including such heavy equipment as tanks and armored personnel carriers), as well as a sophisticated communications network. This varied strength could be justified by the vast expanse of the USSR borders of yesteryear; by the complicated outer and inner borders of the Commonwealth of Independent States (CIS), successor to the Soviet Union; and by the newly complicated borders separating Russia, Ukraine, Belarus, Kazakhstan, the Baltic states, and the rest of the more or less independent republics and states that have emerged from the dissolution of the USSR.

That the Border Guards faced ever-new and more complex tasks following dissolution of the Soviet Union is beyond dispute. What did pose immediate questions was the manner in which the Guards were at first, and quickly, separated from the KGB, and then—almost surreptitiously—reintegrated into the KGB's domestic Russian successor agency, the Ministry of Security. In retrospect, the quick "dissolution" of the KGB following the failed August coup appears to have been a political reflex—a tactic designed to quiet public revulsion against the KGB, to avoid rioting that might have led to actual assaults on KGB offices and personnel, destruction of property, and seizure of files and archives. To diffuse such anger, the KGB was, as it were, deprived of its potentially most powerful arm, that is, the well-equipped Border Guards.

During the weeks following the abortive August coup, the Gorbachev regime implemented this and related policies in rapid succession. Tass first announced (October 14, 1991) that "the KGB department in charge of the Soviet Border Guard troops will soon be transformed into an independent Committee." Early in December, while Gorbachev was still President and the USSR continued to exist as a legal entity, Gorbachev signed a decree that gave legal status to the new "Committee to Guard the USSR State Border" as an agency directly responsible to the President himself.

Although Kremlin events were moving swiftly and dissolution of the Soviet Union was only days away, the Border Guards' deputy chief of staff Major General Victor Zemtsov told the army paper *Krasnaya Zvezda* (December 7, 1991) that the new Committee was an interrepublic organ of state management, defending the interest of the Union and the sovereign republics within it, on the border and in the economic zone. All its activity will be carried out within the limits of powers delegated by the sovereign republics (states). The Committee is responsible for ensuring border policy coordinated with the republics and the effective leadership of all types of activity by border troops." To view this statement in proper perspective, it must be recalled that at that very moment Lithuania, Latvia, and Estonia were clearly determined to assert their national independence totally. Azerbaijan and Armenia were engaged in internal as well as border conflicts; and the USSR's borders to the south—notably with Iran—were developing serious gaps. Just days later, the very existence of the Union of Soviet Socialist Republics (USSR) came to an end, and the Border Guards faced totally unprecedented conditions and tasks.

The replacement of Gorbachev by Boris Yeltsin as the leading personality in the former Soviet Union—Yeltsin having earlier been elected President of the Russian Federation—directly affected the KGB successor agencies. After making an abortive effort to merge the KGB's domestic branch with the Ministry of Interior (MVD), Yeltsin on June 12, 1992, issued a decree titled "On the Formation of the Border Troops of the Russian Federation," which, in effect, returned the Guards to their former KGB control. Itar-Tass reported the next day (June 13, 1992) that such a "unified security system" had been established to guard "the state border and maritime economic zone of the Russian Federation." The text continued as follows:

"Under this document, the [Russian] republic's border troops are placed within the Ministry of Security of the Russian Federation and made up of the personnel of the Committee for Defense of the State Border and the troops subordinate to it. The commander of the border troops is simultaneously a deputy security minister of Russia. The decree lays down that the border troops of the Russian Federation should be guided by international treaties, agreements on border issues made by the member states of the Commonwealth of Independent States, the Constitution of the Russian Federation, the laws of the Russian Federation and legal acts of the former USSR, where they do not contradict Russian Federation legislation."

Media concern about the KGB was renewed by this decree, which put the Border Guards back under their old bosses. And indeed, old bosses they were! The "new" Commander—and Deputy Security Minister— was a veteran of the old Border Guard administration. He was Lieutenant General Vladimir I. Shlyakhtin, born in 1940 in the Rostov region, a graduate of the Soviet Army's Alma-Ata Border Academy. He finished training at the M. V. Frunze Military Academy in 1968 and at the USSR Armed Forces General Staff Academy in 1978. He had served with the KGB Border Guards in three military districts: Transcaucasus, Central Asia, and Transbaikal. During these services, Shlyakhtin rose from dep- uty chief of a Border Guard subunit to district commander; and from 1990 to 1992, he directed the border troops staff. At the time of his appointment as Commander he was fifty-two years old.

Public misgivings were voiced by Sergey Mostovshchikov, writing in *Izvestia* (June 17, 1991) under the headline "BORDER GUARDS RETURN TO THE CHEKISTS' RANKS." Mostovshchikov expressed the view that reintegration of the Border Guards represented "a significant step in a planned campaign to restore to the Russian Security Ministry all the functions the USSR KGB lost after the triumph of democracy." The author quoted "informed sources" as suggesting that Security Minister Victor Barannikov "intends to restore to the Chekists not only the bor- ders, but all the prodigal sons whom the previous KGB chief, Vadim Bakatin, succeeded in driving out of their home."

Shlyakhtin's task included redefinition of Russia's actual borders, a delineation of the borders between Russia and the former republics of the Soviet Union, and—particularly—control over the separations from the Baltic republics and, most likely, from Azerbaijan. He denied that "dead ground" would be created between Russia and Ukraine; such an area would have facilitated border control, but would also dramatize the separation. Even in the Baltic areas, the Border Guards pledged that their controls would not include "plowed strips" or "control strips." And regional commanders in the Northwestern Border District, guard- ing the Latvian and Estonian borders at the Pskov district, told inter- viewers simply that "the usual protection of Russia's territorial economic and political interests along its borders with Latvia and Estonia will be implemented."

While border controls with Latvia and Estonia were relatively clear- cut, those with neighboring Lithuania reflected political, demographic, and economic frictions. But in all these Baltic areas—as in numerous others—potential conflicts over actual borderlines existed. The Moscow paper *Komsomolskaya Pravda* (September 18, 1992) mentioned details that would generally be of concern only to mapmakers and local nationalists: "Lithuania, for example, is not averse to deeming as 'its own' the rayons [districts] on the Kurskaya spit, the city of Sovetsk, and Lake Vistytis; Latvia is not averse to deeming as 'its own' Pytalovsky and Palkingsky rayons in the Pskov Oblast [administrative region] and Estonia is not averse to deeming as 'its own' almost eight hundred square kilometers of Kingiseppsky Rayon in Leningrad Oblast and around fifteen hundred square kilometers of Pechorsky Rayon in Pskov Oblast."

The paper added that, short of actual border changes, "enterprising Balts" had managed to "cart off everything that is not nailed down" in the areas, "with the aid and active assistance of Russian citizens." According to the report, "representatives of the Russian Ministry of Security, the border troops leadership," and other administrators had been unable to halt this removal, mainly of "oil products and ferrous and rare-earth metals," amounting to "hundreds of tons." As the paper said, "an actual state border" would have to be established, covering a Russo-Baltic frontier 985.5 kilometers in length.

Borders are two sided, of course, and so the Baltics and other states found themselves faced with the task of guarding the Russian frontiers on their own side—as well as borders facing outward, at what used to be the Soviet frontier. Of these latter, the Lithuanian-Polish border is perhaps the most heavily traveled and most difficult to control. Belarus (the former Byelorussia) also faced delicate border disputes in the Baltics; while these were pending, Belarus decided to close its borders with Lithuania and Latvia, and to establish customs and other control checkpoints.

To speak of the Border Guards' role and status as a crazy quilt is no colorful exaggeration, particularly since at times and in certain places they had to act on behalf of the Commonwealth of Independent States as well as or separately from their role as Russian Border Guards. At one point, Valentin Gaponenko, commander of the Baltic Border District, described this dilemma to *Izvestia* (March 14, 1992):

"On the whole, we form part of CIS structures. We are subordinate to the Committee for the Protection of the Borders of the Commonwealth. But Latvia, Lithuania, and Estonia are, after all, outside the Commonwealth, and consequently we are guarding a foreign border. Our own border, the Russian border, however, is unsupervised. Until it is properly equipped and guarded, Russia will sustain considerable economic losses. The export of strategic raw materials has become the 'specialty' of dozens of firms in Latvia, Lithuania, and Estonia."

While this situation was certainly temporary, it illustrated the complexity of Border Guard status. Added to the strains on both sides was the hostility toward Russians or "Russian-speakers" in several of the non-Russian republics or states. The historic, political, and cultural roots for such tendencies were all too obvious. For decades, Moscow had treated other republics as lesser beings in one way or another: as suppliers of raw materials; as receivers of benefits from "The Center"; or, to put it more crudely, as "colonial" in economic status or even mentality. Russians in these regions could look upon themselves as an elite whose language was the lingua franca. And indeed, Russian served as a cultural common denominator, as a conduit to the rest of the world— the way English did in India during colonial days and later.

A backlash—much of it tragic—turned some local populations against Russians or Russian-speakers, playing havoc with institutions ranging from schools to mixed marriages. The Border Guards, largely of Russian nationality, were consequently widely regarded as intruders whose prolonged presence was seen as an undesirable remnant of the past. In just one of numerous incidents, on January 5, 1992, someone set fire to a Border Guard post in Rohuneeme, near Tallinn, Estonia, although most of the Guards had left. Andrus Oovel, Estonia's General Director for State and Border Protection, observed that "this is the way some Estonians show their anger for the Border Guards." It was a senseless act, as Estonian Guards were scheduled to take over the facility. Oovel told the Tallinn Radio (September 21, 1992) that he still had only 1,100 local Guards to protect Estonia's borders, instead of the 3,048 necessary. While the country was slowly replacing the Russian Guards, including their patrols in the Baltic Sea, Finland made its Estonian neighbors a gift of three decommissioned patrol boats on August 20, 1991, repainting them in the Estonian national colors.

The lengthy adjustment period in border management brought with it conditions of such large-scale smuggling, circumvention of controls, bribery, and sheer chaos that bureaucracy had to come up with a respectable term when speaking of the situation. It found one: "transparency." Thus, when Major General Yevgeny Bochrov, Commander of Belarusian Border Troops, told *Kasnaya Zvezda* (October 21, 1991) about his problems, the paper gave the story this headline: "BORDER WITH BALTIC REGION LOSES 'TRANSPARENCY.' " In other words, Belarus was beginning to gain control over the six hundred kilometers it shared with Lithuania and Latvia. But even after some two thousand border posts would be installed, the paper's interviewer asked, would the border remain "as formerly, be quite 'transparent' "? Commander Bochrov said he did not see the need for an "iron curtain" at the border. "Real spies and saboteurs," he said, "will not infiltrate Belarus under the muzzles of Border Guards' assault rifles." Like his Russian counterparts, he complained about the continued "export of nonferrous metals, fuels, and lubricants, and works of art from Belarus by legal and illegal means."

Major problems faced Ukraine, which, after Russia, was the largest of the former USSR republics. Almost inevitably, the state's Commander of Border Troops Colonel General Valery Hubenko was a veteran of the KGB Border Guards. He had studied at Soviet military academies, served in the Transcaucasus, the Transbaikal region, and the Far East, and advanced from deputy chief of a border post to chief of Border Guards at an unspecified military district. Indeed, his background closely resembled that of his Russian counterpart, Lieutenant General Shlyakhtin. Hubenko told the Kiev newspaper *Holos Ukrainy* (October 9, 1992) that his troops faced the task of guarding 7,590 kilometers as well as the Black Sea shore of more than 10,000 kilometers. All this required land, sea, and air forces.

Hubenko recalled that his troops had become directly involved during what he called "the conflict in the Dniester region." This was an uprising by Russians and Ukrainians in northwestern Moldova when this republic declared its independence in September 1991. Sections of Moldova north of the Dniester River had been part of the Ukraine before 1944. At that time, Stalin merged the region with newly created Soviet Moldavia, a territory seized from Romania four years earlier. Armed clashes and border migrations occurred when Ukrainians and Russians in the region felt that an independent Moldova would discriminate against them, denigrate them into second-class citizens, and ultimately rob them of their ethnic identity. As Colonel General Hubenko recalled the conflict, "a real war raged near our borders, people died and towns and villages burned." Speaking of the present, he said, "Our main task is to guarantee Ukraine's territorial integrity and the inviolability of our borders." The border troops were aided by units from the Ukrainian Interior Ministry and the Security Service, Ukraine's own newly formed KGB successor agency.

A month later, Colonel General Hubenko spoke of even wider military concerns at Ukraine's borders. He admitted in an interview with the

Kiev paper *Khreshchatyk* (November 16, 1992) that several strategic areas lacked "strict border and customs controls"—a situation that enabled large-scale violations, of which arms smuggling was the most serious. Again he specified the Dniester region as explosive, but also added the Transcaucasus area among territories suffering from "deterioration of the military and political situation." Using the language of military diplomacy, he concluded, "One cannot fail to take into account the existence of 'hot spots' in border areas, and attempts to move armed formations and so-called 'volunteers.' All this creates a threat to the stability of the social and political situation in the border regions of Ukraine, Belarus, and Russia."

Hubenko blamed the "transparency" of crucial Ukrainian-Russian border regions for the almost unrestricted activity of "criminal elements, including citizens of Russia, Georgia, and Azerbaijan. He accused "organized criminal groups"—composed of Ukrainian, Russian, Belarusian, Moldovan, Romanian, Czecho-Slovak, and Polish citizens—of seeking illegally to transport citizens of China, Bangladesh, India, Korea, Sri Lanka, Pakistan, and other Asian countries across Ukrainian borders into Europe.

In Moldova itself, the independence declaration had created severe political stresses. Charges and countercharges were numerous. The Moscow paper *Nezavisimaya Gazeta* (June 5, 1992) quoted the successor to the region's KGB—the Moldovan National Security Ministry—as denying that provocative "terrorist acts" in the Dniester region had been carried out under its "leadership." The paper cited rumors that one activist who had been arrested two days earlier in the town of Tiraspol alleged that several terrorist groups bearing such names as "Black Panther" and "Burunduki" had "their activity coordinated by the Ministry of National Security." On July 20, 1992, the Ukrainian National Guard reported that "well-armed violators of the state border" were crossing from the Ukraine into Moldova "in increasing numbers."

At the same time, Moldovan authorities were accusing the Border Guards of the Commonwealth of Independent States—mainly ethnic Russians—of not doing their job. On June 10 the Moldovan Parliament denounced what it regarded as inaction by CIS Border Guards who were "not fulfilling their assigned mission." According to a parliamentary communiqué, "the number of cases of smuggling, criminal infiltration over the border, and robbery of natural, cultural, and other valuables belonging to Moldova is on the rise." Moldovan President Mircha Snegur stated two days later that Border Guard discipline had "seriously slackened, with cases of desertion ever more frequent." He ordered the Ministry of National Security to "assume command of the border troops." He added that officers who "refuse" such reassignment would be "banned from carrying out their official duties," and that the property of the border posts would be "transferred" to the National Security Ministry.

Since Azerbaijan's borders with Iran were of such strategic importance, and since its open conflict with Armenia was putting an immense strain on both countries, border control was vital. The Azeris' strong national feelings, which had kept the country outside the CIS, favored rapid withdrawal of all types of Russian troops—Border Guards included. On December 16, 1991, Azerbaijani President Ayaz Mutalibov issued a decree establishing a Committee for the Safeguarding of Azerbaijan's State Borders, with "the responsibility of administering the Border Guards deployed within the Azerbaijani territory." The firmness of this announcement ignored the practical difficulties of putting the decree into effect—the replacing of Russian and/or CIS Border Guards, notably at the Iranian frontier; the rapid recruitment and training of a sufficient number of Azeri guards; and the volatility of the borders between Azerbaijan and Iran on the one hand, and actual combat with Armenia on the other hand. Moreover, President Mutalibov was eventually deposed and took refuge in Russia.

Accusations and denials from Russian, Azerbaijani, Armenian, and Iranian sources served to obscure the details of the apparently constant border violations and violent incidents going on. Contradictory reports spoke of the hijacking of fuel trucks, border incursion by armed units, and even fights between rival national border troops. Clearly, the transition period created severe stresses on all sides. On December 27, 1992, Russian Border Guard units turned nineteen frontier posts at the borders with Iran and Turkey over to their Azeri counterparts. The final transfer of border posts was scheduled for August 1993, to coincide with total withdrawal of Russian troops from Azerbaijan.

A particularly explosive situation existed at the border of the Nakhichevan Autonomous Republic, a section of Azerbaijan separated from its main territory by Armenia and sharing a long border with Iran (as, indeed, the region belonged to Persia until 1828). To cite just one incident: on January 15, 1992, two Border Guard officers and four soldiers were taken hostage by what Tass called "Azerbaijani militants." One of the men was killed during an exchange of fire. At about the same time, "armed militants" attacked a border post at a place called Aza, seizing arms and ammunition. The Guards were acting for the Commonwealth of Independent States, and their command acknowledged that "the situation around border troops stationed in the Nakhichevan Autonomous Republic has become extremely dangerous."

By far the most bloody and frustrating border situation in all the ex-Soviet republics existed at the frontier between Tajikistan and Afghanistan. The Tajiks, ethnically close to the Iranians (Persians) in language and cultural traditions, became involved in violent civil conflict between sections that could roughly be categorized as the ex–Communist "establishment" and an emerging Islamic movement that might, or might not, be called "fundamentalist" in outlook and aims. Pulled in various religio-ethnic directions, and radicalized by events across bordering Afghanistan, the Tajik population underwent heart-rending sufferings in 1992 and 1993 that few international television cameras caught—certainly not with the dramatic impact of worldwide attention that was focused on Somalia and Bosnia.

On December 28, 1992, the National Security Committee of Tajikistan (the region's KGB successor agency) signed a decree that would have aided the Russian Border Guards by supplying them with officers familiar with local conditions. The announcement noted that, "as before, the Russian frontier guards are keeping the key to the lock on the southern border of the CIS." Whatever that metaphor may have meant, it came at a time when already some twenty thousand people had been killed in Tajikistan's religiopolitical civil war, and when the border with Afghanistan had become virtually uncontrollable.

Major General Vitaly Gritsan, commander of the Russian Border Guards in Tajikistan, told *Krasnaya Zvezda* (December 1, 1992) that, "however paradoxical it may sound, we are not preventing refugees from crossing from Tajik territory into Afghanistan. In the prevailing situation this may be the only way of avoiding further casualties and the death of many innocent people." He cautioned that, "at the same time, we are informing the refugees that, according to the information at our disposal, nothing good awaits them on the Afghan side."

Unconfirmed reports of the mass shooting of refugees were disseminated by some international news services. On December 22, 1992, the news service Interfax reported from Dushanbe, the Tajik capital, that Russian Border Guards had described continued fighting "between rival Tajik groups in the immediate vicinity of the border with Afghanistan," and that twenty thousand refugees had crowded into the border area. The Guards admitted they were so grossly outnumbered by warring groups, and swamped by the number of migrants, that their own operations had been "paralyzed." Tajik government sources at the same time estimated the number of border-crossing refugees at seventy thousand. Border Guards sought to halt reverse crossings—from Afghanistan into Tajikistan—particularly as they suspected activists of transporting arms and further contributing to the civil war. During various border incidents, Border Guards shot and killed such intruders. In turn, Guards were also killed.

Would the Russian Border Guards, acting either for the CIS or on their own, abandon independent, embattled Tajikistan—in other words, simply throw up their hands at a virtually impossible task? Russia's long-range interests in the stability of this ex-Soviet state, and in its border areas, could not be easily discarded. Major Andrei Aleshin, a spokesman for the Guards in Moscow, told Itar-Tass (November 16, 1992) that a group of officers serving at the Tajik-Afghan border had in fact requested that "redeployment" of the troops be considered. However, Aleshin said, for the time being, "every measure is being taken to guarantee the security and vital functioning of units and subunits guarding the Tajik-Afghan border." That, at least, was the official position at that moment—while the task of guarding the border had, in actual fact, become extremely hazardous and largely ineffective. Russia had pledged to support its Tajik Border Guards financially for a two-year period, ending April 1, 1994. But during the first half of 1993, attacks from bases within Afghanistan had reached a level that overtaxed the Russian troops, and President Yeltsin's patience. One reason given for his dismissal of Barannikov as head of the Russian Ministry of Security, in July, was lack of Border Guard effectiveness at the Tajik-Afghan frontier. The number of Russian dead and wounded had increased to a point where, on August 7, 1993, Yeltsin urged the Tajik leadership to use "measures of reconciliation, not suppression," to end the bloody conflict.

Perhaps the most delicate border situation existed between the former Soviet republics and China. Historically, disagreements over actual frontiers have involved the Chinese claim that Russian czars had imposed "unequal treaties" on China. Moscow and Beijing invested vast resources in manpower and materiel at their borders. On the USSR/Russia's side, this commitment extended far beyond the strength of its Border Guards, and ultimately involved other armed forces. In the summer of 1992, Russian Vice-premier Alexander Shokhin toured the Central Asian states; he negotiated agreements in Tajikistan and Turkmenistan whereby their frontiers would be controlled by Russian Border Guards.

As reported in *Nezavisimaya Gazeta* (July 28, 1991), "By mutual consent, strategic troops in this region are being transferred to Russian jurisdiction."

Russia, Kazakhstan, Kyrgyzstan, and Tajikistan formed a single delegation during border talks in Beijing, the Chinese capital, throughout 1992. According to *Izvestia* (December 2, 1992), the eighth round of these talks ended with an agreement on "how far back troops should be withdrawn." The report stated that the distance would be one hundred kilometers "on each side." The area was to be partly demilitarized—a process that might "take up to the year 2000." At the same time, reports of border incidents—ranging from clashes between fishermen to large-scale smuggling—continued to appear in the Russian media. Considering the length of the border, the variation in terrain, and the complex political-economic situation created by dissolution of the Soviet Union and economic reforms in China, complete enforcement of border controls appeared virtually impossible. Overall, whether under KGB or ex-KGB jurisdiction, the Border Guards had to act in accordance with the regional policies of the Russian government.

At the same time, the very status of the Russian Border Guards within the Ministry of Security placed them into competition with the rest of Russia's armed forces, and into potential conflict with the myriad more or less legal armed units in various independent states. On the one hand, Moscow might prefer to return Border Guards from outlying areas to its own borders; on the other hand, strategic considerations prompted Russia to maintain a wider reach—at times, far beyond its own frontiers.

# 17

# Foreign Intelligence, Modernized

In the spring of 1992, the Moscow Institute of International Relations began a course in contemporary espionage, "Intelligence in the Modern World." The Moscow Institute, known by its Russian initials as the MGIMO and affiliated with the Ministry of Foreign Affairs, has traditionally trained both diplomats and intelligence agents for assignments abroad. More specialized espionage instructions were provided by the Red Banner Institute, renamed in memory of former KGB chief Yuri Andropov and usually simply called the Andropov Institute. What made the new course at the Moscow Institute quite special was the opening lecture on March 17 by the director of the Russian Foreign Intelligence Service (FIS), identified in scholarly fashion as Academician Yevgeny Primakov.

Primakov assured the students that, despite rapid changes in Russian society, its foreign intelligence had not lost impact but had remained "up to the mark." He noted that, in the past, students at MGIMO had to undergo tedious ideological examinations and security checks before they could even register for the course. This practice, he said, no longer reflected the "spirit of the times," and students could now sign up for the course without elaborate ideological screening. "We have to select people who want to work in intelligence," Primakov said, "and who consciously desire to do so. Through optional courses like this one, through this sort of process of familiarization, people can come to us if they want. We will then check them out, and there has to be some weeding-out, but we will nevertheless get the people we want."

Primakov's seminar combined recruiting and public relations efforts. To just about everyone's surprise, not only students but also media representatives attended the lecture, and reports on it appeared in several newspapers. In addition to its director, the Foreign Intelligence Service was also represented by Yuri Kobaladze, chief of its Public Relations Department, and Tatyana Samolis, Primakov's press secretary. The students were told that the course would include presentations by intelligence officers, analysts, and specialists in different geographic and technical fields. Primakov emphasized that the foreign intelligence agency was not only interested in students who were studying foreign affairs, but also in men and women who were specializing in economics, physics, chemistry, and engineering. Introductory intelligence courses— with an eye on recruiting—were planned at other educational institutions. Kobaladze forecast that, "if, as a result of our seminars, about twenty-five people apply to us, or express a desire to work in intelligence, then we will institute courses like this one all over Moscow."

*Nezavisimaya Gazeta* (March 19) recalled that the Moscow Institute had a history of close relations with the KGB: "The intelligence service has given the Institute a number of teachers, and the Institute has given the intelligence service a number of its graduates." In the spring of 1991, one of the MGIMO lecturers was George Blake, who had spied for the Soviet Union while in the employ of British intelligence in West Germany. A British court sentenced him to forty-four years in prison. Blake served six years of this sentence, but then escaped to the USSR and joined the KGB staff; he received the Order of Lenin, the Order of Red Banner, the Order of the Patriotic War First Class, and the Order "For Personal Valor."

While Primakov's talk did not delve into substantive intelligence matters, it did reflect some of his personal attitudes and thoughts concerning future intelligence activities. He acknowledged that intelligence officers were routinely among embassy staffs. "There is a so-called legal intelligence service, worldwide," he said, "working under cover of various institutions and organizations. We are no exception. The intelligence service cannot deprive itself of this opportunity." In this respect, Primakov echoed comments by Vadim Bakatin, who had reaffirmed earlier that the foreign service would continue to accommodate intelligence officers, more or less knowingly. This contradicted the remarks of Boris Pankin, who during a brief period as Soviet Foreign Minister, right after the August 1991 coup, had rashly claimed that intelligence agents would no longer be permitted among embassy staffs.

Eduard Shevardnadze, Soviet Foreign Minister during much of the Gorbachev administration, told *Literaturnaya Gazeta* (January 22, 1992) that the presence of intelligence agents within embassies was part of a "traditional system, and not just with us." He added that, "as long as there is intelligence, there must be a 'cover,' some kind of concealment." However, Shevardnadze felt that there were too many agents camouflaged as foreign service personnel: "I know that in some of our embassies there was an excessive number of 'close' and 'distant neighbors,' 30 percent or more. This seemed abnormal to me. Especially the way this affects diplomacy and the atmosphere in our representative agencies."

How closely would Russian espionage remain linked with its diplomacy? To what degree was Primakov's world affairs background likely to influence the day-to-day operations of future Russian intelligence? And what of the relations between Primakov—the relative newcomer—and the KGB machinery he had inherited? The last of these questions was sharpened when Yevgeny Primakov was appointed chief of Soviet foreign intelligence on September 30, 1991. At that crucial time in Soviet/Russian history, the main criterion for high office in Moscow was proven loyalty to the Gorbachev–Yeltsin center during the August coup attempt. Primakov's position vis-à-vis the Kryuchkov conspirators had been clear-cut: he did not hesitate; he did not delay; he did not sit on any opportunistic fences during the crucial August days. In that respect, his slate was clean, and the doors to a major appointment were open. Why, then, a top KGB job? Did he have any previous intelligence experience?

Lubyanka gossip, at that time, was of two kinds. One group felt that here once again was an outsider, an amateur in the Bakatin mold, who was being brought into the KGB to reform, destroy, or simply ruin it. The second school of gossipers maintained that Primakov had indeed served the KGB in his early years: while a Radio Moscow correspondent in the Middle East, he also served as a KGB conduit whose file carried the code name "Maxim" (which would have been a fairly blatant code name, since his father's name was Maxim). Primakov himself consistently denied any earlier KGB connection. When Andrei V. Karaulov interviewed him for *Nezavisimaya Gazeta* (December 21, 1991), Karaulov said provocatively, "Just do not pretend that you are in intelligence by accident—tell the truth!" Primakov laughed this off. He told Karaulov how funny he thought the remark was, said he considered Karaulov a most cordial interviewer, and added, "But, honest to God, Andrei Viktorovich, I never worked in the KGB, and if anyone thinks that this is the case, he is mistaken."

One might easily accept that Primakov did not actually work "in" the

KGB, that—as the common term has it—he "was not KGB." But that does not rule out almost inevitable intelligence connections, at one time or another, during his lively career. As one reads over Yevgeny Primakov's varied assignments—in the media, in the Communist Party, in the study of world affairs, in diplomacy, and finally within Mikhail Gorbachev's immediate circle of advisers—it seems unavoidable that an alert KGB staff should have utilized his reports and analyses. Nor would such cooperation have been out of line with the ideas of a loyal veteran Communist Party official such as Primakov. After all, he addressed the Nineteenth Congress of the Soviet Communist Party on July 8, 1990, speaking as a candidate-member of the Central Committee's Politburo, stating that he regarded the party's international policies at that time as "not only right but victorious." Shortly after his intelligence appointment, Primakov resigned from the Communist Party.

The new foreign intelligence chief's background was examined critically by a commentator in *Rossiskaya Gazeta* (October 3, 1991), who asserted that it had "long been known" that Primakov was "among the civilian journalists, international affairs specialists, expert economists and historians who had close links with the KGB." The writer added that "the terms journalist and expert can be used without qualification, at least in the sense that they were not just a 'cover'—Primakov did, in fact, publish articles in newspapers and scientific journals." The paper acknowledged that he had served "with much distinction in various countries."

Yevgeny Maximovich Primakov was born of Russian parents in Kiev, Ukraine, on October 29, 1929. During his childhood he spent several unruly years in Tbilisi, the capital of Georgia, where he was a member of a roving street gang of youngsters. Asked about this period, he said during an interview, "I did not kill, and I did not steal. But I actually grew up in the streets." The reason for this unsupervised existence was the schedule of young Yevgeny's mother, a physician, who had to work at two jobs. He did not mention his father. Primakov recalled, "I, generally, was left to myself. But in Tbilisi, everyone grew up on the street; it was that kind of city." Perhaps it was his early exposure to the ambiance of the Soviet South that prompted Primakov to attend the Moscow Institute of Oriental Studies, from which he graduated in 1953. After completing a postgraduate course at Moscow State University in 1956, he worked for three years as a correspondent for the State Committee for Television and Radio Broadcasting. It was during this period that he first served as a correspondent in the Middle East. Then, until 1960, Primakov was a radio editor.

Having joined the Communist Party in 1959, Primakov served on the Chief Editorial Board of the State TV and Radio Committee for two years, beginning in 1960. For the next two years, he was a *Pravda* editor, specializing in Asian and African affairs. Four formative years ending in 1970 were spent in the Middle East, reporting for *Pravda* from several Arab countries, including Iraq. Thus, Primakov's academic studies were supplemented by editing and by reporting from the field. The next steps moved Primakov back in an academic direction, with new pragmatic political applications.

The list of Primakov's scholarly appointments is impressive. In 1970, he was named deputy director of the USSR Academy of Sciences Institute of World Economy and International Relations. He became corresponding member of the Academy in 1974, and was named Academician in 1979. From 1977 to 1985, Primakov was head of the Soviet Institute of Oriental Studies. With the coming of the Gorbachev period, he directed the Institute of World Economy and International Relations from 1985 to 1989. As a member of Gorbachev's inner circle, Primakov served as chairman of the Council of the Union, 1989–1991, and as chairman of the parliamentary group of the USSR, as a member of Gorbachev's Presidential Council, and as an adviser on his short-lived Security Council.

Asked which of his earlier tasks had best prepared him for his top intelligence position, Primakov decided it was that of director of the Institute of World Economy and International Relations, because "I was involved a great deal with situational analysis, with evaluating situations." During his years of close association with Gorbachev, Primakov accompanied the President to five U.S.–Soviet summit conferences, as well as on visits to China and India. Generally, he traveled widely in Europe, Asia, and the Middle East.

Primakov achieved major international attention on the eve of the Gulf War early in 1991, when Gorbachev and Shevardnadze sent him to Baghdad to try persuading Iraq's President Saddam Hussein to withdraw his troops from Kuwait. Primakov's trip was a last-minute Kremlin effort to assert Soviet influence in Iraq. Primakov told Karaulov that the mission failed because Saddam Hussein—whom Primakov had known since 1969—crudely misjudged his own political-military position. The Iraqi ruler had convinced himself that the United States was bluffing—that, as Primakov put it, "they would not hit." Hussein also thought the Soviet Union would never act in concert with the United States, Saudi Arabia would not invite American troops, and neither Egypt, Saudi Arabia, nor Syria would join a coalition with the Americans. In the end, Primakov recalled, "when I met with him, one-on-one, I told him quite frankly, 'Saddam, they will hit you!' " But Saddam Hussein could not be convinced, and the rest was tragic history.

Yevgeny Primakov's career, and his views on himself and on his career track, provide the image of a man whose supporters may be right when they call him "pragmatic," and whose detractors may be equally right when they call him "opportunistic." He has engaged in the practice of what Marxists used to regard as useful "self-criticism." He remembers he wrote articles, as a journalist, that in later years did "not sound quite right." This may sound like a polite way of admitting that he was following Kremlin propaganda lines. "But," he quickly explained, "when I was writing those things, believe me, I was convinced that I was writing the truth." He also confessed that in his student days, while working toward his diploma on a thesis about Arab nationalism, he was supposed to find a suitable quote from one of the "leaders." He used a "dreadful" quotation by Lavrenti Beria—Stalin's notorious secret police chief—contrasting "socialist nations" and "bourgeois nations," to illuminate his point.

Talking to the potential intelligence agents at the Moscow Institute of International Relations (as well as on many other occasions), Primakov spoke of modern intelligence as a "scientific" undertaking. Quite conceivably having worn the hats of spy and scholar simultaneously, he presumably meant that the two professions share methods in the collection and analysis of information; both should aim to be accurate, objective, and reliable. In that sense, the well-trained espionage agent acts like a scholar—and the inquiring scholar has the qualities of a spy. Primakov told the news agency Tass (October 2, 1991) that "intelligence work is a scientific activity." He described the intelligence service as "a large organism, which must increasingly use analytical methods, synthesize and analyze information, and make predictions on its basis." Trends toward scientific methods of analysis, Primakov said, "are not unique to our intelligence service; they also determine the direction of development of intelligence work in other countries."

While cutting back on personnel, Primakov insisted that he was engaged in strengthening and streamlining his agency. By taking officers off unrewarding assignments and moving them to more promising tasks, he sought to increase the overall efficiency of the entire Russian Foreign

Intelligence Service. One of the most costly and time-consuming activities, which ceased under his direction, was the old KGB's biweekly nuclear missile survey. Under this procedure, Soviet intelligence officers were obliged to monitor confidential sources as to whether or not the United States and the North Atlantic Treaty Organization (NATO) were planning a surprise nuclear missile attack on the Soviet Union.

According to Primakov, for more than a decade KGB staffers from all over the globe had been reporting every two weeks to the effect that "there is no visible evidence 'on the horizon' that in the next few days or hours the United States will deliver a nuclear missile strike on the Soviet Union." Primakov cautioned that the missile launch warning system of the Russian Ministry of Defense would remain in effect "until there are no more nuclear missile weapons in the world," but he announced that the KGB system had been discontinued. He said that "a lot of money was spent on this"; instead, the agents who prepared these reports, "the very same people—I do not hide this—could be engaged in more important work."

Primakov defined such "important work" as efforts to "trace processes in the United States and other countries that could objectively lead to a certain destabilization of the situation." He qualified this opaque remark, saying, "I do not have in mind the leading circles. (I do not want to suspect anyone at all.) But, after all, it is necessary to see how those critical technologies are developing (frequently with dual purpose), which, incidentally, could also be exported to third countries. We must know this." This was clearly a reference to Russian intelligence efforts to gain knowledge of confidential technical developments that might have military as well as commercial applications. Primakov added, "Another aspect is the fight against international terrorism. Here, I think, everything is clear. Further, economic intelligence, which helps to study partners and make sure that, to put it crudely, they do not rob us."

Just what did he mean by that? Who were "they"? Who was supposed to be robbing whom? Primakov's spontaneous remark, or slip, suggested that his thinking about Western economic intentions toward Russia did not differ greatly from earlier KGB warnings of the West's supposed predatory schemes. In effect, the secret police had been saying for decades, "We've got to watch them, or they'll outwit and destroy us!" An updated version of this position was provided by Primakov's spokesman—his agency's public relations officer—Yuri Kobaladze, who told Izvestia (May 5, 1992) that Western reports of continued Russian spy activities (for instance, in Belgium and France) were part of an organized campaign. Kobaladze accused "representatives of Western intelligence services" of trying to use "economic pressures to compel the Russian government to drastically reduce, or stop altogether, our intelligence service's activity in the West."

Kobaladze referred to KGB agent Vladimir Konopolev, whose defection had just enabled Belgium to dismantle an extensive espionage network, when he told *Nezavisimaya Gazeta* (April 25, 1992) that "the Americans intend to use Konopolev as an instrument of political pressure on Russia by linking the problem of industrial espionage with the $24 billion financial aid being granted to us." Kobaladze's background suggested that he might have personal knowledge of KGB practices in utilizing media correspondents abroad as part-time agents. Of Georgian background, born in Tbilisi in 1949, Kobaladze attended the Moscow Institute of International Relations. His official biography made no reference to intelligence training, but said he had specialized in journalism. Primakov may have known him from joint work in the State Committee for Television and Radio Broadcasting. Kobaladze, who speaks English fluently, was a Soviet radio correspondent in Great Britain from 1977 to 1984. Before Primakov appointed him to his public relations job, Kobaladze had covered Gorbachev's visits to the United States, Britain, France, and the Malta summit conference.

Although Kobaladze's suggestions that Western intelligence services were using economic blackmail and other pressures might seem dissonant with Primakov's generally conciliatory style, they did fit a basic theme. Primakov, too, tended to echo earlier KGB warnings of alleged foreign manipulations. Even during his introductory talk to students at the Moscow Institute, he suggested that there was an "orchestrated campaign" by the "special services of certain states," designed to achieve international control over nuclear resources within the former Soviet Union. Primakov spoke of sudden widespread publicity in the world press concerning "radioactive raw materials and nuclear weapons components"—publicity organized to "show the hopelessness of the system of storing fissionable materials and other elements used to manufacture nuclear weapons." He said such a campaign was designed "to convince public opinion that international control must be established over this sphere." And he added, "However, for all the chaos in our country, radioactive raw materials and nuclear weapons are under vigorous guard." Primakov cited as proof of the calculated nature of such publicity that press reports "concerning the sale of a consignment of Uranium-235, a small amount of heavy water, and the disappearance of warheads from Kazakhstan appeared at virtually the same time in a fairly coordinated way."

In the same lecture, Primakov admitted that the KGB had planted false accusations that the AIDS virus originated "from secret Pentagon laboratories." But he then alleged that "U.S. special services" had, "in revenge" for this campaign, "cooked up their own version" of the attack on Pope John Paul II, "accusing the Soviet Union of this terrorist act." Primakov failed to recall that speculations on Soviet involvement in the attempted assassination of the Pope circulated in 1981 and 1982, while the KGB's disinformation campaign on AIDS did not begin until the fall of 1985. Putting the best face on it, this mix-up in chronology could merely show a slipup in the FIS research department, while the dramatic "revenge" concept may be attributed to an overeager speechwriter on Primakov's staff.

Primakov survived well the changeover from Mikhail Gorbachev to Boris Yeltsin. He was questioned on this during a meeting with Moscow University's faculty on journalism and the Institute of Asian and African Affairs. After giving a talk on his agency's relations to other former Soviet republics, Primakov was asked how he had managed to make the transition from one top leader to another. He said that the question should actually center on how "professionally useful" an individual was "in relation to work in a particular field." Clearly, he meant that he had proven himself to be a valuable intelligence chief, whether under Gorbachev or Yeltsin. Primakov added, "It is not a question of changing a political front, or desertion from one person to someone else. The intelligence service is depoliticized and activity within it is determined by how well a particular worker carries out the tasks allocated to him." *Nezavisimaya Gazeta*, which reported on the meeting (October 17, 1992), observed that Primakov was "clearly disinclined" to deal with topics involving different personalities; still—ever the diplomat—"he spoke of his good relations with Vadim Bakatin and his respect for his predecessor, Leonid Shebarshin."

Primakov insisted that his agency was "not conducting intelligence work" against the former Soviet republics within the Commonwealth of Independent States. As for republics outside the CIS, he said bluntly, "We are treating them as foreign states." He referred to the status of Lithuania at that time when he said that, "if someone somewhere begins to work against Russia, then we will, of course, take some sort of countermeasures." He drew a line between "imperialist" attitudes and "Russia's national interests." He defined these interests as demanding preservation "of a single economic and military area, along with the full identity of the peoples and full justified desire for autonomous rights; we must preserve our integrity."

On the world scene, Primakov drew attention to his agency when he visited China prior to Yeltsin's visit to Beijing. He also made a secret visit to Yugoslavia in January 1993, during which he was said to have spoken with Serbian President Slobodan Milosevic. *Komsomolskaya Pravda* (January 20, 1993) noted Primakov's previously unreported trip with the observation that "not everyone in the Russian leadership likes the position of those who share the Western viewpoint on the need for a military solution to the [Serbian] problem." The paper asked whether Primakov's trip might point toward "coming changes in Russia's Balkan policy."

Primakov's major public appearance was connected with his agency's 130-page report "The New Challenge after the 'Cold War': The Proliferation of Weapons of Mass Destruction." The Foreign Intelligence Service presented the report at a press conference on January 28, 1993. It listed sixteen countries that had either acquired or showed activity designed to obtain weapons of mass destruction. Primakov stated in his preface to the report that a situation where states possessing nuclear, chemical, or biological weapons may emerge on the perimeters of Russia's border "is unacceptable."

In reply to questions, Primakov said, "As a rule, Russian experts employed in the nuclear weapons industry are not eager to go to any other countries. The danger is posed by specialists working in adjacent areas. They may be used abroad to organize the production of separate parts for nuclear weapons." He added, "Neither we, nor our partners, possess information that our specialists are already working in this area." Primakov said it was wrong to categorize countries as "friendly" or "hostile," and suggested that Israel's position was being ignored by the United States and its NATO allies, which were more concerned about Iraq, Iran, and North Korea. He spoke out against such double standards.

The setting chosen for the press conference publicizing the FIS report was the Press Center of the Russian Foreign Ministry, on Moscow's Zubovsky Boulevard. *Komsomolskaya Pravda* (January 29, 1993) described the presentation as "an unprecedented event in the history of our intelligence service." The meeting was well attended by intelligence officers and foreign service members. The setting and topic illustrated—as did the personality of Primakov himself—continued close links between the Russian Foreign Ministry and the Foreign Intelligence Service. In fact, the tenor of the report, together with such events as Primakov's visit to Milosevic in Belgrade, suggested that the intelligence agency may exert a relatively high degree of influence on the Foreign Ministry and the evolution of its policies. We might add that Primakov—for all his practiced subtleties—has emerged as a representative of an "independent" Russia's foreign policy, with clear demarcation lines toward the United States and the NATO allies.

Primakov made his position explicit on November 25, 1993, when he warned against moves to incorporate Eastern European countries into NATO. Primakov placed the intelligence agency in a policy-making position, allied with Russia's military establishment, as he told a news conference that any eastward "expansion" of NATO would create "the largest military grouping in the world, with a colossal offensive potential, directly at Russia's borders." Such a situation, he added, would call for "a fundamental reappraisal of all defense concepts on our side, a redeployment of armed forces, and changes in operational plans."

# 18

# Top Target: Iran

Leonid Shebarshin would seem to be an ideal guest lecturer at the Moscow Institute of International Relations or the Andropov Institute, the two major schools for young Russian intelligence agents. After all, Shebarshin had directed foreign intelligence operations after years of field work in South Asia, the Near East, and the United States. And yet, his record as KGB Resident in Iran made Shebarshin a highly controversial personality, a man who aroused fierce loyalty as well as severe criticism among his colleagues.

Personalities, performance, policies—these three "Ps" in intelligence operations—are relevant to Moscow's future espionage operations in Iran. For basic geopolitical reasons, Moscow–Teheran relations are likely to be of crucial importance—to these two countries and to the rest of the world, including the United States. The geography is obvious: Iran borders on what used to be the "underbelly" of the Soviet Union. After dissolution of the USSR, Iran became adjacent to several newly independent states. Of these, Azerbaijan, Turkmenistan, Tajikistan, Kyrgyzstan, Uzbekistan, and Kazakhstan had a largely Islamic population; Armenia, engaged in a fierce struggle with Azerbaijan, was mainly Christian.

Almost immediately after the breakup of the Soviet Union, Iran began a diplomatic offensive in the area, including the delicate effort to act as a mediator between Azerbaijan and Armenia in their bloody conflict over Nagorno-Karabakh; this region—a largely Armenian enclave within Azerbaijan—had been the scene of open warfare since early 1988. Whether Iran could succeed in its mediation effort was less relevant than the mere fact that Teheran's intervention was accepted by both sides, earning Iran the prestige of neutrality and statesmanlike detachment.

Mediation between Azerbaijan and Armenia helped to erase memories of Iran as an embodiment of the erratic personality and policies of the Ayatollah Ruholla Khomeini. Throughout 1992, Teheran sent missions to the newly independent states, led by Iranian Deputy Foreign Minister Mahmood Vayezi. The Iranian approach suggested that Teheran sought to fill the vacuum created by the weakening of Moscow's economic support of the area. In particular, Iran sought arrangements to make up for the falling-off of Russian oil supplies; Teheran made similar agreements with Ukraine.

Teheran provided the site for a conference—largely ignored in the West—of the Economic Cooperation Organization (ECO), held on February 16 and 17, 1992, and attended by representatives from Iran, Pakistan, Turkey, Azerbaijan, Turkmenistan, Kazakhstan, Kyrgyzstan, and Tajikistan. Iranian President Hashemi Rafsanjani opened the session with a talk that spoke of turning ECO into a "bridge between North and South." *Izvestia*, the Moscow daily, commented (February 18, 1992) that the meeting represented "a significant geopolitical and economic regrouping in the vast area of the Asian continent, with a population of around one-fourth of a billion people." The paper reported that, while Iran's Foreign Minister emphasized cooperation with Turkey, the Iranian press "was unanimously criticizing Turkey for 'being a pawn in serving the interests of the United States' for the sake of 'imposing a Western model' on the Central Asian republics in order to force the latter to 'shed their Islamic values.' " The next day, *Izvestia* noted that Teheran was using "purely political steps to strengthen its positions in the Iranian-Turkish disagreements within ECO."

Put simply, a triangular rivalry for the Central Asian states had developed: Moscow, Teheran, and Ankara were now competing in an area where Moscow's commanding role had previously been unchallenged. The United States did, in fact, favor Turkey's efforts to counter Iran's attempts at establishing a religiopolitical and economic hegemony among the newly independent Islamic states. At the same time, all these ECO governments, including that of Pakistan, were seeking to establish ties with the competing armed groups that had occupied Kabul, the capital of Afghanistan.

Russia's Foreign Intelligence Service—taking over from the KGB's First Chief Directorate—now had the task of revitalizing its operations in Iran, where it had long and dramatic past experience. The emergence of Yevgeny Primakov as FIS chief illustrated one major shift: the intelligence apparatus was no longer, in actual fact, guided by the Communist Party's Central Committee, but worked hand-in-hand with the Ministry of Foreign Affairs. Dissolution of the Communist Party (after the August 1991 coup attempt) had removed the party's overlord position. It had also done away with another operation: the Central Committee's International Department and its control of Communist parties abroad.

This had been a bone of contention between the KGB and the party for decades. The International Department had inherited the files and functions of the old Communist International (Comintern), which was dissolved during the Stalin era. But Comintern attitudes regarding Russian control, financial support, and ideological and personnel manipulations continued. Former Soviet spies have consistently maintained that the KGB and its predecessor agencies either did not employ Communist Party members as agents or else asked them to resign their membership or, at the very least, disguise their party affiliation. Professional Soviet spies tended to distrust party members as amateurs who were likely to act irresponsibly.

All this had a bearing on KGB operations in Iran, where the Communist Party—using the name Tudeh ("Masses" or "People's") Party—had been outlawed during the reign of Shah Mohammed Reza Pahlavi. Together with other leftist movements (notably, the Mojahedeen and Fedahedeen), it was initially legalized when Khomeini took over in Teheran early in 1979. One account of these events came from Vladimir Kuzichkin, who worked as an "illegal" in the Soviet Embassy in Teheran, spending three morning hours as a consular officer—his cover—and the rest of the time recruiting and directing spies. Kuzichkin stated in his book *Inside the KGB: My Life in Soviet Espionage* that, when Shebarshin took over as KGB Resident in May 1979, he told the staff of KGB chief Andropov's concern that "the Residency has lost almost the whole of its agent network as a result of the revolution," and that he wanted it to be rebuilt in two years. Shebarshin hoped to develop a new network in one year.

Precisely who it was in Moscow who decided that the Teheran KGB should use Tudeh Party members as agents, Kuzichkin never found out. He put the blame on the party's International Department, but it seems unlikely that it could have made the decision without Andropov's approval. When the first Tudeh courier brought a note to the Embassy, placed it on a desk in front of him and put a finger to his lips, Kuzichkin thought the whole charade might be a trap. When he took the message to Shebarshin, the Resident was annoyed, but felt he had to go along with the procedure.

According to Kuzichkin, these notes were written by the Tudeh Party's Secretary General Nureddin Kiyanuri, who had lived in East Germany for twenty years: they referred mainly to the party's allegedly successful attempts to influence Iranian affairs. In contrast to actual developments, the party gave Moscow the impression that it was on the way toward gaining leadership of the leftist movements of the Iranian revolution; it firmly backed Khomeini despite the Ayatollah's undisguised hostility toward the Communists and the Soviet state. Kuzichkin recalled that, when it came to routine agent contacts with the Tudeh Party, "it fell to me to run them," but this "did not suit me at all." Kuzichkin wanted to ask KGB headquarters in Moscow what it thought of this setup, knowing full well "that the 'S' Directorate [Illegal Intelligence] would never agree to my having contacts with a local Communist party." But Shebarshin refused.

As the Khomeini regime cracked down ever harder on opposition groups as well as movements that supported it with some misgivings, the Mujahedeen and Fedahedeen were crushed. After the seizure of the United States Embassy and the taking of hostages, attacks on the British and Soviet embassies also took place. In order to safeguard key documents, Shebarshin and Kuzichkin had them microfilmed and hid the film in a hollowed-out wooden board at the Embassy's "Impulse" station—its communications interception room. When, early in 1982, Moscow–Teheran relations became temporarily more relaxed, Kuzichkin writes, he sought to retrieve the hidden microfilm, but found the hole empty. Under Soviet law, he was liable to seven years in prison for having permitted secret documents to be stolen. Someone, he felt, had stabbed him in the back: "Officially, only Resident Shebarshin knew of the cache, beside myself. Whom else he could have told about it, I did not know. But that no longer mattered. Whoever did it had created an irreversible situation." Kuzichkin maintained that this incident, together with his disillusionment with corruption among Soviet officials and Communist Party leaders abroad, prompted him to defect from the KGB and Soviet society.

Kuzichkin's narrative concluded with a detailed account of his surreptitious trip by car to the Turkish border. He settled in Great Britain; in 1986, he assumed another identity when it became known that a British journalist—a Communist Party member—had been offered

$100,000 by the Bulgarian secret service to kidnap or kill him. Kuzichkin writes "After my disappearance from Teheran, the Soviet authorities adopted the story that I had been abducted by Afghan terrorists." But that is hardly the whole story, particularly where Shebarshin's role is concerned. In an interview with *Izvestia* (October 11, 1991), Shebarshin said, "Kuzichkin was in touch with British intelligence long before defecting from Iran. The Tudeh Party had been doomed. Kuzichkin could neither add to nor detract from its fate."

At least one of Shebarshin's former associates disagreed with his assessment. This KGB insider, who preferred to remain anonymous, told the weekly *Moscow News* (No. 41, 1991) that Shebarshin's performance in Iran had been a failure. He put it this way: "Shebarshin was sent to run the spy network in Iran. He had an excellent chance to display his skills, which were undeniable, in this difficult country. While he was there, there erupted one of the biggest scandals in the recent history of our intelligence." The KGB man alleged that Shebarshin ignored indications that Kuzichkin had become unreliable, but "continued to give him responsible missions." As a result, he said, "valuable agents were revealed and then—as a chain reaction—many Iranians died and a large number of innocent people were executed."

Whatever Shebarshin's role during this crisis, it certainly created a total upheaval in the Soviet Embassy in Teheran. Kuzichkin made his getaway in 1982. On May 3, 1983, the Iranian Foreign Ministry announced that eighteen Soviet diplomats were being expelled, found guilty of "interfering in the affairs of the Islamic Republic [of Iran] by establishing contacts and taking advantage of treacherous and mercenary agents." One of those expelled was Shebarshin. The Tudeh Party was banned once again. Party Secretary Kiyanuri, then seventy-five years old, was arrested in February; he appeared on Iranian television in April and admitted he had spied for the Soviet Union. He was among a number of prominent Tudeh Party members and sympathizers who were executed.

Shebarshin's anonymous critic presented the following version of events: "The recruited Kuzichkin disclosed a valuable network of local agents. The British, who had a stake in complicating relations between Iran and the USSR, smuggled this information to the Iranians. The result was the rout of the Tudeh Party. It had been rumored that, by his arrogant and unwise behavior, Shebarshin prodded Kuzichkin toward betrayal. Be that as it may, Kuzichkin simply disappeared. It is known that Shebarshin did not respond to this at once, did his best to defend him, and rejected the idea that he might have been recruited by the British. Shebarshin also misinformed the leadership, persuading them that, most likely, Kuzichkin had been killed. Later, Kuzichkin reappeared, alive and in sound health, in Britain. This whole story is well known in the Committee [of State Security-KGB]. As an agent, Shebarshin committed a number of unforgivable errors."

These accusations did not sit well with Shebarshin. He told the editors of *Moscow News* that "none of the claims made by the anonymous author about me personally is consistent with reality." The paper (No. 46, 1991) interviewed Valentin Bratersky, who had earlier served in Afghanistan and came to Teheran in 1980 as KGB Deputy Resident. According to Bratersky, who retired from the KGB in 1990, Shebarshin was in Moscow when Kuzichkin failed to report for work. Bratersky sent a telegram to Kryuchkov, then head of KGB foreign intelligence, telling him of the mysterious disappearance. When Shebarshin returned to Teheran, he maintained that Kuzichkin "had been killed, cut into pieces and thrown into the sewerage system." The Embassy, with the help of Iranian secret service, traced Kuzichkin's car to the Turkish frontier. Bratersky said, "I believe that the car was driven away by someone else, and he himself left Teheran on one of three flights that left that day. I suggested Shebarshin try and check the passenger list. Possibly Kuzichkin disappeared under someone else's name, yet such an attempt had to be made. Shebarshin kept putting this off and did nothing as a result."

At last speaking for himself in a summary of his position, Kuzichkin addressed the People's Deputies of Russia in October 1990 as follows:

"In February 1979 Iran was rocked by an Islamic revolution. As early as March 1979 members of the Communist People's (Tudeh) Party of Iran, who had sat tight for years in the USSR and GDR [German Democratic Republic], started returning to Iran. Then Soviet party leadership sent them to Iran in the capacity of Trojan Horse, so that at an opportune moment the pro-Soviet forces would have a base for capturing power in the country. However, as early as the summer of 1979, it became clear to the network of KGB residents in Teheran that the Tudeh Party had no hope of success whatsoever. We had no doubt that the Tudeh Party was doomed to physical extermination in the near future. Residents informed the Centre [the KGB's Moscow headquarters] of this, yet the warnings were disregarded. The fact was that the actions of the Tudeh Party were guided not by the KGB, but by the International Department of the CPSU Central Committee.

"The unimaginable and undisguised stealing by government officials and party leaders in the Soviet colony in Iran, their involvement in sordid affairs of the Tudeh Party, the death of absolutely innocent Soviet soldiers in Afghanistan, and complicity, even if indirect, in whipping up war hysteria weighed heavily upon my soul.

"In those times, the times of Brezhnev's rule, a person in my position had no special alternatives with respect to the methods of struggle. It was pointless to openly defy the authorities, for I would have become one more nameless victim of the Soviet regime. And so I had to choose the only path possible at that time—the path of the West. . . . As far as Russia and the Russian people are concerned, however, I am clean and innocent before them, and I have been and remain a Russian Patriot."

In 1986, after discovering there was a price on his head, Kuzichkin had gone into hiding. But two years later the telephone suddenly rang in his wife's Moscow apartment. It was the night of April 17, 1988. As Galina Kokosova recalls the conversation, she heard Kuzichkin's voice: "Hallo, Galya, do you recognize me?" She answered, quite automatically, "Yes, of course, I do. Hallo, Volodya." Kuzichkin was calling from England, but his first question was, "Have you paid the share for the flat?" And then, "How do you feel?"

Kuzichkin surely assumed that the KGB would overhear their conversation. He then said: "I am not guilty of anything. But all this time I have begged your forgiveness. Do you think that I need this? I was tripped up by the KGB people. I can't help you in any way. Your life is very hard, I know. But at least you're at home." His wife then asked, "You eat prison meals, don't you?" To which he replied, "No, more like a pension. Galya, do you want to come here?" That was a question he repeated fifteen minutes later. She said, "No, I don't." He laughed with pleasure: "Atta boy!" They carefully talked about trivia, about the home, their dog. But he also urged her, "Write to Gorbachev!"

Well, Gorbachev left, and Yeltsin took over. And in August 1991 after the Communist Party was closed down, Kuzichkin wrote to Boris Yeltsin, asking that his case be reexamined to open the way for his return to Russia: "Now that the CPSU rule has been permanently overthrown, thanks, among other things, to your personal heroism, new and happier times are starting for Russia. With regard to this, esteemed Boris Nikolayevich, I sincerely request you reconsider my case and enable me to become a useful citizen in a new, free and democratic Russia."

Putting aside all matters of bureaucratic gossip, it is evident that the Russian Foreign Ministry's link with the country's intelligence service has created a new pattern of emphasis on Near Eastern and South Asian developments. Intelligence director Primakov brought expertise in Islamic and Arab affairs to his new position; Shebarshin's service period in Pakistan and Iran gave him a unique background in areas of vital current interest to Russia. On the other hand, Kuzichkin's defection to the West marks him—despite his knowledge of Farsi and of the Iranian politicocultural scene—as an unlikely candidate for future intelligence assignments.

Initially, at any rate, Russian intelligence operations concerning Iran will have to be radically different from those of the past. Earlier, Moscow clearly hoped that the overthrow of the Shah had opened the door toward successful infiltration of the revolutionary movements, using Iranian Communists and agents of influence, and eventually leading to a Teheran regime as closely linked to Moscow as the misbegotten Soviet-controlled governments of Afghanistan. Once Khomeini was firmly in power, Moscow sought to exploit his aggressive campaign against the United States, the "Great Satan."

With the Soviet Union dismantled and Khomeini gone, a more flexible Teheran regime faced a defensively anxious Russia as well as potential economic, religiocultural, and political allies on Russia's southern rim. Teheran's short-range and long-range projects—all subject to continuous monitoring by Moscow's foreign intelligence staff—included the following:

*Ukraine.* After talks between Ukrainian President Leonid Kravchuk and Iranian Foreign Minister Ali Akbar Velayati, plans were made for Ukraine to replace its shortfall of Russian oil with imports from Iran. In turn, Ukraine could offer such raw materials as manganese and iron ore, help with industrial installations, and shipments of certain food categories. The sale of armaments by Ukraine to Iran was also considered.

*Tajikistan.* Of all the former Soviet republics, Tajikistan has the closest ethnic links with Iran; its Tajik population has Persian roots, and Tajik (Farsi/Persian) was declared the state language in 1990. About 80 percent of its five million inhabitants are Sunni Moslems, in contrast to Iran's Shiite population. Tajikistan's Communist leadership sought to hang on even after the breakup of the Soviet Union. Prominent among the Communists' opponents was the Islamic Renaissance Party. When diplomatic relations were established between Teheran and Dushanbe, Tajikistan's capital, in January 1992, a joint communiqué emphasized the two countries' "common language, traditions, and cultural ties." On the Islamic New Year's Day—March 21—direct air service between Dushanbe, Teheran, and two other Iranian cities was established. A highway, and a railway connection through Turkmenistan, were planned. As a producer of uranium, Tajikistan was of strategic importance to any nation intending to build nuclear armaments. Tajikistan was also a potential weapons exporter.

*Turkmenistan.* Turkmen President Saparmurad Niyazov met with Iranian President Hashemi Rafsanjani in Teheran in October 1991. They announced simplified border crossing procedures between the two countries, as well as "development of transportation, border trade, the joint construction of dams on border rivers, and cooperation in the spheres of culture and science." Iran agreed to replace Russia as Turkmenistan's supplier of oil, to import Turkmen gas, and to help build a pipeline across its territory that could carry Turkmen gas to Turkey and Pakistan. Turkmenistan planned its own oil refinery, rather than depend on the Russian refinery at Tyumen.

*Kyrgyzstan.* Iranian approaches have been limited in Kyrgyzstan under President Askar Akayev, who hoped to encourage his country's economic contacts with the United States, Europe, and Far Eastern countries (such as South Korea). In late November 1991, an Iranian delegation headed by Foreign Minister Velayati briefly visited Bishkek, the Kyrgyz capital. The Iranian mission met with parliamentary representatives as well as President Akayev. The two countries signed a memorandum of understanding on economic, cultural, and trade cooperation.

*Kazakhstan.* Following the pattern of its overall diplomatic-economic activities throughout the area, Iran's Deputy Foreign Minister Mahmud Vayezi visited the Kazakh capital city of Alma-Ata on January 31, 1992, spoke of the "common historical and cultural background of our two countries," and signed several agreements. One of these documents dealt with the opening of an Iranian bank in Kazakhstan; another agreement foresaw deals in petroleum and petroleum derivatives, as well as Iran's assistance in oil exploration, transportation of goods between the two countries' ports at the Caspian Sea, and opening of an Iranian Trade Center in Alma-Ata.

*Uzbekistan.* Relations between Iran and Uzbekistan developed at a slower pace than those with other Islamic republics in the area. Erkin Khodzhiev, chairman of the committee on economic reform of Uzbekistan's Supreme Soviet, visited Teheran early in 1992. On his return, on February 13, he reported that Iran was "ready to invest in the economy of Uzbekistan," but he did not provide details. Khodzhiev, who had led a parliamentary delegation to the Iranian capital, said that they had only discussed "economic cooperation," rather than direct investment. At that time, Uzbekistan was still in the process of preparing the ground for foreign economic activities, including currency regulations, customs duties, and export-import categories.

*Azerbaijan.* Aside from its mediation efforts in Azerbaijan's conflict with Armenia, Iran took an intensive interest in the country's affairs. Hostile as well as interlocking ethnogeographic traditions have long existed between Teheran and Baku, Azerbaijan's capital (traditionally a major oil-producing center). While Azerbaijan's leadership underwent several changes, its apparent eagerness to tighten relations with Teheran remained constant. On the one hand, Baku enlisted Iran's support in its conflict with Armenia; on the other hand, it felt the need for new ties to supplement its frayed links with Moscow. Teheran, in turn, sought to project its image as a benign, pious but unthreatening neighbor. Propagandistic machinery was quickly put in place, including television, radio, and telephone communications from Teheran; an Iranian cultural center was established in Baku. As in the case of Kazakhstan, an Iranian bank branch was planned for the Azerbaijani capital, as were air connections between Baku and Teheran (via Tabriz), and marine traffic between Baku and Enzeli, an Iranian port on the Caspian Sea. Of political-strategic interest was Iran's opening of a consulate in the Azerbaijan region of Nakhichevan, a predominately ethnic Iranian enclave wedged between Armenia and Turkey; Iran also sent food supplies to the enclave.

So much for Iran's increased impact on the so-called Islamic states on Russia's rim; all of them also contain substantial non-Islamic minorities, including ethnic Russian (or, "Russian-speaking") populations that experienced political and economic stress during the breakup of the Soviet Union. While mediating the explosive status of Azerbaijan's mainly Armenian enclave of Nagorno-Karabakh, Iran sought to give the appearance of acting in an evenhanded manner. It even approached Armenia in much the same way it approached that country's neighbors, although a good deal more low-key. Iran agreed to supply Armenia with enough oil and natural gas to meet one-third of its needs. Armenian representatives visiting Teheran came away with the assurance that a bridge over the Araks River, which separated the two countries, would be built quickly. Iran also promised direct air connections with Armenia's capital, Yerevan, as well as mutual banking arrangements. In a move that carefully balanced Iran's action in Nakhichevan, an Iranian delegation brought twenty-two tons of medicine and food to Armenia—a gift from

Iran's Armenian community, with the Iranian government providing transportation.

Another non-Islamic state on Iran's diplomatic itinerary was Georgia. Negotiations began with President Zviad Gamsakhurdia. When he was deposed, they continued with his successors; and on February 6, 1992, the two countries signed a five-point memorandum that established diplomatic contacts between them. In terms similar to arrangements elsewhere, the document established a commission to deal with "co-operation in the spheres of transport, industry, fuel and gas (particularly in the supply of Iranian natural gas and transportation), power engineering, agriculture, and trade," and it called for economic, scientific, and technical contacts.

While Russian intelligence must be concerned with Iran's efforts to replace Moscow—economically and, in diverse ways, politicoculturally—at Russia's southern rim, it needs to be particularly concerned about the results of closer relations between Ukraine and Iran. As elsewhere, the falling-off of Russian oil supplies, or the increase in Russian oil prices, prompted the Kiev government to look for other, cheaper sources. The much-traveled Iranian Foreign Minister Ali Akbar Velayati visited Ukrainian President Leonid Kravchuk in Kiev on January 21, 1992, carrying diplomatic greetings from Hashemi Rafsanjani and stating that the two countries shared "great economic, scientific, and cultural potential."

Russia's uneasiness over Iran's high-powered campaign was reflected in a Radio Moscow commentary (January 23, 1992), which stated, with reluctant tolerance, that "no one should be jealous or suspicious of direct relations between Ukraine and Iran"—except for "one condition: Kiev and Teheran should not cooperate against a third country." Obviously, the third country in this case could only be Russia. It required no shrewd reading between the lines to see an element of spite toward Moscow in the cordial Iran–Ukraine alliance. In fact, quick defiance of Russia's newly tightfisted oil policy could be detected in virtually all the agreements with Iran. The Radio Moscow commentary concluded that agreements "for the sake of cooperation" were acceptable, but "if relations are established to solve temporary political problems, at the expense of others, that is quite different."

The emergence of Teheran as an oil superpower—replacing Moscow in its own backyard—clearly presented a potential threat to Russia's political and economic future. In tandem, Russia's Foreign Ministry and the Foreign Intelligence Service had to make plans to meet this challenge on a long-range basis. For the intelligence establishment, this meant developing a new corps of area specialists, linguists, and technicians who could pick up where their predecessors left off. Among these predecessors were veterans such as Leonid Shebarshin, whose experiences in Pakistan and Iran could not be easily replaced. And a professional like Vladimir Kuzichkin—fluent in Farsi and intimately familiar with Iranian society—represented years of training and a huge investment. Could Primakov rebuild Russia's Iranian intelligence operation without the likes of these two men? Primakov himself, with his knowledge of Arabic and some Farsi, was likely to keep the Iranian target firmly in focus.

Shebarshin and Kuzichkin dramatized the dilemma faced by the KGB in its latest incarnation: its "new, improved" Foreign Intelligence Service. In the case of Shebarshin, dismissal was simply prompted by a run-in with Bakatin—a clash of personalities—that followed Shebarshin's failure to protest the August coup while it was under way; but then, most of the KGB staff was sitting on the fence at the time, and only the top-level conspirators were actually fired. Still Kuzichkin's appeal to Yeltsin, asking to return to Russia, was likely to fall on deaf ears. To his former colleagues, and much of the Russian public, his dramatic defection permanently branded him as an outcast.

The new generation of Iran specialists faces tasks quite different from those of the Shebarshins and Kuzichkins of yesterday. Where an earlier generation of intelligence agents could plan on infiltrating a foreign society at the top, hoping to influence cabinet members, military commanders, and key opinion-makers by bribe or manipulation, Russia's new covert operations in Iran would have to be in the category of "active defense," a sophisticated holding operation. On many functional levels, the best defense should be a "benign offense," too subtle to be recognized. Moscow must certainly know that, at the same time, Iran is upgrading its own secret services at home and abroad, placing agents inside the newly independent states—and, of course, within Russia itself.

# 19

# Under Whatever Name

The KGB by any other name will still be the KGB. That old self-created air of omniscience, of faceless danger, of power beyond control will surround the Russian and other ex-Soviet secret services for decades to come. Some of this has odd psychological roots: there seems to be a basic human fear and fascination with secrecy, conspiracy, visible and hidden, with real and imagined enemies. The temptation to blame the KGB for disastrous events in which it had played no role, to blame it for crimes of which it was—to use the incredible term—quite innocent, is ever present. In their days, the KGB and its multi-initialed predecessors have been guilty of too much to require embellishment.

The KGB's oddly pathetic public relations campaign—covered in chapter 3—was yet another effort to change masks. Throughout the seven decades of the Soviet secret service, it has undergone multiple switches in names and administration. From CHEKA through GPU and OGPU, then later as NKVD and, finally, KGB, the agency passed through a history so bloody, so convoluted, and at times so self-devouring as to elude the fantasies of the most imaginative of fiction writers.

This brief history of the KGB just before and after its official "death" is proof of the secret police machinery's ability to adapt even to its official demise. Its central task remained its own survival, its own immortality, and a public and official belief that the secret service's existence was as essential as air or water. In addition, leaders everywhere seem to be fascinated with access to inside information obtained through forbidden channels; with gossip, whether in trivia or in momentous decisions; with secret knowledge about enemies and allies.

One of the tragic ironies of Russian literature during the height of

Moscow's thought control was the KGB's interest in the work of reputed anti-Soviet writers. These writers might never see their work in print, but they could know that KGB agents were intercepting it, reading it— and possibly even discussing it with the authors they were investigating. This tragic cat-and-mouse game disappeared when political censorship was lifted; but with the fading of its antagonists, much of the Russian literary community also lost its verve and daring.

For decades, the "Western imperialists" and, in particular, "American capitalism" were the main targets of Soviet secret operations. Well into the Gorbachev era, the KGB enlisted members of the U.S. armed services to reveal military secrets, while it gathered mountains of classified and unclassified data from around the world—data that could never even be completely translated, much less analyzed or utilized by Soviet science and the military.

Against that sprawling background, a policy of cutting back to essentials, of modernizing the ex-KGB, is making it more efficient. It need no longer act as a gigantic vacuum cleaner, sucking up information from every direction, seeking to be all knowing or at least all collecting. As we have seen, virtually every former Soviet republic has retained a KGB or a KGB-like apparatus for its own national purposes. Internally, these regional KGBs can be assumed, with a high degree of certainty, to be tools in local power struggles. Externally, their tasks must differ greatly, as each republic seeks to establish its identity within the former Soviet Union as well as in global society. Several areas, such as Armenia and Azerbaijan, are undergoing serious military and economic challenges that go far beyond the capacities of the secret services. In many of the republics—Lithuania, for example—the fear of some form of Russian "recolonization" has absorbed much of the local KGB's attention.

The future role of the KGB in the states that used to form the Soviet Union—and let's continue calling it the "KGB" for now, as many do in the former USSR—starts with defining each agency's position. And that position is dictated by the status of Russia in relation to the former Soviet republics, and their relations to each of the other former republics. Technically, the Russian Ministry of Security is exclusively concerned with internal Russian matters. Why, then, did the Ministry's former head, Victor Barannikov, visit and make agreements with other republics? Aren't these states—being outside Russia—within the domain of Russia's Foreign Intelligence Service?

This dilemma is more than an old-fashioned bit of rivalry between two bureaucracies. It reflects the unresolved relationships between these republics, states, nations—whatever you want to call them! The truth of the matter is that external problems vitally affect internal Russian security. Take the unique case of the original Checheno-Ingush Autonomous Republic, inhabited by 1.3 million Moslems, and now part of the Russian Federation. On November 8, 1991, Russian President Boris Yeltsin issued a ten-point decree declaring a "state of emergency over the whole territory." In defiance of Russia's move, on November 26 the local Supreme Soviet declared the region's "independence." The Russian parliament, strongly supported by Vice-president Alexander Rutskoi, voted that Russia put a stop to the Chechens' challenge and "take immediate steps to restore law and order in this republic." Rutskoi called the independence forces "a gang which is terrorizing the population." Among other decisive moves, these forces seized the KGB building in Grozny, the capital. One KGB officer, Lieutenant Kayupov, was wounded; rifles, ammunition, and grenades were stolen.

Yeltsin's decree and the Russian parliamentary resolution were firmly opposed, however, by Victor Ivanenko, then head of the Russian KGB, in a statement he made on October 10. Within days, the newly appointed Chechen President Dzhakhar Dudayev passed a retroactive decree, effective November 1, "On the State Sovereignty of the Chechen Republic." The Chechen parliament abolished the KGB, replacing it with the region's own security service. Moscow's Radio Rossii (November 9, 1991) quoted local KGB staff members as saying that, by disbanding their service, the Chechen parliament "will, intentionally or not, help to undermine the fight against serious crime and play into the hands of representatives of corrupt elements and Mafia organizations." The authors of the statement emphasized that they would remain KGB staff members. Interfax reported that Dudayev had given former KGB officers twenty-four hours to register with the republic's Defense Council; those who failed to do so "by 9 P.M., Moscow time, on November 14, would be persecuted." Chechen militia arrested a KGB officer, Major Victor Tolstenev, on November 12. He was apparently authorized to carry a handgun, but the arresting individuals considered his possession of a weapon to be a crime. According to Tass (November 14, 1991), Chechen radio commentators stated that "the people would judge him"; his body "was delivered to the mortuary" that same night.

Communications between Grozny and Moscow were seriously disrupted. In Moscow, the KGB denied Chechen reports that its regional KGB had stormed Grozny's central telephone exchange. When rioting broke out in Grozny, Russian KGB chief Ivanenko told the press service

Interfax (November 10, 1991) that he—like other Russian law-enforce-ment officials—had only learned about a "state of emergency" in the Chechen region from Vice-president Rutskoi. The two men had visited the Chechen area the previous month. Ivanenko emphasized that he had "always opposed the use of force against the [Chechen] republic's national movement." That same day, Dudayev told a news conference that Moscow—and specifically, the KGB—had played a "provocative role" during the unrest, but that military units of the Russian Interior Ministry and of the KGB had "left the republic safely, without firing a shot."

From then on, the Chechen region under the combative leadership of Dudayev (a former Soviet Air Force general) existed in a state of erratic limbo. While Russia did not acknowledge Checheniya's independence, Dudayev appealed for support in other Transcaucasus regions—includ-ing neighboring Georgia—and among Moslems generally. The former Checheno-Ingush region was further disrupted when Dudayev backed a purely Chechen republic, forcing the Ingush to go their own political way. With Russia's North Ossetia and Georgia's South Ossetia as neigh-bors, Dudayev found numerous opportunities to express strong opin-ions on a variety of religio-ethnic, military, strategic, and global topics. Inevitably, on April 8, 1992, a Chechen Ministry of Security was estab-lished to replace the KGB; Salman Aldakov, a close associate of Dudayev, was named Security Minister.

Well, then, was Checheniya—as it has increasingly been called—a "foreign" country that would be subject to monitoring by Russia's For-eign Intelligence Service? Or did it remain technically "domestic," and therefore within the realm of Russia's Ministry of Security? Probably the latter, as Moscow does not recognize the Chechens' declaration of inde-pendence. But consider the fact that Lithuania, which is not even a mem-ber of the Commonwealth of Independent States, was clearly regarded as a foreign power by the Moscow intelligence community. Does the same principle apply to Latvia and Estonia? And what about Azerbaijan, which originally failed to join the CIS, and where foreign intelligence chief Primakov was personally accused of interfering in internal affairs?

The reconstituted Russian KGB must see its field of operations in a series of concentric circles. The innermost circle would have to be the Ministry of Security's purely domestic operations, ranging from the much-publicized fight against crime to the more elusive monitoring of individuals suspected of "criminal" activity (however that be defined) or of engaging in subversion of an economic, political, or military nature, possibly in the employ of one of the foreign special services. A huge menu of tasks, to be sure! And yet, as the Chechen example illustrates in a tragically dangerous way, ethnic stresses within Russia itself must call for the Ministry of Security to include the actual or potential antagonisms of a great variety of religionationalist groupings.

Beyond this already very wide domestic circle serviced by the Ministry of Security can be found the still wider circles that are of interest to the Foreign Intelligence Service. What should be its priorities? Where do the lines of its duties begin, and where do they end?

The image of concentric circles representing "Russia's security interests" was used by Sergey Rogov, deputy director of Moscow's United States and Canada Institute. Writing on the topic, "Does Russia Need Its Own National Security Policy?" in *Nezavisimaya Gazeta* (March 6, 1992), Rogov noted that Russia's relations with the former Soviet republics were "of prime, priority importance." He warned that "the greatest danger today is that of being dragged into territorial and national conflicts," and he added that "friendly and preferably allied relations" with these neighboring states should be established. Rogov noted that "tens of millions of Russian citizens live there."

An additional circle of Russian security interests, in Rogov's view, encompassed the "regions such as Eastern Europe, the Near East, and the Far East, which were traditionally part of the USSR's sphere of interests." Although Russia is now "separated from these regions (except for the East)," he added, "certain former republics may find themselves under the influence of regional power centers, like China and Iran," and "conflicts in these regions could lead to Russian involvement." As Rogov wrote, "Relations with China and Japan may to a considerable extent determine" the economic development of Siberia; "if relations with its great neighbors in Asia deteriorate, Russia may miss this opportunity."

Rogov viewed the West—"primarily the United States and Western Europe"—as an additional "circle" of Russian security interests. He urged that Russia participate in the European and North Atlantic "integration process" or run the risk of "lagging hopelessly behind the developed countries." If that were to happen, he concluded, "Russia's 'Eurasian' nature will inevitably take on an increasingly Asian tinge."

Such strategic considerations must determine the tactics of Russia's Foreign Intelligence Service. It was natural, therefore, that the FIS as well as the Ministry of Security form part of a new Interdepartmental Foreign Policy Commission of Russia's Security Council. Interfax reported (January 26, 1993) that the new Commission had been created to "coordinate international actions connected with the work of the various Russian ministries and departments." Among other agencies involved were the Ministry of Foreign Affairs and the Ministry of Defense. The Commission was scheduled to meet at least once a month. Primakov and Barannikov both attended one of the first meetings of the new Commission, on March 3, 1993.

Public discussion of crucial international problems highlighted long-range intelligence problems. In 1993, at a time when Russia sought to restrain the United Nations (and specifically, the United States) from taking strong action against an aggressive Serbia, Moscow's attention was also directed toward other danger points. President Turgut Ozal of Turkey—speaking in Baku, Azerbaijan, at the conclusion of a twelve-day tour of Central Asia (and three days before his death of heart failure in Ankara)—warned Russia (April 14, 1993) that Azerbaijani intercepts indicated that Russian transport planes were supplying Armenian forces.

Shortly before, a "high-ranking Russian diplomat" was quoted by Interfax (March 4, 1993) as saying that his country's "future relations with Iran and Pakistan will depend on whether these states take into account Russia's interest in Central Asia, above all in Tajikistan." The diplomat stated that "Tajik Islamists undergo training in Afghanistan, a country much influenced by Pakistan and Iran."

The multiplicity of intelligence problems faced by Primakov's agency was certainly not unique; its dilemma was shared by every other security service in the world, from Israel's Mossad to Germany's Bundesnachrichtendienst (BND). In the United States, the administration of President Bill Clinton asked Congress for an increase in the overall intelligence budget, while reducing general military expenditures. The end of the Cold War not only had created numerous new nations, but had also vastly increased the complexities faced by intelligence-gathering agencies—ranging from language studies, and general regional specializations, to new risks and opportunities in recruiting agents.

Russia's Foreign Intelligence Service faced these tasks with substantial resources; it had survived the breakup of the KGB virtually intact. Leonid Mlechin reminded readers of Moscow's monthly *New Times* (June 1992) that the First Chief Directorate of the KGB (foreign intelligence) had been "separated from the rest of the organization's staff, both structurally and in terms of responsibility for the KGB's seventy-year record." Primakov, according to Mlechin, "misses no opportunity" to tell the news media about "sweeping reforms" in his agency, "but no radical changes in the intelligence service are in evidence so far." Mlechin added, "The Foreign Intelligence Service is among the organizations authorized by the recently adopted Criminal Investigation Act to tap telephones, open private letters, put suspects under police surveillance, search flats, and carry out arrests."

According to Mlechin, the FIS had to shift its attention from the Western industrialized countries and focus on the former Soviet republics and on the nations of Eastern Europe and the Middle East. As he put it, "our intelligence officers now packing their trunks in Paris, Bonn, or Tokyo might proceed straight to Kiev, Tashkent, and Baku, bypassing Moscow." This, of course, was an ironic oversimplification; espionage skills useful in industrialized nations might well be handicaps in other areas. The article added that, "in the former republics of the USSR, intelligence networks are being set up anew. Moscow cannot rely on the personnel of the republics' state committees: as likely as not, those men will rather work against Russia." And one afterthought: "Security Minister Victor Barannikov has already set up a large interior counterintelligence division, whose job it is to expose 'enemies in our own midst.' His men will naturally try to keep tabs on Academician Primakov's department, too."

The two most outspoken ex–KGB officers—Leonid Shebarshin and Oleg Kalugin—remained the agency's voluble critics. Shebarshin, who once was head of the KGB's foreign intelligence service, told *Rossiskaya Gazeta* (June 29, 1992) that "a concerted campaign is being waged," largely by "the Americans," which seeks "to force Russia either to abolish its intelligence service completely, or to reduce it to a state where it is unable to function properly." He urged quite diplomatically—as "a task of national importance," and "for the sake of the future"—that Russia's intelligence service be retained unweakened.

Shebarshin's charges, repeated by other KGB traditionalists and by Russian media sources, were largely based on a study exploring the "Forging of a U.S.–Russian Partnership," published by the Washington-based Heritage Foundation (June 12, 1992). The paper noted that the KGB "remains in operation," while "divided into two services, and renamed the Ministry of Security and the Foreign Intelligence Service." It stated that "despite this facade, its structure and personnel will be drawn primarily from that of its Soviet predecessor," and suggested that, "if a true intelligence service is needed, it should be established from a new beginning." Cited for this information were U.S. intelligence officials who had found that "the level of KGB operations in the U.S. has not decreased since the demise of the Soviet Union and has even increased in the areas of military intelligence and defense technology." The study urged that "continued KGB operations in the U.S. and elsewhere" be regarded as "incompatible with Russia's desire to establish close relations with the U.S.," adding, "This type of spying is unacceptable for a country receiving assistance from the West." Moreover, The Annual Report of the U.S. Attorney General for 1991 had noted that, although "the Soviet republics have started to restructure the domestic responsibilities of the KGB," the U.S. Federal Bureau of Investigation had confirmed that "the KGB and its military counterpart, the GRU, continued to operate in the United States."

Shebarshin, in his interview with *Rossiskaya Gazeta*, made this forecast:

"It would be crazy and dangerous to think about a return to the era of confrontation. However, I am absolutely certain that the day will come when Russia will grow strong, when it will be in a position to carry out a genuinely dynamic and independent foreign policy, geared exclusively to its national interests. Like any other power, it will inevitably have to resort not only to overt means of realizing its aims, but also to the assistance of covert friends and supporters. These can only be found by the intelligence service."

Shebarshin's former colleague General Kalugin addressed a conference, "The KGB: Yesterday, Today, and Tomorrow," which took place in Moscow from February 19 to 21, 1993. Kalugin maintained that the essence and character of Russia's security services had not changed decisively. He reported that the Ministry of Security employed 140,000 people, and that the combined staffs of the two major intelligence agencies added up to "almost half a million." The conference irritated the Ministry of Security sufficiently enough that it asked former Russian KGB chief Ivanenko to withdraw from the meeting. In its final resolution, the conference concluded that "state security bodies of the Russian Federation should cease to exist in their present form, and with their current composition of executive officers." The resolution also said, "We believe that the development of a democratic process in the country is impossible while state security services continue to perform functions of state management." According to the resolution, attempts to reorganize the KGB after August 1991, "in order to bring its activities in line with the law, have failed." The conference called for an "effective mechanism of parliamentary and judicial control over the activity of security services."

Vadim Bakatin—talking to the press at the conference—said that the KGB "cannot be more democratic than the society of which it is part." While he agreed that it would be "naive to claim that the special services have become democratic," he said that one should guard against "exaggerating the danger" they might present. Bakatin emphasized that a "developing democracy" should "not be at war with its security organs; we already have more than enough battle fronts, and we don't need another one."

Within the KGB itself, and certainly among leading officers of the Foreign Intelligence Service, Shebarshin's views—so diplomatically and elegantly phrased—were most likely to be applauded. The expectation that Russia's power will increase, and its future interests will demand experienced covert support, is likely to be at the core of any long-range intelligence planning. Emphasis on military intelligence, or on technological and industrial espionage, might fluctuate with changing world conditions and the political pressures felt by the Russian government. In addition, conflict and disintegration among the outlying republics must inevitably disturb Moscow and tempt it into action. And while national leaders in several republics have spoken fearfully of a new Russian "colonialism," the concept of a United Nations-backed "trusteeship" over ungovernable countries has presented an inviting formula.

Such a mechanism was outlined by the historian Paul Johnson in a provocative article, "Colonialism's Back—and Not a Moment Too Soon," in the *New York Times Magazine* (April 18, 1993). Johnson proposed a temporary trusteeship by a major power, under UN auspices, over countries such as Somalia and Liberia. It could be imagined that, under such a formula, Russia might seek to obtain a trusteeship over an ungovernable Tajikistan for a period of some five to twenty-five years, to restore order and assure political and economic stability. That one or another ex-Soviet republic might, more or less reluctantly, call on Moscow to settle regional conflicts is to be expected -- much as Russians might find themselves both attracted and repelled by the role of a loved-and-hated policeman-ruler. But the Russian Foreign Intelligence Service would certainly be called upon to analyze such delicate situations, formulate blueprints, and possibly engage in related covert actions. If the concept of a UN trusteeship would appear too cumbersome or unreliable, the intelligence service might well fall back on a more traditional approach: assuring, by overt or covert means, the emergence of governments consistently favorable to Moscow.

As we have seen, it was within a period of a few months that the

KGB officially died but was quickly reborn. Once Russia decided to take over the essential parts of what had been the USSR KGB, the continuity of the agency was assured. The KGB departments underwent the administrative changes that the dissolution of the Soviet Union demanded, but retained their basic structures and personnel. The development of national security services throughout the former USSR was remarkably rapid. When young nations emerged from World War II, it seemed that each one wanted to assert its own identity either with a major industrial project, such as a hydroelectric dam, or with a national airline. When the Soviet Union dissolved, each emerging nation seemed intent on having its own KGB—if possible, overnight. The psychological need for an agency that engages in conspiracy and secret power plays appears to be universal. And so, a reborn KGB will continue to live on, under whatever name.

# Selected Bibliography

Andrew, Christopher and Oleg Gordievsky. *KGB: The Inside Story of Its Foreign Operations*. New York: HarperCollins, 1990.

Azrael, Jeremy R. *The KGB in Kremlin Politics*. Santa Monica, Calif.: Rand/UCLA Center for the Study of Soviet International Behavior, 1989.

Barron, John. *KGB: The Secret Work of Secret Agents*. New York: Reader's Digest Press, 1974.

————. *KGB Today: The Hidden Hand*. New York: Reader's Digest Press, 1983.

Bower, Tom. *Maxwell: The Outsider*. New York: Viking, 1992.

Corson, William R. and Robert T. Crowley. *The New KGB: Engine of Soviet Power*. New York: William Morrow, 1985.

Deriabin, Peter and T. H. Bagley. *KGB: Masters of the Soviet Union*. New York: Hippocrene Books, 1990.

Dziak, John J. *Chekisty: A History of the KGB*. Lexington, Mass.: Lexington Books, 1988.

Ebon, Martin. *The Andropov File*. New York: McGraw-Hill, 1983.

Hyde, Montgomery. *George Blake, Superspy*. London: Constable, 1987.

Kessler, Ronald. *Moscow Station: How the KGB Penetrated the American Embassy*. New York: Scribner's, 1989.

Knight, Amy. *The KGB: Police and Politics in the Soviet Union*. Boston: Allen & Unwin, 1988.

Kuzichkin, Vladimir. *Inside the KGB: My Life in Soviet Espionage*. New York: Pantheon Books, 1990.

Levchenko, Stanislav. *On the Wrong Side: My Life in the KGB*. McLean, Va.: Pergamon-Brassey's, 1988.

Myagkov, Aleksei. *Inside the KGB*. New Rochelle, N.Y.: Arlington House, 1976.

Rahr, Alexander. *A Biographical Dictionary of 100 Soviet Officials*. Boulder, Colo.: Westview Press, 1989.

Romerstein, Herbert and Stanislav Levchenko. *The KGB against the "Main Enemy."* Lexington, Mass.: Lexington Books, 1989.

Rositzke, Harry A. *The KGB: The Eyes of Russia*. Garden City, N.Y.: Doubleday, 1981.

Wolton, Thierry. *Le KGB en France*. Paris: B. Grasset, 1986.

# Index

**About the Author**

MARTIN EBON served with the U.S. Office of War Information during World War II. He was subsequently on the staff of the Foreign Policy Association and, during the Korean War, was with the U.S. Information Agency. Ebon has lectured on world affairs and communist tactics, in particular, at New York University and the New School for Social Research. He is the author or editor of more than sixty books, and his numerous articles have appeared in such publications as the *New York Times*, *Psychology Today*, and the *International Journal of Intelligence and Counterintelligence*.